2G
Spectrum Scam

BY THE SAME AUTHOR

Ayodhya Ram Temple and Hindu Renaissance

Economic Development and Reforms in India and China

Hindus Under Siege: The Way Out

Sri Lanka in Crisis: India's Options

Terrorism in India: A Strategy of Deterrence for India's National Security

Rama Setu: Symbol of National Unity

Corruption and Corporate Governance in India: Satyam, Spectrum and Sundaram

Hindutva and National Renaissance

India's China Strategic Perspective

Virat Hindu Identity: Concept and its Power

Building the Sri Rama Temple in Ayodhya

The Ideology of India's Modern Right

2G
Spectrum Scam

Subramanian Swamy, Ph.D. (Harvard)

Member of Parliament, India
Former Union Cabinet Minister for
Commerce, Law & Justice, India

HAR-ANAND
PUBLICATIONS PVT LTD

Reprint, 2020

Published by Ashok Gosain and Ashish Gosain for
HAR-ANAND PUBLICATIONS PVT LTD
E-49/3, Okhla Industrial Area, Phase-II, New Delhi-110020
Tel: 41603490
E-mail: info@haranandbooks.com/haranand@rediffmail.com
Shop online at: www.haranandbooks.com

Printed in India

PREFACE

Corruption in law in India is now a major concern because of the gigantic and mind-boggling amounts illegally appropriated in the Satyam, IPL, CWG, and 2G Spectrum scams. By all objective criteria, India today has by far one of the most corrupt governance.

More than three years ago in autumn 2008, I had begun to study the dimensions of two gigantic financial scams, Satyam and Spectrum, which had plagued the nation, and published my researches as a book *Corruption and Corporate Governance in India: Satyam, Spectrum and Sundaram* (Har-Anand Publications, 2010).

As I had pointed out in that book, my interest was stoked by the forgery that became apparent in the divestment of equity stake in Swan Capital Company by Anil Dhirubhai Ambani, the owner of ADAG, in favour of the DB Realty Company, reportedly on the then Telecom Minister A. Raja's behest.

I had written to the Prime Minister a letter dated November 29, 2008, for Sanction under Section19 of the Prevention of Corruption Act (1988) to prosecute Telecom Minister A. Raja – by filing a private complaint before the Designated Sessions Court. Thus began my venture into the 2G Spectrum Scam. The PM's procrastination led me to the Supreme Court. Thereafter, a Bench of Justices Singhvi and Ganguli, by their meticulous reading of the briefs and documents filed and by their crisp orders and directions, have changed the national public mood from despair and despondency to hope and expectation. The international media has today, therefore, changed its perspective about India, from a Banana Republic in the making, to a vibrant and functioning democracy of live institutions.

This judicial intervention came none too soon. An international watchdog committee conducted a study on the illicit flight of money from

India, perhaps the first ever attempt at shedding light on a subject steeped in secrecy, and concluded that India has been drained of $462 billion (over Rs 20 lakh crore) between 1948 and 2008. The amount is nearly 40 per cent of India's gross domestic product.

The unanimous view throughout the world today is that corruption is no more the inevitable grease or speed money to be tolerated in any system but is a cancer that will cause death of a society by continuous debilitation--unless it is cured at an early stage.

However, India although is a signatory to the UN Convention Against Corrupt adopted by the General Assembly in October 2003, it has not yet ratified the Convention. The Convention, however, came into force on December 14, 2005 when 38 countries ratified it. Its asset recovery provision is very appealing, and yet the Indian Government is not yet moved to ratify the Convention.

Corruption misallocates resources from the meritorious to the unworthy, the immoral, the criminal, the powerful or the illegitimately rich. Optimality conditions of trade for transactions thus are altered and transaction are effected sub-optimally. Moreover, since merit is regarded inferior to power, most transactions then lead to sub-optimally produced sub-standard goods and services, which could not otherwise have been sold open market without retribution from law enforcement.

The Indian financial system also suffers from a hang-over of cronyism and corruption that have brought the government budgets on the verge of bankruptcy. This too needs fixing. India's infrastructure requires about $150 billion dollars to make it world class, and the education system needs 6 per cent of GDP instead of 2.8 per cent today. But an open competitive market system can find these resources, provided the quality of governance and accountability is improved. Obviously, a second generation of reforms are necessary for all this.

The bitter truth thus is that India's corporate world's success stories are founded on fudged accounts and on undisclosed and unreported funding through blackmoney held by corrupt politicians and notorious criminals.

The goal of a transparent governance cannot be achieved unless there is accountability in governance; such accountability requires transparent and ethical reporting of the finances of an organization.

This book is a case study of India's most recent and the world's biggest corruption scandal ever. The most acceptable estimate of the loss to the national exchequer is about Rs. 1.76 lakh crores [about $40 billion], and a bribe payment of Rs. 60,000 crores [about $ 14 billion].

In getting to the bottom of this scandal I am, and indeed the nation is indebted to the thoroughly professional studies done first by the CVC, then by the CAG, followed by the magnificently documented Justice Shivraj Patil Committee Report, and finally by the complete and masterly expose by the Dr. Murli Manohar Joshi – led Public Accounts Committee of Parliament contained in the as yet Draft Report dated April 30, 2011. So stung by the revelations in this Report were the high and mighty in public offices, that they used their brute majority in the committee to block the Draft from being formally forwarded to the Lok Sabha Speaker for being laid on the Table of the Houses of Parliament.

I treat all these Reports as national resources in the struggle against corruption and exposing the 2G Spectrum Scam. Hence, I have borrowed heavily from these Reports. This book is, therefore, dedicated to these Constitutionally ordained institutions of the nation and their contribution to the expose of the 2G Spectrum Scam.

Intellectually, I am deeply indebted to *Pioneer* news-daily correspondent and spartan sleuth J. Gopikrishnan; patriotic and courageous whistleblower Ashirvatham Achari; and to my wife and tenacious researcher Dr. Roxna Swamy. Many others too helped me along but that list is too long for me to ensure that all names are recorded. Of course, no one else but I am responsible for the contents of this book.

SUBRAMANIAN SWAMY

Contents

Chapter I

The Definition and Impact of Corruption

Corruption in India is now a major concern because of the gigantic and mind boggling amounts illegally appropriated in the Satyam, IPL, CWG, and 2G Spectrum scams. By all objective criteria, India today has relatively by far one of the most corrupt governance.

Definition of Corruption

A 2005 study done by *Transparency International* (TI) in India found that more than 75 per cent of the people had first-hand experience of paying bribe or peddling influence to get any type of job done in a public office. Taxes and bribes are a daily life fact, common between state borders; Transparency International estimates that freight carrying trucks pay annually US$5 billion in bribes.

For 2010, India was ranked way down in the list of countries in Transparency International's *Corruption Perceptions Index,* which rank itself was a big drop from the preceding decade. Flushed with unaccounted illegally acquired cash in almost all walks of life in India, have become increasingly criminalized.

Criminalization of Indian politics arises from the use of unaccounted funds by criminals in elections, and hence is a major as well as a serious problem for our democracy. In July 2008, *Washington Post* reported that nearly a fourth of the 540 Indian Parliament members faced criminal charges, "including *human trafficking,* immigration rackets, embezzlement, rape and even murder."

An international watchdog committee conducted a study on the illicit flight of money from India, perhaps the first ever attempt at shedding light on a subject steeped in secrecy, and concluded that India has been drained of $462 billion (over Rs 20 lakh crore) between 1948 and 2008. The amount is nearly 40 per cent of India's gross domestic product.

Bribery remains rife in many countries, totaling about $1trillion globally every year. It is not anymore just petty palm-greasing for speedier file movement on the bureaucrat's table. We are now in a world of billion dollar Ponzi schemes and political patronage for the same.

The unanimous view throughout the world today is that corruption can no more be condoned as the inevitable grease or speed money to be tolerated in any system but is instead a cancer that will cause death of a society by continuous debilitation—unless it is cured at an early stage.

The problem of corruption thus needs to be solved by governments while they still can. Corruption is a challenge not only for public officials but even in implementing economic reforms in a globalized framework. Although there is much open discussion in the last decade, corruption despite the global anti-corruption and awareness-raising campaigns, has *not* declined worldwide.

Corruption, as we find now, is however not unique to developing countries, nor has it declined on average globally with rising prosperity. In fact, some developing countries, such as Chile and Botswana, do exhibit lower levels of corruption than some fully industrialized nations.

The cost to society of bribing a bureaucrat to obtain a permit to operate a small firm pales in comparison with, say, a telecommunications conglomerate that corrupts a politician to shape the rules of the game granting it monopolistic rights, or an investment bank influencing the regulatory and oversight regime governing them.

Corruption thus occurs when a certain party, unable to compete in a transaction on merit, uses its wealth or power to bypass that merit. Corruption is, therefore, inherently bad for the efficient functioning of any economic system. It blurs the incentive to perform and discourages relying on merit as a means to success.

Corruption generally therefore is any inducement, or bribe, to do (or not to do) anything that the bribe giver wants from the bribe taker who otherwise will not do or will do. By this broad definition, even dowry payment is corruption. Bribe can be non-monetary such as promotion in a job or fast clearing of a file.

For our purposes here, it is 'corruption in law' that we are concerned with, which is misuse of public office for private gain either for oneself, family or friend. This represents a governance failure. It can manifest in owning assets disproportionate to known sources of one's income. It is prosecutable in India under the Prevention of Corruption Act (1947) that was re-cast in 1988, which any citizen can set into motion subject to some safeguards such as Sanction. Corruption is also sue-able under the case laws of the Supreme Court under the Doctrine of Public Trust, as malfeasance in office.

A more drastic law on the anvil under pressure from the civil society at large, is to be known Lok Pal Act. It obviates the requirement of sanction, and institutes an independent prosecutor.

However, India although is a signatory to the UN Convention Against Corruption adopted by the General Assembly in October 2003, has not yet ratified the Convention. The Convention however came into force on December 14, 2005 when the 38 countries ratified it. Its asset recovery provision is very appealing, and yet the Indian Government has not yet moved to ratify the Convention.

IMPACT OF CORRUPTION

Corruption misallocates resources from the meritorious to the unworthy, the immoral, the criminal, the powerful or the illegitimately rich. Optimality conditions of trade for transactions thus are altered and transaction are effected sub-optimally. Moreover, since merit will then be regarded inferior to power, most transactions then lead to sub-optimally produced sub-standard goods and services, which could not otherwise have been sold in the open market without retribution from law enforcement.

More than three years ago in autumn 2008, I had begun the study the dimensions of two gigantic financial scams, Satyam and Spectrum, which had plagued the nation, and published my researches as a book *Corruption and Corporate Governance in India: Satyam, Spectrum and Sundaram* (Har-Anand Publications, 2010).

As I had pointed out in that book, my curiosity was fired by the fraud and forgery that became apparent in the sudden divestment of equity stake in Swan Capital Company by Anil Dhirubhai Ambani, the owner of ADAG, in favour of the DB Realty Company reportedly on the then Telecom Minister A. Raja's behest. Why? There hangs the Spectrum Scam tale.

I had written to the Prime Minister a letter dated November 29, 2008, for Sanction under Section19 of the Prevention of Corruption Act (1988) long before anyone else had, seeking to prosecute Telecom Minister A. Raja by filing a private complaint before the Designated Sessions Court. Thus began my venture into the 2G Spectrum Scam. The PM's procrastination led me to the Supreme Court. Thereafter, a Bench of Justices Singhvi and Ganguli, by their meticulous reading of the briefs and documents filed and by their crisp orders and directions, have changed the national public mood from despair and despondency to hope and expectation. The international media has today, therefore, changed its perspective about India, from a Banana Republic in the making to a vibrant and functioning democracy of live institutions.

This judicial intervention came none too soon. An international watchdog committee conducted a study on the illicit flight of money from India, perhaps the first ever attempt at shedding light on a subject steeped in secrecy, and concluded that India has been drained of $462 billion (over Rs 20 lakh crore) between 1948 and 2008. The amount is nearly 40 per cent of India's gross domestic product. This flight, the study pointed was accelerating in amounts. The 2G Spectrum Scam caused the nation to lose $46 billion, i.e., about 10 per cent of the total flight since 1948, in just one transaction.

The unanimous view throughout the world today is that corruption is *no more* the inevitable grease or speed money to be tolerated in any system but is a cancer that will cause death of a society by continuous debilitation— unless it is cured at an early stage.

However, India although is a signatory to the UN Convention Against Corrupt adopted by the General Assembly in October 2003, it has not yet ratified the Convention. The Convention however came into force on December 14, 2005 when 38 countries ratified it. Its asset recovery provision is very appealing, and yet the Indian Government is not yet moved to ratify the Convention.

Corruption misallocates resources from the meritorious to the unworthy, the immoral, the criminal, the powerful or the illegitimately rich. Optimality, conditions of trade for transactions thus are altered and transaction are effected sub-optimally. Moreover, since merit is regarded inferior to power, most transactions then lead to sub-optimally produced sub-standard goods and services, which could not otherwise have been sold in the open market without retribution from law enforcement.

The Indian financial system also suffers from a hang-over of cronyism and corruption that have brought the government budgets on the verge of bankruptcy. This too needs fixing. India's infrastructure requires about $150 billion dollars to make it world class, and the education system needs 6 per cent of GDP instead of 2.8 per cent today. But an open competitive market system can find these resources provided the quality of governance and accountability is improved. Obviously, a second generation of reforms are necessary for all this.

The bitter truth thus is that India's corporate world's success stories are founded on fudged accounts and on undisclosed and unreported funding through black money held by corrupt politicians and notorious criminals.

This goal cannot be achieved unless there is accountability in governance, such accountability requires transparent and ethical reporting of the finances of an organization.

Hence, corrupt transactions result in the sale and purchase of goods or services of inferior quality, which is detrimental to the nation. Moreover, offices lose their legitimacy once they indulge in corruption, undermining people's trust in the political system along with the decline in the power of office to stem the rot of corruption. Colombia and Mexico are living examples of this. In the past, flourishing empires have collapsed because of financial and moral corruption.

One of the worst problems with corruption in India is the creation of "black money," money that is used in such transactions and is obviously unreported, hence is neither taxed nor is it spent openly. It travels to secret bank accounts abroad, or, worse, is used by the corrupt to indulge in gross luxurious consumption and bribery.

While this in itself harms the country, it also has the effect of raising the profitability of non-essential and luxury industries, which in turn

attract future investment to these industries. This essentially crowds out investment in other, more essential industries.

In India, the luxury goods sector, directly and indirectly receives 70 per cent of the national investment. Black money also funds elections and hence there is no accounting. It tempts the receiver to stash and salt away part of the campaign funds. Since elections leads to political power of those funded, future governments become bribe-compliant and protect the crooked. Such black money stock also creates inflation by enabling easy finance for hoarding of supplies even as the GDP growth rate accelerates.

Corruption, therefore, impacts on economic development of a nation in five dimensions:

(1) Decisions taken for corrupt motive sub-optimises the allocation of scarce national resources and hence in the long run lowers the rate of growth in GDP. It also encourages buccaneers instead of innovative entrepreneurs.

(2) By the use of bribe money which escapes the tax net and is mostly stashed away in banks abroad or in trunks in safe houses, is deployed in luxury goods purchase, ostentatious life, splurging in five star hotels, real estate, and on partying. This raises demand for luxury production and services, and in turn distorts investment priorities. In India, 70 per cent of the investment goes directly or indirectly to sustain the luxury sector.

(3) Unaccounted bribe money is lent to hoarders and speculators who then cause artificial shortages and thus inflation and property bubbles.

(4) Since those who indulge the most in corrupt activities would be in public office, they enact laws to not only to safeguard the booty by lax criminal investigations and prosecutions, but to enable earning interest or return on the bribe money. The invention of Participatory Notes (PNs) and the Mauritius Tax and Capital Gains exemption treaties is aimed at that sordid objective [see below].

(5) Corruption enables beneficiaries to involve foreign governments seeking influence and criminal gangs resident abroad to launder money and provide protection.

Hence, as a country becomes industrialized, its governance and corruption challenges do not disappear. They simply morph and become more sophisticated. It becomes a complex phenomenon than just transfer of a briefcase stashed with cash in a Swiss bank. The formation of shell companies in tax haven islands makes the tracing of the money trail very difficult.

Now subtler forms of "legal corruption" also exist e.g. an expectation of a future job for a regulator in a lobbying firm, or a campaign contribution with strings attached. In many countries this may be legal, even if unethical. In industrialized nations, undue influence is often legally exercised by powerful private interests, which in turn influence the nation's regulations, policies and laws.

This has dire consequences: witnessed in the various forms of corruption underlying the current global financial crisis that started in the U.S.. Concrete examples abound as given below:

First, Freddie Mac and Fannie Mac spent millions of dollars lobbying some influential members of Congress in exchange for, among other things, lax capital reserve requirements for these mortgage giants.

Second, AIG's derivatives unit located in London managed to fudge its accounts helped by lax regulatory oversight, and took wild risks that brought down AIG's empire of 100,000 employees in 130 countries thus catalyzing the global financial crisis.

Third, giant mortgage lenders such as Countrywide Financial Switch were permitted to regulators, so as to fall under the lax oversight of the Office of Thrift Supervision [and paid for by the regulated banks and in turn which also supervised AIG's derivative unit!].

Fourth, During a G-5 meeting at the Securities and Exchange Commission in April 2004 the largest investment banks persuaded the SEC to relax its regulatory oversight and allow a much larger amount of debt than the norm.

Finally, Madoff's giant Ponzi scheme, points to subtler forms of corruption. The SEC knew Madoff, who had served on the commission's own advisory committee, was then misleading it in how he managed the funds of his customers. Yet the SEC failed in detecting the Ponzi scheme till billions of dollars were lost.

Therefore, corruption ought to include acts that may be legal in a strict narrow sense but where the rules of the game have been bent or permitted "scotched earth" techniques. Would this broader view of corruption result in different corruption ratings of nations? No doubt about that. For example, over the past few years, traditional measures of corruption, such as the Corruption Perceptions Index of Transparency International, place the U.S. among the least corrupt nations in the world (currently ranking No. 18 among 180 rated countries).

In 2004, Dr. Daniel Kaufman of Brookings Institution, Washington D.C. had calculated an index of "legally corrupt" manifestations (measured through the extent of undue influence through political finance and powerful firms influencing politicians and policy making) and found that the U.S. rated in the bottom half among the 104 countries surveyed! The U.S. was rated 53rd, a few ranks below Italy. Netherlands, Norway, Denmark and Finland exhibited low levels of "legal corruption" (ranking Nos. 1 through 4, respectively). Chile was rated 18th. Also rating better than the U.S. were countries like Botswana, Colombia and South Africa!!

This is happening along with new expanding role of government in new and sophisticated areas of governance. But in order to restore confidence, citizens, entrepreneurs and bankers need to generate renewed trust in the financial system. Transparency is, therefore, the key. Transparency and Accountability cannot co-exist with Corruption.

In this context, the World Bank, in which nations are represented as members in the governing body, had decided to make public the names of all companies that have been debarred from receiving direct contracts from the Bank Group under its corporate procurement program. This change was made in the interest of fairness and transparency and aligns with the disclosure practice for companies that provide goods and services directly to the Bank with the current policy governing procurement on Bank financed projects in developing countries. In parallel with the Bank's disclosure of the names of companies and individuals debarred on Bank financed projects from now on, the Bank Group will publicly list the names of companies debarred from its corporate procurement for 'palm greasing' and other corrupt practices.

A complete list of the 111 companies and individuals currently debarred from participating in Bank-financed projects are available in www.worldbank.org. It shows that UK leads the list with 37 companies, while India has now entered this list with three companies.

SUBVERSION OF THE INDIAN FINANCIAL SYSTEM BY CORRUPTION

The Indian financial system also suffers from a hang-over of cronyism and corruption that have brought the government budgets on the verge of bankruptcy. This too needs fixing. India's infrastructure requires about $150 billion dollars to make it world class, and the education system needs 6 per cent of GDP instead of 2.8 per cent today. But an open competitive market system can find these resources provided the quality of governance and accountability is improved. Obviously a second generation of reforms are necessary for all this.

This goal cannot be achieved unless there is accountability in governance such accountability requires transparent and ethical reporting of the finances of an organization. For this, the ICAI's "Concept Paper on Convergence with IFRS in India" is worth reading. India thus needs to adopt increasingly the International Standards of Financial Reporting and Disclosure Standards for attracting FDI.

But that is not the practice today. For example, though SEBI has made compliance for listed companies the Corporate Governance Guidelines mandatory and effective from January 1, 2006, about one-fourth, i.e., 1,213 listed companies have not complied for the period ending March 31, 2008. Yet there has been no action by SEBI, which can under Clause 49 of the Listing Agreement de-list these companies. There is instead a collusion of greedy promoters and chartered accountants. The latest Satyam scandal is only a storm signal of the general and widespread collapse of the values of a corporate system. These failures of governance arises from greed. Greed flourishes where there is no spirituality.

Similarly, as I have pointed out in my earlier writings, the Participatory Notes (PN) which account for 55 per cent of the foreign funds into the Stock Market in India have no requirement to comply with even the SEBI disclosure rules, and are obviously meant for laundering black money of politicians, industrialists and even including those of terrorists. Even after Tarapore Committee ridiculed the PNs the SEBI had to keep silent because the Finance Minister favoured P-Notes to launder ill-gotten money of his and his masters. The lack of ethics and patriotism thus appears maximum inside the government today.

One of the most scandalous frauds on the financial system of India thus is the derivative called P-Notes. Along with the "round tripping" of illegal funds, i.e., unaccounted funds of Indians sent to Mauritius by the hawala route and then the illegal funds being brought back to India, taking advantage of the concessions under the Double Taxation Avoidance Treaty, e.g. exemption of Capital Gains tax, both in India and in Mauritius.

In 2002, India and Mauritius extended the controversial Indo-Mauritius Double Taxation Avoidance Treaty (DTAT) first signed in 1983. Under this treaty no resident of Mauritius would be taxed in India on capital gains arising out of sale of securities in India. In other words, capital gains arising out of sale of shares of securities for an Indian would normally be subject to Capital Gains Tax but, if investments are routed through Mauritius, they would be exempt from the said tax in India. After the DTAT was signed, the Government of Mauritius too abolished capital gains tax in their country. So, in effect, there are no taxes on Mauritius-based FIIs investing in India. After the UPA came to power, Mauritius has emerged as the largest foreign investor in India. *The tax losses to India as a result of the DTAT are estimated at a fabulous Rs. 4000 crores to date.*

These two devices: P-Notes and DTAT have managed financial buccaneers to rig the Indian stock market giving windfall gains of billions of dollars to racketeers, and ruin for the middle class.

An example of this is when some foreign investors sold stocks aggregating to Rs.18,000 + crores on just 2 days viz. January 23 and 24, 2008. I quote a media report of that time: "In the third week of 2008, the Sensex experienced huge falls along with other markets around the world. On January 21, 2008, the Sensex saw its highest loss of 1,408 points at the end of the session... The next day, the Sensex index went into a free fall. It hit the lower circuit breaker a minute after the markets opened at 10 AM. Trading was therefore suspended for an hour. On re-opening at 10.55 AM, the market saw its biggest ever fall when it hit a low of 15,332, down 2,273 points. However on "reassurance" from the Finance Minister of India, the market came back to close at 16,730 with a loss of 875 points." Today, the Sensex is below 10,000. Who are the beneficiaries?

In his address to the 43rd Munich Conference on Security Policy on February 11, 2007, M. K. Narayanan, the National Security Advisor to the Government of India, listed out the various ways by which terrorists in India were funded. He admitted: "Instances of terrorist outfits manipulating the stock markets to raise funds for their operations have been reported. Stock exchanges in Mumbai and Chennai have, on occasions, reported that fictitious or notional companies were engaging in stock market operations. Some of these companies were later traced to terrorist outfits." This is a truly shocking admission.

Thus, so the Government of India is well aware that terrorists are parking funds in Indian ventures. Yet the Finance Ministry has done nothing about the system of P-notes, which gives terrorists the additional benefit of anonymity while making hefty investments in the Indian market, which could later be used to fund terrorist activities against the Indian people in India! According to conservative estimates, there are over Rs. 2,50,000 Crore Rupees worth of P-notes issued abroad by FIIs and brokers being actively traded in the Indian market! At present P-Notes fuels about 53 per cent of all foreign investments in the stock markets of India.

The nation is, till date, not aware of any details whatsoever of the investors who seek to invest through P-Notes, which under the regulations, permits such investors to remain anonymous. This is unprecedent for any democratic nation. Also the people have no data on Indian plutocrats who are re-routing their unaccounted money through Mauritius, cleverly avoiding Capital Gains Tax both in that country and ours by taking advantage of the Indo-Mauritius Double Taxation Avoidance Treaty.

While an Indian citizen in India has to provide his/her address proof, photo ID proof, PAN details, etc to open even an ordinary savings bank account in a local bank, foreign investors can hide their identity under a sub-account by making use of Participatory Notes to route their investments, often running into hundreds of crores. The main reason for the popularity of a P-note is in fact the anonymity it provides. P-notes are instruments issued by registered Foreign Institutional Investors (FIIs) to overseas investors who wish to invest in the Indian Stock Market without registering themselves with the market regulator—the Securities and Exchange Board of India (SEBI). Almost all top FIIs like Fidelity Investments, Merrill Lynch, Morgans Stanley and Credit Lyonnais issue P-notes, a derivative without parallel in the world.

As stated earlier, concerned about the possibility of influx of large quantities of terrorist funds into India through this route, SEBI had asked the FIIs to disclose the identities of the holders of P-notes. But there was no compliance. Surprisingly, the Finance Ministry did nothing about this. Investment though the P-notes route are believed to be largely responsible for the sudden, unexplained fluctuations in the stock-market indices, including the huge falls which have even resulted in suicides in Dalal Street. As a consequences, our Stock Markets are rigged by anti-national forces directly or indirectly.

Repeatedly pressed by patriotic persons, the Finance Ministry however has failed to answer why this special exemption to P-Notes is being provided especially when:

(i) The Tarapore Committee appointed by the Ministry had recommended that P-Notes be abolished in the national interest and financial stability.

(ii) The National Security Adviser of the Government, M. K. Narayanan stated publicly that terrorists were making money on the Indian Stock Exchanges by using derivatives (like P-Notes).

(iii) The former SEBI Chairman Damodaran during his tenure had written several times that P-Notes being outside the normal disclosures rules was playing havoc with the stability of the Stock market and also leading to its manipulation. But Damodaran was given marching order.

(iv) A Tribunal headed by a sitting Delhi High Court Judge had in an Order on May 15, 2008 exonerated Goldman Sachs of compliance of SEBI regulations on disclosure, and instead fined the SEBI a sum of Rs.1 lakh for asking for disclosure!

Union Finance Ministry had in a press note claimed: "FIIs are regulated entities; SEBI being the regulator… FIIs are required to report at the end of every month, in the prescribed format, all the information relating to P-notes issued by them including the names of subscribers to the said P-notes" [rebuttaldated June 5, 2008 of a press statement].

From this, one has to assume that SEBI has the names and details of all the foreign investors who have invested in India through these P-Notes. If this is the stated position, the Union Finance Ministry ought to furnish answers to the question about the identity of P-Notes owners.

But the Union Finance Ministry has refused to publish the list of P-note holders, along with their details and the amount of investment, on its website, or on the website of SEBI, or anywhere else.

P-notes are subscribed to by a company but the Union Finance Ministry does not track the names of the owners/promoters of beneficiaries of that company. Hence the company in question could well be promoted or funded by an Osama bin-Laden, a Dawood Ibrahim or by the late Velupillai Prabhakaran? If so, how to ensure that narco-terrorist money does not find its way into the Indian Stock Market, as the National Security Advisor M. K. Narayan had feared?

M. Damodaran, who had headed SEBI, had told the *Business Standard* (in September, 2007), that he was not "entirely confortable" that one-fourth of the market was being held by anonymous P-note investors. He told me personally so too the same thing.

The idea to introduce P-Notes and the Mauritius round-tripping facility for *hawala* route for illegal funds of politicians, criminals and terrorists was the brain child of the NDA Finance Minister Yashwant Sinha— of Gold Auction fame of 1991. Some of us may remember that, on the projected assumption of office by Dr. Manmohan Singh the UPA Government on May 18, 2004, it was greeted with a steep fall in the Indian Stock Market (Sensex fell by 567.74 points). It was *later* found that UBS Securities Asia Ltd, which is a SEBI registered FII dealing through its SEBI registered proprietary sub-account Swiss Finance Corporation (Mauritius) Ltd, *had sold stocks* in the Cash Market segment to the extent of Rs. 188.35 crores. SEBI decided to investigate. During the investigation, SEBI called for further information from UBS relating to its major P-note clients in terms of their addresses, the names of their directors, fund managers, major shareholders, top five investors etc., UBS did not furnish the information citing reasons such as client confidentially. This is a substantiated allegation that I am making, since I am basing it on what is contained in SEBI Order No.WTM/GA/1/STD/5/05.

But the Union Finance Ministry has taken no action since May 2004 [when the UPA Government assumed office] to arm SEBI with appropriate legal teeth to face such situations in future. On the contrary, it took P-Notes out of the purview of SEBI much to the dismay of the members of the Tarapore Committee on Financial Reforms.

The Report of the Expert Group on Encouraging FII Flows and Checking the Vulnerability of Capital Markets to Speculative Flows of the Reserve Bank of India, sent to Dr. Ashok Lahiri, Chief Economic Adviser, Department of Economic Affairs, Ministry of Finance, Government of India states: "The Reserve Bank's stance has been that the issue of Participatory Notes *should not be permitted.*"

In this context we would like to point out that the main concerns regarding issue of PNs are that the nature of the beneficial ownership or the identity of the investor will not be known, unlike in the case of FIIs registered with a financial regulator. Trading of these PNs will lead to multi-layering which will make it difficult to identify the ultimate holder of PNs. Both conceptually and in practice, restrictions on suspicious flows enhance the reputation of markets and lead to healthy flows."

This capacity for mischief by using P-Notes was revealed when foreign investors had sold stocks on January 23 and 24, 2008, aggregating to Rs.18,600 crores. Who are these people who sold stocks in such massive quantities, which led to an unprecedented fall of the Indian stock market on these two days, leading to unprecedented huge losses to the ordinary Indian investors, even leading to suicides by several investors who lost all? And why? Soon thereafter, new mysterious buyers with P-Note holders arrived and bought these stocks at crashed prices. And because of the Mauritius routing for the purchase, no capital gains could be levied.

SEBI in fact had, in September 2006, slapped a fine of Rs.1 crore on Goldman Sachs Investment (Mauritius) for the latter's failure to report the issuance of P-notes to the Mauritius-based Magnus Capital Corporation Ltd (see Annexure). This was considered a violation of the declaration to furnish regular statements to SEBI on the P-notes issued by them. However, on May 5, 2008, the Securities Appellate Tribunal (SAT), set aside SEBI's order against Goldman Sachs Mauritius. It opined that SEBI was not at all justified in asking FIIs and their sub-accounts to file undertakings of the kind prescribed in the revised reporting format contained in the circular of August 8, 2003. It also overturned SEBI's fine of $1 crore, and instead asked the official market regulator SEBI to pay Rs.1 lakh to Goldman Sachs for harassing them!!

The case is not only a slap on the face of SEBI, but also a clear indication that the Union Finance Minister's claim that investments from abroad are being adequately monitored by SEBI is false and deliberately misleading.

CORRUPTION AS A GRAVE NATIONAL SECURITY THREAT

India's security-external, internal and economic- is far more important than the personal likes and dislikes of people in power. The nation is reeling under unprecedented recession. The people are floored by the spiraling crisis. Development is lopsided, with the rich getting richer and the poor getting poorer. The stock market, which had touched dizzy heights a year ago, has fallen by over 11,000 points in this period. Terrorism is on the rise with no monetary constraints and there are clear indications that these anti-national activities are being funded from abroad. Yet the Government of India does nothing. It is time for all right-thinking, patriotic citizens to sit up and take notice. We have to act now. Tomorrow might be too late. We might become another Colombia.

In the US, following 9/11, a law titled *Uniting and Strengthening America by Providing Appropriate Tools Required to Intercept and Obstruct Terrorism Act* (2001) more commonly known as the *USA Patriot Act,* was enacted. The key area where tightening was done was with relation to the inflow of foreign funds. The American reasoning was that any terrorist activity requires huge funds to flourish. And if the inflow of funds dries up, the terrorism dies out or at least loses its momentum. The Federal Reserve Board (the American equivalent of the RBI) authorities minutely audited accounts of every bank. Every investment into the country was investigated. The source of funds were traced to ascertain whether the money was legal or not.

In the United Kingdom, on March 30, 2006 the Terrorism Act was passed in the aftermath of the July 7, 2005 London bombings. This law creates new offences related to terrorism, and amends existing ones. The

British Government considered the law a necessary response to an unparalleled terrorist threat, notwithstanding criticism from human rights activists.

In comparison, in India, acts of terrorism are taking place with monotonous regularity, everywhere. Practically, every State in the country has experienced the phenomenon of senseless, wanton violence. Crowded trains and railway stations, bus stands, bazars, places of worship, tourist destinations, even India's Parliament House have been used by sundry terrorist outfits as their playground, often with devastating effect. So many innocent people have died. So many valiant personnel from our security forces have also perished. And what does the Indian Government do?

It abrogates the *Prevention of Terrorism Act of* 2002 (POTA)! It opens the doors to unchecked entry of all sorts of funds from abroad in the name of globalization, enabling terrorist outfits from abroad to not only fund terrorism in India but to also cripple India economically. This is nothing short of economic terrorism. Much has already been said about the scrapping of POTA, and I shall not go deeper into this now. It is the open door policy for foreign funds about which of interest here.

The bitter truth thus is that India's corporate world's success stories are founded on fudged accounts and on undisclosed and unreported funding through black money held by corrupt politicians and notorious criminals.

But he was assassinated and that booty has gone to his named beneficiary and which has grown since then Rs. 25,000 crores. Indians have about $1.5 trillion in Swiss banks alone, not to mention Liechtenstien, Isle of Man, Cayman Islands, Macao, etc. All this money can be brought back by legal methods within two months, but who can cast the first stone today?

Earlier, this money used lie in the bank vaults, but now thanks to Participatory Notes [PNs] and the Mauritius route, this money is returning to India and in the BSE to earn windfall profits. Even terrorists are funding Indian corporates via the share purchases through the PNs. According to me, the BSE has become the most rigged stock market in the world after the Shanghai exchange.

This kind of money enables politicians and business persons to carry cash around the world for pleasure, and sometimes caught with it. For example, on September 27, 2001, a young politician and his girl friend were arrested by the FBI at Boston's Logan airport with $160,000 in cash, without declaring it to the US Customs. US law requires cash at hand of more than $10,000 to be declared. But he was let off after nine hours in FBI custody as a result of political intervention.

With a thousand crore rupees as legal tender, much as Rs.10 is for the middle class, politicians and criminals have entered to finance the Indian corporate world. That rotten core of our growth story is the real threat to the nation's security. Any enemy of India can thus ruin the nation by leveraging the financial web that fuels our greed for more profits and search for short-cuts to satisfy that greed. Satyam's real truth is just that, and not the criminality and betrayal of trust by Raju. That root cause has to be addressed and removed before the nation goes under, as we did go from the height of our prosperity in 1200 A.D. to utter poverty in 1947. Such a depressing event can happen again if there is compliance, capitulation and conspiracy of silence to fraud.

How is it possible for accountants not to know what was going on? What about the glossy business magazines and pink and costly financial newspapers which kept quiet on Dr. Sarma's complaint and Metro Rail chief Sridharan's outrage at the Maytas fraud? They must have all known but chose to look the other way at soft targets. On whom did the 185 Fortune 500 companies, which were Satyam's clients, rely for clearance? What about the 24/7 TV news channels which threw a fit by the minute on the security cover given to politicians. Why did they refuse to see this nexus? Was it their greed, or cowardice, since corporates are hard targets?

The dimly visible good news is that even today the vast majority of Indians are moral and honest. Hence, the Satyams, Harshad Mehtas, and others should wake those of us up who can do something and galvanize collectively into action. Democracy and national integrity are not spectator sports like a cricket match. Nor can we be running commentators only. Each of us is a player, and have to determine what we can do for the country. That is the truth about Satyam.

Hence, of all the frauds in India, the P-Notes cum Mauritius Treaty are the most sinister and anti-national of scams. It obviously had patronage of the Delhi establishment since neither the Congress Party not the BJP wants to speak about it. This collusion is at the root of the corruption in the nation.

Business ethics, if practiced faithfully, could be contrary to organizational growth that is fueled by profit maximization contradictions that are required to be resolved if India is to become a developed country. But there are political compulsions that have to be overcome. Political compulsions that exist are due to electoral politics since the poor in India constitute about 40 per cent of the electorate. They are also more conscientious voters and turn out in much higher percentages to vote in elections than do the better—off sections. A reformer political leader to succeed in elections will not only have to practice ethical norms but also design reforms in such a way that these poor can perceive gains to them as quickly as the vested interests, who are entrenched in the power structure to see their losses.

This is not a easy task since gains from ethical behaviour and spiritual values come with a time lag, while loss of "rents" from controls and quotas that have been vested, are immediate upon implementing de-regulation. Thus the rentier class living off scams is better organized to fail efforts to root out corruption. They usually engage the best lawyers for fighting it out in courts.

This is the crux of the challenge of governance.

Chapter II

The 2G Spectrum Licence Fraud

More than three years ago in autumn 2008, I had begun the study regarding the dimensions of two gigantic financial scams, Satyam and Spectrum, which had plagued the nation, and published my researches as a book *Corruption and Corporate Governance in India: Satyam, Spectrum and Sundaram.*

WHAT IS THE SCAM ?

My curiousity was fired by the fraud and forgery that became apparent in the sudden disinvestment of equity stake in Swan Capital Company by Anil Dhirubhai Ambani in favour of the DB Realty Company reportedly on the then Telecom Minister A. Raja's behest. Why? There hangs the Spectrum Scam tale.

I wrote to the Prime Minister a letter dated November 29, 2008, for Sanction under Section19 of the Prevention of Corruption Act (1988) to prosecute Telecom Minister A. Raja by filing a private complaint before the Designated Sessions Court which soon opened the can of worms that the '2G saga' is.

This proposed complaint made a reference to Swan Telecom being awarded a 2G Spectrum licence despite a bar that no licence can be given if an existing licence holder had 10 per cent or more equity share. The UAS guideline provided "no single company/legal person either directly or through associates shall have substantial equity holding in more than one licensee company in the same service area." The ceiling for substantial equity was notified at 10 per cent.

Reliance Communication, through its subsidiary Reliance Telecom, held more than 10 per cent (and not 9.9 per cent as claimed by Reliance) of equity shareholding of Swan Telecom. It had also been certified that Reliance Communication or its subsidiary Reliance Telecom did not hold any shares in Tiger Trustee, the company which held 90 per cent of the shares of Swan Telecom. It also claimed that preference shares is not capital but more in the nature of debt and cannot be added to equity shares for the purpose of computing the percentage shareholding.

This is how it happened:

Swan Capital was the original name at the time of incorporation and it's name was changed to Swan Telecom on 15/2/07 since the company was needed for the telecom sector. The company needed a capital on paper of over Rs. 1,100 crores to comply with minimum capital requirement norms for applying for license in the thirteen circles.

Swan Telecom was registered as Swan Capital Pvt Ltd, was incorporated on July 13, 2006. One share was allotted to Himansu Agarwal and 4999 shares to Powersurfer Interactive (India) Private Limited and that the address of both the shareholders was Reliance Energy Centre, Santa Cruz (East) Mumbai 400055.

In addition another 5,000 shares was subscribed by Reliance Energy Management Services Private Limited with the same address. The persons signing the Memorandum and Articles were all having the same address of Reliance Energy Centre, Santa Cruz (East) Mumbai 400055.

The promoters of Reliance Communications held more than 66 per cent of the shares of the company throughout the period of the scam that is from March 2, 2007 to December 16, 2007. Refer to the filings on the shareholding pattern of Reliance Communication with the National Stock Exchange.

The UASL guideline means that not only the company cannot hold more than 10 per cent in another company but that the promoters of the company too cannot hold more than 10 per cent of the shares in another company with a license. It definitely means the latter because if it was the former then Tatas, Mittals and the Ambanis , not to forget the Essars (who incidently are in a similar Swan Telecom-like situation) would float companies by the dozens and corner as many licenses as possible.

It is true that more than 90 per cent (90.09 per cent to be precise) of the shares of Swan Telecom were held by Tiger Trustee Pvt Ltd [Refer Auditors' Report for March 31, 2007 and March 31, 2008].

Dr. Subramanian Swamy Ph.D. (Harvard)
President, Janata Party
Minister for Commerce, Law & Justice (1990-91)
Chairman (with Cabinet rank), Commission on Labour Standards and International Trade (1994-96)
Member of Parliament (1974-99)
Professor of Economics, Indian Institute of Technology, Delhi (1969-91)
Faculty, Harvard University (1963-69, 1985-86, 2001-08 Summer)

JANATA PARTY
A-77, Nizamuddin (East) New Delhi - 110 013, India
Phone +91 24353805 Fax +91 24357388
Mobile +91 9810194279 +91 9940203333
Website www.janataparty.org, www.indiaright.org
E-mail swamy@post.harvard.edu
swamy39@gmail.com

November 29, 2008.

Prime Minister,
Government of India,
New Delhi.

Sub: Permission of Sanction u/s 13, Prevention of Corruption Act (1988).

Sir,

The Chief Vigilance Commissioner vide letter dated November 15, 2008 had issued a Show Cause Notice to Telecom Minister A. Raja, who had allotted new licences in 2G mobile services on a 'first come, first served' basis to two novice telecom companies, Swan and Unitech. His move is a complete violation of Clause 8 of the Guidelines for United Access Services Licence issued by the Ministry of Communication and Information Technology Development of Telecommunication, Government of India (No.10-21/2005-BS.I(Vol.II)/49, dated December 14, 2005), thus causing a loss of over Rs.50,000 crores to the Government, and consequently according pecuniary benefit to others illegally.

Clause 8 has been violated as follows: While Anil Dhirubhai Ambani Group (ADAG), the promoters of Reliance Communications (R Com), had more than 10 per cent stake in Swan Telecom, the figures were manipulated and showed as 9,99 per cent holding to beat the said Clause. The documents available disclose that on March2, 2007, when Swan Telecom applied for United Access Services Licences, it was owned 100 per cent by Reliance Communications and its associates viz. Reliance Telecom, and by Tiger Trustees Limited, Swan Infonet Services Private Limited, and Swan Advisory Services Private Limited (see Annexure 1). At one or the other point of time, employees of ADAG (Himanshu Agarwal, Ashish Karyekar, Paresh Rathod) or its associate companies have been acquiring the shares of Swan

Telecom itself. But still the ADAG manipulated the holdings in Swan to reduce it to only 9.99 per cent. Ambani has now quietly sold his shares in Swan to Delphi Investments, a Mauritius based company owned by Ahmed O. Alfi, specializing in automobile spare parts. In turn, Swan has sold 45% of its shares to UAE's Emirates Telecom Corporation (Eti Salat) for Rs.9000 crores! All this is highly suspicious and not normal business transactions. Swan company got 60% of the 22 Telecom licenced areas at a throw away price of Rs.1650 crores, when it was worth Rs.60,000 crores total.

Rcom has operations in the same circles where the application for Swan Telecom was filed. Therefore under Clause 8 of the Guidelines, Swan should not have been allotted spectrum by the Telecommunication Ministry. But the company did get it on Minister's direction, which is an undue favour from him (Raja. There was obviously a quid pro quo which only a CBI enquiry can reveal, after an FIR is registered. There is no need for a P/E, because the CVC has already done the preliminary enquiry.

It has to be investigated whether two officers of the Department of Telecom – RJS Kushwaha and D. Jha, who were opposed to showing undue favour to Swan Telecom – were transferred just prior to the allotment of the spectrum.

BSNL, which has never done any roaming agreement with any operator, was forced to do a roaming agreement with Swan Telecom, ironically BSNL does not extend this facility to any other operator. It is quite clear from the agreement that those who are at the helm of affairs of BSNL worked in favour of Swan Telecom. Quite surprisingly, the 2G spectrum licences were priced at 2001 levels to benefit these private players. That was when there were only 4 million cellphone subscribers; now it is 350 million. Hence 2001 price is not applicable today.

Immediately after acquiring 2G spectrum licences both Swan and Unitech sold their stakes to foreign companies at a huge profits.

While Swan Telecom sold its stakes to UAE telecom operator Etisalat, Unitech signed a deal with Telenor of Norway for selling its share at huge premiums.

In the process of this 2G spectrum allocation, the government received only one-sixth of what it would have got had it gone through a fresh auction route. The total loss to the exchequer of giving away 2G GSM spectrum in this way – including to the CDMA operators – is over Rs.50,000 crores and is said to be one of the biggest financial scams of all times in the country.

While approving the 2G licences, Minister Raja turned a blind eye to the fact that these two companies do not have any infrastructure to launch their services. Falsely claiming that the Telecom Regulatory Authority of India had approved the first-cum-first served rule, Raja went ahead with the 2G spectrum allocation to two debutants in the Telecom sector. In fact earlier TRAI had discussed the spectrum allocation issue with existing services providers and suggested to the Telecom Ministry that spectrum allocation be made through a transparent tender and auction process. This is confirmed by what the TRAI Chairman N. Misra told the CII organized conference on November 28, 2008 {Annexure 2}. But Raja did not bother to listen to the TRAI either and pursued the process on 'first come, first served' basis, benefiting those who had inside information, causing a loss of Rs.50,000 crores to the Government. His dubious move has been to ensure benefit to others at the cost of the national exchequer.

According to an uncontradicted report in CNN-IBN news channel of November 26, 2008, you are said to be "very upset with A. Raja over the spectrum allocation issue". This confirms that an investigation is necessary, for which I may be given Sanction so that the process of law can be initiated.

I therefore write to demand the grant of Sanction to prosecute Mr. A. Raja, Minister for Telecom of the Union of India for offences under the Prevention of Corruption Act. The charges in brief are annexed herewith {Annexure 3}.

Warm Regards

Yours sincerely,

(SUBRAMANIAN SWAMY)

Encls: a/a

However, the clean chit given to Swan Telecom *vide* MoCA letter in file no 3/92/2010/CL-II dated December 24, 2010 has been issued with the approval of the Corporate Affairs Ministry (last line of the letter). Thus, by giving Swan Telecom a clean chit the Ministry of Corporate Affairs (MoCA) and its senior officers are involved in a criminal conspiracy to cover up for Anil Ambani.

The GSM license for which application was made by Swan Telecom was not pan India but for only those circles in which Reliance Communication did not have GSM license. The application was made for thirteen circles as Reliance Communication had GSM license for Bihar, Himmachal Pradesh, Kolkatta, Madhya Pradesh, Orissa, West Bengal. The fact that licenses for only thirteen circles were applied for and that only those circles in which Reliance had GSM license was excluded shows that the ADAG group was the owner and in control of Swan Telecom through its proxy directors.

Second and more important, the company needed to have capital and reserves of over 1,100 crores in the balance-sheet to apply for the license for 13 circles, according to the fee that was paid in 2001 in the bidding process for the fourth operator.

Whether the ADAG group clairvoyant powers of anticipating the future telecom policy of A. Raja of allotting licenses on 2001 prices on a first-come first-serve basis or were a conspirator in dictating the policy can be decided by the quantum of investment made in Swan Telecom and the circles for which the application made seven months before the policy was announced.

The dilemma was to get 1,100 crores in Swan Telecom and also not apparently violate the licensing norms of an existing telecom company not owning more than 10 per cent of the shares in another telecom company.

The money was there in the public-listed company Reliance Communication from where it had to be re routed. It was not there in any of the privately held ADAG companies. The old model of using money from the public listed company and retaining control off the shares by privately held company was used. While 90 per cent of the money was invested by a subsidiary of Reliance Communication, a public-listed company (1,002 crores), a little less than 10 per cent of the shares of Swan Telecom were allotted to the ADAG group subsidiary of Reliance Communication. This was done by Reliance Communication subscribing to preference shares at 8 per cent interest at an unimaginable premium of 99,900 per cent. for an amount of Rs. 992 crores.

The rest of the shares 90 per cent were allotted to a company registered on June 20, 2006 as Tiger Traded Private Limited which was rechristened as Tiger Trustee with the approval of the Registrar of Companies (will be referred to as Tiger Trustee to avoid confusion).

It is this company which in effect was the owner of Swan Telecom, which has been ignored in the investigation by the MCA deliberately. In fact, it is this company which is at the root of the fraud and bribe giving. It is, therefore, not surprising that the Minister has chosen to ignore the holding company of Swan Telecom—Tiger Trustee—while giving a clean chit. The omission is deliberate, *mala fide* and smacks of a *quid pro quo.*

Tiger Trustee registered address was Reliance Energy Centre, 3rd Floor, Santa Cruz (East), Mumbai 400055. It had two directors—Ashok Karyekar and Paresh Rathod. The residential address of both the directors was Reliance Energy Quarters, Chembur. While Ashish Karyekar held directorship in 13 companies of the ADAG group whose name began with Reliance, Parash Rathod was a director in 12 ADAG companies.

The paid up capital of Tiger Trustee was one lac. The capital remained at one lac, till October 17, 2007, that is well beyond the unrevised cut off date of October 1, 2007 for applying for fresh telecom (UAV) license. Tiger Trustee owned 90 per cent of the share capital of Swan Capital, while contributing only 10 per cent of the funds and the balance was contributed by the public-listed ADAG company Reliance Communication subsidiary.

Given the address of the holding company Tiger Trustee , the directors and their addresses, the paid-up capital of mere one lac and the fact that over 1,000 crores of money was siphoned off from the public-listed company (in spite of the so-called independent directors) into Swan Telecom to make it complaint with capital norms; can there be any doubt that Swan Telecom was anything but a Anil Ambani Company?

If Anil Ambani was not the owner of Tiger Trustee, then who could it be? This is because Anil Ambani will invest 1,000 crores either to benefit himself or someone involved as a crony or *benami*. To date none of the people involved in the cover up have answered the question as to who was the owner of Tiger Trustee from March 2, 2007, the date on which the application was filed to October 18, 2007, the date on which pan-India license was given to Reliance Communication and on which date the company Tiger Trustee was transferred to Balwa and Goenka for a paltry investment of 4.99 crores? That was the bribe for the license given to Reliance Communication on October 18, 2007, one day before the policy was announced.

Swan Telecom thus was a shell company, incorporated, owned and controlled by the ADAG group. It was among the various shell companies that the Reliance group keeps on forming for multifarious activities depending on what is the requirement of the day. Most of them are investment companies in which the ownership is to be layered so that the identity of the true owner has to be concealed as India is the ultimate destination of hot money and crony capitalism. It is the vehicle through which the political masters are bribed and become part owners of the business they help to benefit through their illegal decision-making process.

It is because of this reason alone that these shell companies are formed and kept ready in time of need. They can also be the vehicle of major frauds and bribes. In fact, transfer of Swan Telecom was the bribe paid for the license given to Reliance Communications on October 18, 2007 and it was transferred to the *benami* of the politicians on the very same day.

Thus began my investigation into the biggest scam of not only Indian but the world.

The Spectrum scam has, of the two, turned out to shock the nation's conscience as nothing else so far has done. Why? Because it promises to sully Indians' global ticket to modern status because unlike Satyam, the Spectrum Scam catches the Union Cabinet's hand in the till with all the top corporate big-wigs as complicit.

In recent times, India has emerged as one of the most dynamic, promising and fastest growing telecom markets in the world. It has third largest overall telecom network and the second largest wireless network in the world. Mobile telephony and thus Spectrum have played a vital role in the stupendous growth of the telecom services in India. The 2G spectrum scam of this huge magnitude ironically was the outcome of the huge rise in demand since 1991 for mobile phone services in the country.

The four "pillars" of the scam are: *First,* the low pricing of the spectrum by Telecom Minister Raja by choosing to peg the Spectrum (including the entry fee) price at the 2001 discovered level, which was about one-tenth the 2008 price, when the Spectrum was allotted to nine companies. This enabled the licensees to get a huge windfall, and the Treasury thereby lost notionally a monumental record-breaking Rs. 176,000 crores.

Second, the artificial and fraudulent system of First-Come First-Served (FCFS), wholly unsuited for efficient allocation of any scarce resource, to grant licenses for spectrum allotment, which thereby ensured that a favoured few of the Telecom Minister A. Raja, got the licences on a tip-off in advance from him, and thus the pay-offs for the favour shown to them by the Minister.

Third, the arbitrary pre-poning of the cut-off date from October 1, 2007 and announced on January 10, 2008 thereby reducing unreasonably and with *mala fide* intentions, the number of applications.

And *fourth,* the complete bypassing of the constitutional scheme of checks and balances, such as the TRAI Act, the Telecom Commission and the Transaction of Government Business Rules framed under the Constitution, to ensure that at no stage the predetermined choice of companies for licence allotment of Minister Raja and his beneficiary colluders, are not challenged.

The approximate and estimated Rs. 60,000 crores in bribes paid out of the windfall gains of nine companies (notionally estimated at Rs. 176,000 crores), was shared amongst the "stakeholders" according the importance of the patronage provided by them. Principally, *this is the scam*—public offices have been misused to cause a huge financial loss to the nation, to acquire wealth at public expense for self, family and friends, and even by recklessly compromising national security.

WHAT IS SPECTRUM?

The word 'Spectrum' basically refers to a collection of various types of electromagnetic radiations of different wavelengths that is the medium for transmission of data. Radio frequency Spectrum is a limited global natural resource with a high economic value, due to its heavy demand in the telecommunication sector. It is a finite but non-consumable natural resource. But it will be wasted if not used efficiently. In India, the radio frequencies are being used for around forty different types of services like space communication, mobile communication, broadcasting, radio navigation, mobile satellite service, aeronautical satellite services, defence, communication etc.

In India, the Cellular Mobile Service Providers (CMSPS) use two types of technologies *viz.* Global System for Mobile Communication (GSM) and Code Division Multiple Access (CDMA). The allocation of Spectrum to the CMSPs depend on the type of technology they use.

GSM is a digital mobile telephony system which uses a variation of Time Division Multiple Access (TDMA) and is widely used world over. It operates in the 900 MHz or 1800 MHz frequency band. CDMA technology allows many users to occupy the same time and frequency allocations in a given band/space. As its very name implies, CDMA assigns unique codes to each communication to differentiate it from others in the same Spectrum bands. It operates in the 800 MHz and 1900 MHz bands. Presently 25 MHz Spectrum in 900 MHz band (890-915/935-960 MHz) and 75 MHz in the 1800 MHz band (1710-1785/1805-1880 MHz) are earmarked for the GSM services. Spectrum for the rollout of 3G services (voice, data and video were allotted through e-auction in the 2.1GHz (1920-1980/2110-2170 MHz) band.

All the above bands were historically allotted to the defence for their mobile and point to point communication needs in India. Therefore, their cooperation was also required to make the bands available for commercial use. To facilitate the same, the Government of India have been allocating funds from time to time to provide Optical Fiber Cable (OFC) for use by the defence and consequent vacation of Spectrum for commercial purposes.

Some of the important and typical characteristics of the radio frequency Spectrum are as below:

(i) Unlike other natural resources, radio frequency spectrum is not consumed upon its usage. It is also liable to be wasted if it is not used optimally and efficiently. Radio frequency spectrum usage is, therefore, to be shared amongst the various radio services and must be used efficiently, optimally and economically in conformity with the provisions of national and international laws.

(ii) Use of radio frequency spectrum is susceptible to overlapping interference and requires the application of complex engineering tools to ensure interference free operation of various wireless networks.

(iii) Radio frequency spectrum does not respect international geographical boundaries as it is spread over a large terrestrial area.

The limitation of the radio frequency Spectrum is mainly due to the following factors:

(i) Propagation characteristics of different types of radio waves.

(ii) Availability of technology and equipment for different types of radio frequency spectrum applications.

(iii) The suitability of frequency bands for specific applications.

Efficient allocation of Spectrum is therefore important and necessary to ensure interference free operation for each radio service. All nations share the electromagnetic Spectrum and reserve their right to its unlimited use. However, with a view to facilitating international telecommunication cooperation to support trade, transportation, communications and mutual protection against interference, all the countries have agreed to an International Telecommunication Convention. Thus, Spectrum frequencies for the use of various countries are allocated by the International Telecommunication Union (ITU) at the 'World Radio Communication Conferences' which are held every three/four years. The last conference was held in 2007. Allocations are made on a regional basis and for different types of services. It is mandatory for all the countries to adhere to these allocations. India comes in the region number three.

For the purpose of Spectrum allocation, each member country submits its proposal to the ITU, based on their requirements and priorities for opening of the bands. During the conferences, all the proposals are discussed and decisions are accordingly taken for opening of the bands for new services or extension of the existing bands. These decisions are reflected in the International Frequency Allocation Table of the radio regulation and other regulatory provisions for use of the bands which forms the basis for allotment by the member countries.

Each frequency band is shared amongst various radio services but the sharing is possible only with the use of similar systems. Sharing is also possible by way of geographical separation, time-sharing through technical solutions like smart antenna and intelligent radio system. In India, the radio frequencies are confined between 9 KHz and 400 GHz.

The Wireless Planning and Coordination (WPC) Wing in the Ministry of Communications and Information Technology (Department of Telecommunication) created in 1952 is responsible for Spectrum Management, Wireless licensing and frequency assignments. WPC is divided into major sections like Licensing and Regulation (LR), New Technology Group (NTG) and the standing Advisory Committee on Radio Frequency Allocation (SACFA). SACFA makes the recommendations on major frequency allocation issues, formulation of the frequency allocation plan and making recommendations on various issues related to the ITU to sort out the problems referred to the Advisory Committee by various wireless users.

The National Frequency Allocation Plan (NFAP)–1981 forms the basis for identification of the frequency bands to be allocated for various major users, Spectrum utilization and development and manufacturing of wireless equipment in the country. The NFAP was earlier officially considered as a classified document. But the New Telecom Policy 1999 decided that it should be made a public document and the Spectrum allocation should be made in a transparent manner.

On January 1, 2000, the DoT made the NFAP a public document after due consultations with all the stakeholders. The NFAP is reviewed periodically by the DoT and currently the NFAP, 2008 is in vogue. The Plan contains the service options in various frequency bands for India and also provides the channeling plan in different bands. Frequency bands allocated for certain types of radio services in India are as under:

	Frequency Band		Services
(i)	9 KHZ - 525 KHZ	-	Martine, Aeronautical Navigation, Medium Wave Broadcasting.
(ii)	525-1625 kHz	-	Marine and Aeronautical Navigation, short wave broadcasting, Amateur (Hour) radio and Cordless Phones.
(iii)	1.6-30 MHz	-	Fixed, Mobile, Maritime, Broadcasting.
(iv)	30 -87.5 MHz	-	Fixed Mobile , Broadcasting, Aeronautical Navigation.
(v)	87.5 - 108 MHz	-	FM radio.
(vi)	109 - 173 MHz	-	Aeronautical Mobile (R), Radio Navigation and Outdoor Broadcast vans.
(vii)	174 - 230 MHz	-	Television Broadcasting.
(viii)	230 - 450 MHz	-	Radio Astronomy, Fixed Mobile Aeronautical, Radio Navigation, Radio Pegging.
(ix)	450 - 585 MHz	-	Broadcasting.
(x)	585 - 698 MHz	-	Fixed Mobile.
(xi)	698 - 806 MHz	-	Fixed Mobile.
(xii)	806 - 960 MHz	-	GSM & CDMA mobile services (2G), Trucking.
(xiii)	960 - 1710 MHz	-	Mobile satellite, Fixed Mobile Radio Location, Radio Navigating Satellite, Aeronautical Mobile.
(xiv)	1710 - 1930 MHz	-	GSM Services (2G), Fixed Mobile.
(xv)	1930 - 2010 MHz	-	Fixed Mobile.
(xvi)	2010 - 2025 MHz	-	Fixed Mobile.
(xvii)	2025 - 2110 MHz	-	Satellite and Space Operation, Fixed Mobile.
(xviii)	2110 - 2170 MHz	-	3 G, Fixed Mobile.
(xix)	2170 - 2300 MHz	-	Fixed Mobile.
(xx)	2300 - 2400 MHz	-	BWA, Fixed, Mobile.

(xxi)	2483.5 - 2500 MHz	-	Fixed, Mobile.
	2500 -2690 MHz	-	MSS. BWA, BSS.
(xv)	3300 - 3600 MHz	-	ISP, Satellite.
(xvi)	3600 - 10000 MHz	-	Space research radio navigation, Satellite Communication.
(xvii)	10000 - 14000 MHz	-	Satellite Communication and DTH services.
(xviii)	14000 -23000 MHz	-	Fixed, Mobile Satellite.
(xix)	23000 -24000 MHz	-	Radio Location.
(xx)	24000 – 27000 MHz	-	Aeronautical, Radio Navigation.
(xxi)	2690 -3200 MHz	-	Radio Location.
(xxii)	3400 - 7125 MHz	-	Satellite Communication.
(xxiii)	7125 – 10000 MHz	-	Fixed Microwave links, X-Band Radar.

SPECTRUM LICENCE ALLOCATION POLICY

Before the mobile telephony came into existence in India, there was hardly any commercial value of Spectrum, rather it was practically none. That is why in the 1980s, it was allocated to various Departments without any charge. The demand for Spectrum was felt in 1994 when in accordance with the National Telecom Policy 1994, the Telecom service sector was for the first time opened up for private sector participation to complement the efforts of the Department to raise additional resources through increased international generation and adopting innovative means like leasing, deferred payments etc. The Licensing of Cellular Mobile Services in accordance with the objectives enunciated in NTP–1994 was initially done in two phases.

In the first phase, two Cellular Mobile Telephone Service (CMTS) licences were awarded in November 1994 in each of the four Metro Cities of Delhi, Mumbai, Kolkata and Chennai on a Beauty Parade basis which meant that the Spectrum prices to be fixed in such a manner so as to ensure its optimum utilization by awarding it to the user(s) who scored the highest against a group of present criteria such as rural coverage or the fulfillment of the roll out obligations. Licence fee for the

above two licences was predetermined. Spectrum Charges and Royalty for use of Spectrum were payable separately.

In the second phase, the two CMTS licences were awarded in December, 1995 in 18 Telecom Circles/Licence Service Areas based on a competitive bidding process. Bids were for licence free spread over 10 years licence period. It did not include Spectrum charges for which a separate wireless operating licence was to be obtained and Spectrum Charges were payable separately at applicable rates. In addition, right of the Government was reserved to operate the cellular mobile services as the third operator.

So far as award of Basic Service Licences was concerned, tenders were invited in January 1995 through bidding process and licence fee was payable over a period of 10 years. The Basic service licences with five companies were signed with effective date as September, 1997 and with one company as effective date from March, 1998.

The Industry became sick under the above cited fixed licence regime to be paid upfront every year regardless whether any revenues were made or not. In other words, the service providers made high bids and huge investments in the hope of large growth of business which did not materialize. The commitments for high licence fee could not be honoured because of inadequate revenue generation. It necessitated a relook and review of the existing Telecom Policy.

Accordingly, a High Level "Group on Telecom" was constituted by the Government to make recommendations on (i) the proposed New Telecom Policy, (ii) Issues relating to existing licences of Basic and Cellular services and suggest appropriate remedial measures within the framework of the New Telecom Policy and (iii) Issues relating to the Telecom Regulatory Authority of India (TRAI).

The recommendations of the Group on Telecom (GoT) on changes in the Telecom policy and to resolve the problems of the existing operators were considered by the Union Cabinet who approved the New Telecom Policy–1999. **The NTP–1999 became effective from April 1, 1999. The main objectives of the NTP–99 was to: (a) Create a modern and efficient telecommunications infrastructure taking into account the convergence of IT, media, telecom and consumer electronics and thereby propel India**

into becoming an IT superpower. (b) Strengthen research and development efforts in the country and provide an impetus to build world-class manufacturing capabilities. (c) Achieve efficiency and transparency in spectrum management. (d) Protect defence and security interests of the country.

NTP–99 thus stipulated the availability of affordable and effective communications for the citizens and open up the telecom sector to a greater competitive environment in both urban and rural areas providing equal opportunities and level playing field for all the players. Resolving the problems of the existing licensees was also envisaged under the NTP–99.

The New Policy framework categorized the Cellular Mobile Service Providers, (CMSPs), Fixed Service Providers (FSPs) and Cable Service Providers collectively referred to as the "Access Service Providers."

But the NTP–99 stipulated that the Government would invariably seek TRAI's recommendations on the number and timing of new licences before taking decision on issue of new licences in future. Thus NTP – 99 made it clear that before taking any decision on the issue of new licences, the Government shall seek the recommendations of TRAI on the number and timing of the new licences. Similarly, the entry of more operators in a circle/service area is required to be based on the recommendations of TRAI which was to review this requirement every two years. The NTP – 99, with a view to providing relief to the Access Service Providers who were facing financial troubles, brought in the revenue sharing regime which contemplated payment of one time entry free and licence fee based on revenue share.

In September, 2003, a Group of Ministers on Telecom matters was constituted under the Chairmanship of the Finance Minister vide the Cabinet Secretariat Memo dated September 10, 2003. The Terms of the References (TORs) of the GoM included the issue to "Chart the course to a Universal Licence."

The GoM on October 31, 2003 approved the October 27, 2003 recommendations of TRAI on Unified Access Service Licence (UASL) regime. The Cabinet considered the recommendations of the GoM on October 31, 2003 and *inter-alia* approved the following:

> The scope of NTP-99 may be enhanced to provide for licensing of Unified Access Services for basic and cellular licence services and unified Licensing comprising all telecom services. Department of Telecommunications may be authorized to issue necessary addendum to NTP-99 to this effect. The DoT was authorized to finalize the details of implementation with the approval of the Minister of Communications & IT in this regard including the calculation of the entry fee depending on the date of payment based on the principle given by TRAI in its recommendations.
>
> If new services are introduced as a result of technological advancement, which require additional spectrum over and above the spectrum already allotted/contracted, allocation of such spectrum will be considered on payment of additional fee or charges; these will be determined as per guidelines to be evolved in consultation with TRAI.

Based on the above Cabinet decision, an addendum to NTP-99 was notified on November 11, 2003. Guidelines for Unified Access (Basic and Cellular) Services Licence were issued on the same date. The Guidelines *inter-alia* stipulated that "with the issue of these Guidelines all applications for new Access Services Licence shall be in the category of Unified Access Service Licence." The UASL regime envisaged the provision of wire line, fixed and limited mobile wireless, full mobile wireless and cellular mobile telephone services under one licence on payment of the prescribed entry fees.

On November 17, 2003, DoT decided to accept and process the UASL applications similar to the manner adopted for Basis Service Licence. On November 24, 2003, the Minister of Communications and Information Technology reportedly approved the approach of granting UAS licences on First-Come-First Served basis as the announced guidelines had made it open for new licences to be issued on continuous basis at any time and Spectrum was to be allotted subject to availability.

Thus, signing of UASL did not guarantee allotment of Spectrum. Service providers intending to provide wireless services were required to apply to the WPC Wing for allocation of Spectrum after obtaining UAS licence.

Meanwhile after enhancement of FDI in the Telecom Sector from 49 per cent to 74 per cent, the DoT issued revised Guidelines for UAS licences on December 14, 2005. These guidelines *inter-alia* stipulated that:

- Licences shall be issued without any restriction on the number of entrants for provision of Unified Access Services in a Service Area.
- The applicant will be required to pay one time non-refundable entry fee, annual licence fee and Spectrum charges on revenue share basis as specified by the WPC Wing.

The above Guidelines issued on December 14, 2005 remain the extant Guidelines for grant of new UAS licences till today. Prior experience in the Telecom Sector was no more a prerequisite for grant of telecom service licence. As per the condition of UAS license, initial Spectrum of 4.4 MHz+ 4.4 MHz was to be allotted for GSM based systems and a maximum of 2.5 MHz+ 2.5 MHz Spectrum to be allotted for CDMA based systems, on case by case basis and subject to availability. Incremental Spectrum beyond the initial allotment was linked to the subscriber base achieved by an operator.

As per the existing policy, radio frequency Spectrum allotted to wireless service providers are charged based on usage. There is no upfront charges payable at the time of allotment of Spectrum. Though there is a one time non-refundable entry fee for obtaining UASL, operators intending to provide wireless services are eligible for 4.4 MHz of GSM or 2.5 MHz of CDMA Spectrum, depending upon the technology they choose for roll out. Incremental allotment of Spectrum is subject to achieving a definite subscriber base.

The Wireless Planning and Coordination (WPC) Wing in the Ministry of Communications and Information Technology (Department of Telecommunication) created in 1952 is responsible for Spectrum Management, Wireless licensing and frequency assignments. WPC is divided into major sections like Licensing and Regulation (LR), New Technology Group (NTG) and the standing Advisory Committee on Radio Frequency Allocation (SACFA). SACFA makes the recommendations on major frequency allocation issues, formulation of the frequency allocation plan and making recommendations on various issues related to the ITU to sort out the problems referred to the Advisory Committee by various wireless users.

Since 2004, the Department have been issuing new Unified Access Service Licences and allotting 2G Spectrum on continuous and first-come-first served basis. Between 2004 and 2007, 51 new UAS licences were issued after the introduction of the UAS licensing regime on November 11, 2003. This continued till 2007.

2G SPECTRUM ALLOCATION AND LICENCES

On April 13, 2007, when Dayanidhi Maran was still MoC & IT the DoT made a reference to TRAI stating that the policy on UASL was finalized in November, 2003 based on the recommendations of TRAI and 159 licences had been issued so far for providing Access Services (CMTS/UAS/Basic) in the country with 5-8 Access Service Providers in each service area.

These service providers were mostly providing wireless services using GSM/CDMA technology. There was, therefore, substantial demand on spectrum as any Indian company fulfilling the eligibility criteria could apply for UAS licence.

TRAI submitted its recommendation son August 28 of that year, and suggested "No Cap" on the number of players and also recommended no auction of spectrum in the 800, 900 and 1800 MHz bands [see Table below]. The Authority also recommended grant of spectrum under combination of technology. The TRAI in its recommendations advocated that all UAS licences were eligible for 6.2 MHz of 2G spectrum but that there would be a separate one time licence fee and a spectrum fee. This was rejected arbitrarily and illegally by the Telecom Minister Raja.

Subsequently, TRAI in Para 2.55 of the its recommendation dated August 28, 2007 on 'Review of license terms and conditions and capping of number of access providers,' relating to delinking of spectrum from licence, stated as below:

> 2.55. Today the spectrum allocation follows grant of UAS License. On payment of a certain entry fee, the applicant is given the license and subject to availability, he is given a certain amount of spectrum in the 2G band. **In case the applicant does not require this spectrum for providing the access service, he may want to use only wire-line or may want to provide services using some other spectrum, e.g. BWA, there is no clear cut path for him. He is required to pay the full license entry fee.** The Authority in the past has also recommended that the license fee should be separate from the spectrum fee. With the advent of new technologies where spectrum other than 2G band will be used, resolution of this issue is becoming critical. **As recommended earlier, the Authority again reiterates that spectrum should be de-linked from the licensing regime.** There is also a need to clearly specify the license fee charges without spectrum. The Authority is of the view that license fee charges should be on a reduced scale to facilitate penetration of telecom services. **Bifurcating present entry fee in to license fee and spectrum charge is difficult.** It is also a fact that entry fee determined in 2001 does not bear any relationship to present spurt in the telecom market. Keeping in mind that spectrum is a scarce resource, **the Authority recommends that the DoT should examine the issue early and specify appropriate license fee for UAS licensees who do not wish to utilize the spectrum.**

The DoT, however, demurred stating that against this background, delinking of pricing of spectrum from issuance of licences had not taken place *so far*, but assumed it would be so. This dichotomy between licence fee and Spectrum price suggested and assumed by the TRAI was glossed over, fudged and obfuscated in press briefings while the media also remained clueless about it. While the TRAI recommendations are binding on DoT, any recommendation can be flouted if upon a review sought by the DoT the TRAI declines to delete or modify it. But without seeking such a review, the DoT cannot flout or disregard any TRAI recommendations. But this is precisely what was done and hence there was a violation of the TRAI Act.

Incidentally, the TRAI had also given its recommendations on Spectrum issues including Spectrum pricing earlier on May 13, 2005:

(i) "As in the existing framework the Spectrum charges should continue to have two components: one time Spectrum charge and annual Spectrum charge." (Para 4.1)

(ii) "In UASL, the one time Spectrum charges and entry fee for license have not been separated. In other words, the entry fee includes one time Spectrum charge also." (Para 4.3.3)

(iii) "Existing method of annual Spectrum charge in terms of percentage of revenue share should continue" (Para 4.5.1).

(iv) "Keeping in view the objectives of growth, affordability, penetration of mobile services in semi-urban and rural areas and also the aspect of Spectrum charges, Authority further recommends that existing ceiling on annual Spectrum charges of 6 per cent AGR should be brought down to 4 per cent of AGR." (Para 4.5.2)

(v) "The presently used subscriber base dependent Spectrum allocation procedure is useful in situations where there is constraint in the availability of Spectrum." (Para 2.2.6)

(vi) "The present criteria of allocation of additional Spectrum is different for GSM and CDMA operators. The TRAI, therefore, recommends that the subscriber based Spectrum allocation criteria for both GSM and CDMA should be revised. The revised criteria should also keep in mind the expected results from intensive efforts to get more Spectrum released and the resulting availability picture of Spectrum. Further, these criteria should be made to gradually move in the direction wherein they become technology neutral. If the Government so desires, TRAI jointly with TEC can assist WPC to formulate a revised criteria." (Para 2.3.3).

The DoT, however, when questioned on oath, mentioned to the Public Accounts Committee of Parliament that TRAI in its recommendations dated May 11, 2010 on "Spectrum Management and Licensing Framework" had recommended that all future licences should be unified licences and that spectrum *be delinked from the licence.* TRAI had further, on May 18, 2010, requested the Government to await its recommendations on spectrum pricing, *which were still awaited.*

SPECTRUM PRICE DETERMINATION

As stated above, the Group of Ministers (GoM) on Telecom Matters was constituted under the Finance Minister's chairmanship (vide Cabinet Secretariat's memo dated September 10, 2003) consisting of the Minister of Defence, the Minister of Law and Justice, Commerce and Industry, Communications and Information Technology and Disinvestment, Minister of External Affairs, and Minister of State (Independent Charge) of the Ministry of Information and Broadcasting.

The GoM held five meetings. In their fifth and final meeting held on October 30, 2003 the GoM had *inter-alia* recommended that "**the Department of Telecommunications and the Ministry of Finance would discuss and finalize Spectrum pricing formula, which will include incentive for efficient use of Spectrum as well as disincentive for sub-optimal usages.**" Thus, Spectrum pricing issue was to be decided in consultation within the Ministry of Finance and *hence the Finance Minister had a joint responsibility with the Telecom Minister in deciding the spectrum price.*

Asked to state specifically by the Public Accounts Committee of Parliament [PAC] the level at which the decision was taken to change the terms of References of the GoM – 2006—to take Spectrum pricing out of the purview of the Union Cabinet altogether, and instead associate only the Minister of Finance in the discussion and finalization of Spectrum pricing with the Telecom Minister [MoC & IT], the Department of Telecommunications [DoT] replied that the revised Terms of References which excluded the "Spectrum Pricing" from Cabinet decision was issued by the Cabinet Secretariat *vide* their letter dated December 7, 2006.

The Prime Minister Dr. Manmohan Singh being prevailed upon by the then MoC & IT, Dayanidhi Maran, agreed to take the issue completely out of the purview of the Cabinet decision making.

The Department of Telecom, in fact, has stated in answer to a question from the PAC that the issue of Spectrum pricing *was independently discussed at length* between Ministry of Finance and DoT between January and July 2008. The then Finance Secretary and the then Secretary, DoT also met a number of times between February and June

2008. Meetings to finalize the price were then held between the then Finance Minister P. Chidambaram and the then Minister of Telecom Raja on January 30, 2008; May 29, 2008; and June 12, 2008.The letter sent and Note submitted by Finance Minister P. Chidambaram dated April 15, 2008 to MoC & IT Raja clearly brings out that the former concurred with the latter on setting the Spectrum licence price cum entry fee at the price discovered in 2001 [Annexure].

In his speech in the Rajya Sabha on February 24, 2011, the Prime Minister clearly stated:

> ...The Government's policy of the pricing of Spectrum was taken on the basis of a Cabinet decision of 2003 which specifically left the issue to be determined by the Ministry of Finance and the Ministry of Telecommunication. Contrary to the assertion of the Leader of the Opposition, the record clearly shows that the then Minister *while he initially had a different view which he communicated to me on January 15, 2008, subsequently consulted the Minister, Telecommunication and the two Ministers worked an agreed formula on Spectrum charges which was reported to me in a meeting on July 4, 2008.* Furthermore, this decision that was put to me by the two Ministers was in line with the recommendation of TRAI in its Report of August 2007. In that Report the TRAI had clearly stated that only 3G Spectrum should be auctioned and the policy for 2G Spectrum should continue on the same basis as hitherto.

The Cabinet Secretariat on being asked by the PAC to state the reasons for not constituting a GoM for looking into the policy issues arising out of and for processing a large number of applications for grant of the UAS licences, and for ignoring the suggestions of the Ministers of Law and Justice as well as Commerce and Industry, the Cabinet Secretariat replied that Groups of Ministers (GoMs) are appointed by the Cabinet, the Standing Committees of the Cabinet, or the Prime Minister for investigating and reporting to the Cabinet on such matters as may be specified. When any of the aforesaid authorities take a decision to constitute a GoM, Cabinet Secretariat issues the requisite orders.

No facts on record are available with the Cabinet Secretariat relating to any advice/orders to form a GoM on the issue referred to in the question. *Vide* PMO ID dated November 27, 2006, Cabinet Secretariat was informed that the PM had approved a revised ToR in respect of this GoM. The necessary modifications to the ToRs of the GoM were brought about by Cabinet Secretariat memorandum dated December 7, 2006.

This is in keeping with the fact that the Group of Ministers (GoMs) are appointed by the Cabinet, the Standing Committees of the Cabinet, or the Prime Minster for investigating and reporting to the Cabinet on such matters as may be specified; and, when any of the aforesaid authorities take a decision to constitute a GoM, the role of the Cabinet Secretariat is limited to issuing the requisite orders.

Thereafter, on receipt of the letter of the then Finance Secretary, dated April 19, 2007, asking for inclusion of "Spectrum pricing" in the ToRs of the GoM, Cabinet Secretariat, vide its communication dated May 17, 2007, advised both the Department of Economic Affairs (DEA), Ministry of Finance (MoF) and DoT that the issue may be discussed and resolved at the level of Secretaries and thereafter the Cabinet Secretariat be advised about the decisions taken in the matter. This advice was consistent with the decision of the Union Cabinet, dated October 31, 2003, that Spectrum pricing issues may be discussed and finalized between DoT and MoF. Nothing further was heard from DEA on this issue thereafter.

The PAC asked the reasons for overlooking the mandatory pre-condition of the Transaction of Business Rules while deciding on Spectrum pricing and allocation particularly when the Finance Minister had specifically desired that these issues be included in the ToR of 2006. In reply, the Cabinet Secretariat stated that the Union Cabinet, in its meeting held on October 31, 2003, had, *inter-alia*, approved the following: "2.1.2 (3) The Department of Telecom and Ministry of Finance would discuss and finalise Spectrum pricing fomula, which will include incentive for efficient use of Spectrum as well as dis-incentive for sub-optimal usages...."

As mentioned earlier, the then Finance Secretary (Ashok Jha) wrote a letter on March 28, 2007 (Annexure-XX) to the then Secretary, DoT (D. S. Mathur) requesting inclusion of the Spectrum pricing issue in the ToRs of the GoM. Mr. Mathur replied on April 2, 2007 (Annexure-XXI)

Tel +91-11-2371 9898
Fax +91-11-2371 1514
e-mail : dsmathur@nic.in

D. S. MATHUR
सचिव Secretary

भारत सरकार
संचार एवं सूचना प्रौद्योगिकी मंत्रालय
दूरसंचार विभाग
संचार भवन, नई दिल्ली-110 001
Government of India
Ministry of Communications &
Information Technology
Department of Telecommunications
Sanchar Bhawan, New Delhi-110 001

DO No. L-14047/1/2006-NTG
April 2, 2007

Dear Shri Jha,

Kindly refer to your DO letter No 3/11/2003-Infra dated 28th March 2007 concerning the TOR for GOM on vacation of spectrum and raising resources for the purpose.

2. In this context, I may mention that DOT had proposed a draft TOR for the GOM in January 2006, which focused on the issues relating to vacation of spectrum in a time-bound manner for the growth of telecom sector, making available funds for relocation of existing systems and use of digital technology.

3. The TOR issued by Cabinet Secretariat in February 2006 included certain other issues, including spectrum pricing, which are within the normal work carried out by this Ministry. The Hon'ble MOC&IT had written to the Hon'ble PM accordingly in February 2006, requesting that the Terms of Reference may kindly be modified as suggested in our original proposal. The revised TOR were issued by Cabinet Secretariat in December 2006. I hope this clarifies the matter.

With regards,

Yours sincerely,

(D.S.Mathur)

Shri Ashok Jha
Finance Secretary
Ministry of Finance
North Block
New Delhi

turning down the request. On June 6, 2007 and again on November 22, 2007 the then Finance Secretary (Dr. D. Subbarao) wrote to Mr. Mathur on the same line to which Mr. Mathur did not agree as conveyed by his letters dated June 15, 2007 and November 29, 2007 respectively.

In the above context, the Committee desired to know from Dr. Subbarao as to what happened after Mr. Mathur's reply of November 29, 2007. Dr. Subbarao submitted in evidence: "Maybe, there was no exchange of correspondence, but there were certainly discussions going on between the Secretary [Telecom] and myself on these matters."

Asked to furnish evidence of such discussions, Dr. Subbarao submitted:

> Sir, there may not be a paper trail, but there was certainly discussion going on. Sir, as you know- you have been a Minister yourself-in the Government, not everything is on paper or reduced to writing. Maybe there was some note file endorsements, but I cannot recall them because the note file is not here. but I recall that we were continuing to talk to the Telecom Ministry.

The Public Accounts Committee then queried whether oral communications between two Secretaries of different Ministries on such important issues was professionally appropriate. The then Finance Secretary and now Governor, RBI submitted: "I do agree that leaving communication between two Ministries at the oral level is a bad professional practice. But it does happen all the time because of pressure of work and other things. we shall certainly try to improve that."

Asked to pinpoint what was exactly the pressure of work, Dr. Subbarao replied:

> This was in the month of December and we were getting into budget and there were so many concerns at that time. It is not as if I was completely, fully engaged on this issue, but I do recall that we were talking to them even as there were other commitments on our time. I cannot really say that I had specifically asked them why they did not supply the information that I had called for.

Expressing their surprise, the PAC asked whether it was prudent to ignore such great source of revenue, more so when the Ministry of Finance was engaged in the budget exercise. In reply, the then Finance Secretary Dr. Subbarao submitted:

> Sir, to infer that we had ignored the issue or abandoned the issue, I think, would be incorrect and inappropriate. I agree that we had not reduced all that was taking place in oral communication into writing. That certainly was a lapse. But I do recall that discussions were taking place as much as time allowed. We were deeply conscious that this has revenue implications. In fact, it is the revenue implications which in the first instance triggered our effort to motivate revisiting the stance of Spectrum pricing.
>
> Actually, the burden of my argument at this time is that had we known that some event was going to take place on the 10th of January, in November, we would have been certainly more active. But we did not know, Hon. Member had said it was coming out in the papers, etc. Indeed, it was. But it was not certainly clear to me or to our Ministry. Nobody told me that all this is actually going to lead to the culmination by issue of licences on a particular date. We thought that it was still open-ended and that there was room for discussion, and that we will not reach the point where we should conclude that discussions had broken down and we must take it to another higher forum.

The PAC also wanted to know whether it was not the duty and responsibility of the Finance Ministry to ensure that the ToRsof the GoM entrusted with them with the task of discussing and finalizing the Spectrum pricing issue, were adhered to. In reply, the then Finance Secretary, deposed:

> Sir, I submit that I was trying to fulfill that responsibility of carrying out the Terms of Reference. Yes, I admit that there was no written record of everything that was happening, but efforts were being pursued. Certainly, we would have doubled our efforts, if we knew

> that there was a deadline approaching. We did not know at that point of time that licences would be issued and the terms of engagement would change.

Asked to state whether the matter was brought to the notice of the Cabinet Secretary or the Finance Minister, Dr. Subbarao deposed: "I do not recall having said specifically that we should go back to the Cabinet that I cannot really say without seeing the file. But I should have briefed the Finance Minister about the on-going discussions."

In response to another specific query on D.S. Mathur's June 15, 2007 letter, Dr. Subbarao submitted: "I have seen this reply now of June 15 of Shri Mathur, but I do not recall having seen this ... it indeed the letter was received, I do not recall having briefed the Finance Minister."

The Committee then desired to know whether at any point of time, the Finance Ministry consulted TRAI or obtained the opinion of the Law Ministry. In response, Dr. Subbarao submitted: "I do not think we have done that. *That would be, as you said, a systemic lapse.*"

The Committee asked whether that meant that due diligence was not applied. Dr. Subbarao said: "In a way, yes, sir. I would have to admit that...."

In response to specific query as to whether giving Spectrum in 2001 on the DoT's reasoning of increasing competition and teledensity was appropriate, Dr. Subbarao submitted: "If indeed competition and welfare maximization were the issues, then the purpose of welfare maximization was not served if you had actually allowed some licence holders to then sell equity."

Dr. Subbarao then summed up obliquely castizing the Telecom Ministry decision:

> There is an argument to be made that if your forego revenue, you can gain on the welfare side like creating teledensity and providing telecom access to lower income people. Providing them opportunities would not only enhance growth but also made them more inclusive. But I think that has to be an explicitly objective and indeed, if that was the objective, we should have weighed the costs and benefits of

D.O. NO. 10709/FS/2007

Dr. D SUBBARAO

FINANCE SECRETARY
DEPARTMENT OF ECONOMIC AFFAIRS
MINSITRY OF FINANCE
GOVERNMENT OF India
New Delhi

November 22, 2007

Shri D S Mathur
Secretary
Department of Telecommunications
Ministry of Communications and Information Technology
Sanchar Bhavan
New Delhi

Dear Shri. Mathur,

1. During the presentation on the Spectrum Policy to the Cabinet Secretary on 20 November 2007, you had mentioned, among other things, that: (I)three CDMA operators were given crossover license for GSM operations; (II) the fee for this license was determined at Rs.1600 crore (for all India operations with pro-rata determination for less than all India operations); and (III) that one of the licensees has already paid the license fee.

2. The purpose of this letter is to confirm if proper procedure has been followed with regard to financial diligence. In particular, it is not clear how the rate of Rs.1600 crore, determined as far back as in 2001, has been applied for a license given in 2007 without any indexation, let alone current valuation. Moreover, in view of the financial implications, the Ministry of Finance should have been consulted in the matter before you had finalized the decision.

3. I request you to kindly review the matter and revert to us as early as possible with responses to the above issues. Meanwhile, all further action to implement the above licenses may please be stayed. Will you also kindly send us copies of the letters of permission given and the date?

Best regards

Yours sincerely,

Sd/-

(D SUBBARAO)

> foregoing a certain amount of revenue against what would be the retune by way of increasing teledensity. We had not done that at any point of time. We were always arguing on the basis of level playing field rather then on the basis of nay growth dimensions this might have subsidise that and if they have chosen to do that, then, as a civil servant, it would have been beyond my remit to contest that.

Referring to the June 15, 2007 letter of D.S. Mathur, the former Secretary, DoT, to Dr. D. Subbarao, the former Finance Secretary wherein Mathur indicated that since Spectrum pricing and charges for the use of Spectrum was a dynamic issue, it was to be reviewed and considered from time to time in the context of the changing technology and international best practices, in consultation with TRAI, the Committee asked the Ministry of Finance to furnish details thereof. In reply, the DEA stated that the said letter did not appear to have been received and processed on the file of DEA, as per records.

The Public Accounts Committee then desired to know from the DEA as to how the file relating to the correspondence between Dr. Subbarao and Shri Mathur was closed after November, 2007. In reply, the DEA stated that after receiving the D.O. No. 20-165/2007-AS-1 dated November 29, 2007 from D.S. Mathur the then Secretary, DoT, a self contained note had been prepared by Shyamala Shukla Director (Infrastructure) on December 17, 2007. The note has been marked to JS (O.T.) and AS (EA).

There are, however, no notings thereafter and the file has not been processed further. Why? A copy of the notings of Ms Shyamala Shukla is enclosed here with (**Annexure-XXVI**).

In his note dated January 15, 2008, the then Finance Minister wrote to the Prime Minister:

> Spectrum is a scarce recource. The price for Spectrum should be based on its scarcity value and efficiency of usage. The most transparent method of allocating Spectrum would be through auction. The method of auction will face the least legal challenge. If Government is able to provide sufficient information on availability of Spectrum,

that would minimize the risks and, consequently, fetch better prices at the auction. The design of the auction should include a reserve price.

The Finance Minister's same note to the Prime Minister reads further:

This leaves the question about licensees who already hold Spectrum over and above the start up Spectrum. In such cases, *the past may be treated as a closed chapter and the payments made in the past for additional Spectrum (over and above the start up Spectrum) may be treated as the charges for Spectrum for that period [sic].* However, prospectively, such licensee should pay for the additional Spectrum that he holds, over and above the start up Spectrum, at the price discovered in the auction. This will place old licensees, existing licensee seeking additional Spectrum and new licensees on par so far as Spectrum charges are concerned.

The Prime Minister in his interaction with the Editors of the Electronic Media on February 16, 2011 said:

This was also discussed with the Finance Ministry because in terms of the Cabinet decision of 2003 the pricing and allocation of Spectrum was to be settled between the Ministry of Finance and the Telecom Department. Initially, of course, the Finance Ministry did ask for a high price of Spectrum but after many discussions, the two ministries agreed that as far as 2G is concerned, we have to live with the present system particularly with regard to the amount of Spectrum that is built and embedded into a license agreement. *So this is the background why I did not proceed further with this matter of pricing of Spectrum, because if the Ministry of Finance and Ministry of Telecom both agree and they have the obligation of the Cabinet Decision of 2003 to decide on the matter* and also since TRAI is an expert body and Telecom Commission has experts, if all of them are of the same view, I did not feel I was in a position to insist that auctions must be insisted.

On the question of Sale of Spectrum, the Prime Minister further clarified:

> I thought ... it was then the prevailing practice and Raja was continuing that policy, that as far as who gets licenses, the first come first serve policy, how it was implemented, that was never discussed with me. Licenses was not matter which got referred to me or to the Cabinet that was the decision exclusively of the telecom minister. Now subsequent events have shown that Companies sold their equity but I was told that they had not sold it to shareholders. They have sold it in a manner to dilute the equity of the promoters.

On being asked by the PAC to state as to whether he brought the matter of the extremely low price of Spectrum to the notice of his Minister, the Telecom Secretary Mr. Mathur submitted: "The Minister had been requested at least twice by us to reconsider the matter and bring the rates at which the licences were to be given up-to-date."

Asked to state specifically whether he apprised the Minister that side tracking the Ministry of Finance would lead to the violation of the Cabinet decision of 2003, Mr. Mathur responded: "I may not have used those words but I did bring it to the notice of the Hon'ble Minister that we may have to go to the Cabinet for that."

When the Minister did not agree, the PAC asked, whether it was brought to the notice of the Cabinet Secretary or the Principal Secretary to the Prime Minister. In response, Mr. Mathur replied: "I submit to you that I brought it to the notice of the Cabinet Secretary and the notice of the Principal Secretary to the Prime Minister not once but several times."

Asked to state whether it was done in writing, Shri Mathur submitted: "Orally, in October-November."

According to Audit of the C&AG, the Ministry of Finance was insisting on the issue of inclusion of Spectrum pricing in the ToR of GoM constituted for Spectrum vacation since early 2006. In June 2007, Finance Secretary had informed the DoT that the matter had been discussed at Hon'ble Finance Minister's level and Ministry felt that a sound policy on Spectrum pricing was required.

Note on Spectrum Charges

The first licenses for cellular mobile telephone services were awarded in 1994 for 8 cellular operators in four metro cities. The operators were bound by a ceiling tarrif and call charge, and were required to pay a license fee spread over ten years. The annual payment ranged from a minimum of Rs.1 crore in the first year to Rs.24 crore per year in the seventh year for various metros. More licenses were awarded in 1995 based on a bidding process. The bids were based on license fees spread over a ten year license period but did not include spectrum charges. Charges for spectrum were payable separately and these licensees were charged for spectrum at Rs.4,800 per voice channel and Rs.1200 for each additional station.

2. In the year 1999, NTP-99 was announced. The existing operators (including basic services operators) were permitted to migrate to provide cellular mobile services with effect from 1st August 1999 on payment of "license fee" and "spectrum charges". At this point of time, the following three charges were levied:-

(i) entry fee - based on a bidding process;
(ii) charges for spectrum (at the present rate);
(iii) revenue sharing (collected as a license fee).

3. In 2002, licenses were issued to a fourth cellular operator based on bidding for the entry fee.

4. On 27th October 2003, TRAI recommended that the existing entry fee charged from the fourth cellular operator would be the entry fee for the new Universal Access Services License (UASL) regime.

contd...

5. Cabinet approved the recommendations of the TRAI with regard to implementation of the Universal Access Services License regime (for basic and cellular services) and authorised DoT to finalise the details of implementation including the calculation of the entry fee depending on the date of payment based on the principles given by TRAI in its recommendations.

6. A GoM constituted for the purpose made certain recommendations. Cabinet approved the recommendations on release of adequate spectrum, namely,

(i) DoT and MoF would discuss and finalise the pricing formula for spectrum which will include incentive for efficient use of spectrum;

(ii) the allotment of additional spectrum would be transparent, fair and equitable; and

(iii) the long-term (5-10 years) spectrum requirements would be worked out by DoT.

7. It is therefore clear that there are three separate concepts:

(i) entry fee;

(ii) charges for spectrum;

(iii) revenue share.

8. (i) **Entry Fee:** The present entry fee is based on the highest bid received in 2001, namely, Rs.1,651 crore if operating over the entire country. DoT has taken the stand that entry fee is **not** in the nature of spectrum charges or license fees.

(ii) **Charges for spectrum**: Currently, spectrum charges are fixed at 2 per cent, 3 per cent or 4 per cent of Adjusted Gross Revenue (AGR) depending upon the spectrum bandwidth. The rate goes up from 2 per cent to 4 per cent as the bandwidth increases from 4.4 + 4.4 MHz to 10 + 10 MHz. There are two more rates of 5 per cent and 6 per cent for higher bandwidth, but spectrum in this range has not yet been allotted.

contd...

Start up spectrum is allocated as part of the license. Initial allotment is up to 4.4 + 4.4 MHz for TDMA based systems and up to 2.5 + 2.5 MHz for CDMA based systems. It is also provided that additional spectrum may be considered after ensuring optimal and efficient utilisation of the spectrum allocated.

(iii) **Revenue share** (also described as **license fee**): Currently, revenue share is a percentage of AGR. With effect from 1.4.2004, the share is 10 per cent for category 'A', 8 per cent for category 'B' and 6 per cent for category 'C'.

9. This note does not deal with the need, if any, to revise entry fee or the rate of revenue share. This note deals with spectrum charges for 2G spectrum.

10. **Spectrum is a scarce resource.The price for spectrum should be based on its scarcity value and efficiency of usage. The most transparent method of allocating spectrum would be through auction. The method of auction will face the least legal challenge. If Government is able to provide sufficient information on availability of spectrum, that would minimize the risks and, consequently, fetch better prices at the auction. The design of the auction should include a reserve price.**

11. The auction could be for a "one-time payment" for the additional spectrum or "an annual rent" for the additional spectrum. Once the price is discovered, additional spectrum should be allocated to all bidders at that price.

12. In addition, if a licensee sells his license (including the spectrum) to another person, it could be stipulated that the licensee should share with the Government a part of the premium/profit gained by him through the sale.

contd...

13. This leaves the question about licensees who already hold spectrum over and above the start up spectrum. In such cases, the past may be treated as a closed chapter and the payments made in the past for additional spectrum (over and above the start up spectrum) may be treated as the charges for spectrum for that period. However, prospectively, such licensee should pay for the additional spectrum that he holds, over and above the start up spectrum, at the price discovered in the auction. This will place old licensees, existing licensee seeking additional spectrum and new licensees on par so far as spectrum charges are concerned.

(P. Chidambaram)
Finance Minister
15.1.2008

PRIME MINISTER

April 21, 2008

Dear

As you are aware, based on your non-paper on spectrum charges, Finance Secretary has held discussions with Secretary, Ministry of Communications & Information Technology. Based on those discussions, I enclose a non-paper containing our views on issues relating to 2G spectrum and issues relating to 3G/WiMax Spectrum.

2. After you have had an opportunity to examine the same, may we meet and discuss and reach some conclusions? These conclusions could then be presented to the Hon'ble Prime Minister.

With regards,

Yours sincerely,

(P. Chidambaram)

Shri A. Raja
Minister for Communications &
Information Technology
Electronics Niketan
CGO Complex, Lodhi Road
New Delhi – 110 003

Encl: a/a.

SPECTRUM ISSUES – NON PAPER
(Copy of DoT's non-paper is attached)

Issues relating to 2G spectrum

I. Spectrum Usage Charges

Spectrum Usage Charge is currently linked to bandwidth and the rate of charge is a function of the quantum of spectrum allocated to an operator. DoT, in their communication dated February 08, 2008, (copy attached) had agreed to change the existing system in favor of a percentage of AGR based on Circle specific rates, which reflects the scarcity value of spectrum and envisages a premium for Circles with higher volumes of business. However, in their present formulation, as indicated in their non-paper, DoT is persisting with the bandwidth linked levy, albeit with a higher percentage charge on each range of bandwidth.

DEA is of the view that the revised methodology as indicated in the February 8, 2008 letter of DoT should be pursued.

The existing rates, proposed rates of DoT and recommendation of DEA in this regard are depicted in the Table below.

Current position	
Bandwidth Range (MHz)	**% of AGR**
Upto 4.4	2%
4.4 - 6.2	3%
6.2 - 8.0	4%
8.0 - 10.0	4%
10.0 - 12.5	5%
12.5 - 15.0	6%

Proposal of DoT (non paper)	
Bandwidth Range (MHz)	**% of AGR**
Upto 4.4	3%
4.4 - 6.2	4%
6.2 - 7.2	5%
7.2 - 8.2	5.5%
8.2 - 9.2	6%
9.2 - 10.2	6.5%
10.2 - 11.2	7%
11.2 - 12.2	7.5%

Proposal of DEA	
Circle Category	**% of AGR**
Metro I (Delhi, Mumbai)	8%
Metro II (Kolkata)	8%
Category - A	8%
Category - B	6%
Category - C	4%

II. Pricing of 2G Spectrum

DoT is agreeable to pricing of spectrum beyond 4.4 MHz but wants this deferred till auction of 3G and WiMax is completed.

An "in principle" decision on this issue may be taken at this stage itself, with the details to be worked out later.

III. Revision of Spectrum Entitlement criteria

Under the current regime, any allocation of spectrum beyond the initial start-up of 4.4 MHz is linked to the subscriber base; as soon as an operator reaches a prescribed subscriber base, additional spectrum corresponding to the increased subscriber base is allotted to him subject to availability of spectrum.

TRAI have examined the existing subscriber base criteria and concluded[1] that the present spectrum allocation criteria needs to be immediately reviewed as it is not spectrally efficient and does not take into consideration "the present technology innovations for increasing spectral efficiency". A revised subscriber base criteria has been proposed for implementation in the interim, while asking that a specialized multi disciplinary Committee be set up to frame a new long term spectrum allocation criteria[2].

The above recommendations of TRAI may be taken up for immediate implementation in the interest of enhancing efficiency of spectrum usage and encouraging technological innovations.

---

[1] August, 2007 Report on "Review of license terms and conditions and capping the number of access providers"; Para 2.57; p 37 of the Report.

[2] Paras 2.61, 2.62; pp 38-39 of the Report.

April 17, 2008

Issues relating to 3G/WiMax spectrum

IV. Allocation of 3G spectrum

Two options have been recommended by DoT:

i. Auction within existing UAS license holders – at present, there are about 10 license holders per circle.

ii. Open Global auction (ICB).

In the opinion of DEA, the first option as above is not workable. However, International Competitive Bidding (ICB) model may be used, with the following conditions:

i. Mandatory "roll out" clause already exists – spectrum is withdrawn and bid payout is forfeited if roll out does not take place within a year. This may be re-iterated.

ii. Conditions for pre-qualification may be specified, to ensure that the competition is restricted to serious contenders – details of such conditions, e.g., prior exposure to the sector, net worth criteria etc can be worked out in due course.

V. Allocation of WiMax Spectrum

Issues and options are the same as for 3G; only the number of existing players will be about 16 as WiMax auction is open to ISPs as well. DEA of the view that the same methodology as recommended for allocation of 3G spectrum may be used herein as well.

2770 | FS/08
2/4

Spectrum Charges

Sl No.	MHz	Spectrum Charges Existing	TRAI	Proposal 1	MHz
1	Upto 4.4	2%	2%	3%	Upto 4.4
2	4.4 to 6.2	3%	3%	4%	4.4 to 6.2
3	6.2 to 8.0	4%	4%	5%	6.2 to 7.2
				5.5%	7.2 to 8.2
4	8.0 to 10.0	4%	5%	6.0%	8.2 to 9.2
				6.5%	9.2 to 10.2
5	10.0 to 12.5	5%	6%	7%	10.2 to 11.2
				7.5%	11.2 to 12.2
6	12.5 to 15.0	6%	7%		

*	Increased spectrum charges may give an additional revenue of about Rs.1000 crore
3 G Spectrum	For allocation of 3 G spectrum following two option are available:

or
1 Auction within existing UAS licence holders. At present there are about 10 licence holders per circle
2 Open global auction.

WIMAX	For allocation of ~~3G spectrum~~ WIMAX (BWA) (Broadband Wireless Access) following two option are available:

or
1 Auction within existing UAS and ISP licence holders. At present there are about 10 licence holders per circle
2 Open global auction. 700 MHz - 5.5 GHz

3G
WiMAX | Which is the preferred auction route?

[illegible] 3/4

AS (EA) 2/4/08 Note pls.
JS (T) - 07

MINISTRY OF FINANCE
Department of Economic Affairs

21/AS(EA)/08
10/1/2008

Subject: Spectrum Policy.

References: (i) Letter No.10709/FS/2007 dated 22.11.2007 from FS to Secretary, Telecom.
(ii) Reply received from Secretary, Telecom – D.O.No.20-165/2007-AS-I dated 29.11.2007.

FM had instructed that the prolific Press reports over the last two months relating to pricing of spectrum and the "Telecom Wars" may be tracked.

02. The Press reports relate to a variety of issues. These include:

- DoTs decisions on the pending applications for Licenses (for which a deadline of September 25th was declared on October 1st 2007 by DoT);
- 2G and 3G Spectrum: the quantum available, the methods of allocation and pricing thereof;
- DTH and Broadband coverage;
- TRAI recommendations on the subject at different times on the above;
- Views of Competition Commission on number of players in Telecom.

The common theme underlying all the issues relate to a range of technologies now available under the rubric of Telecom - from telephony, video, television to broadband DTH etc. (In other words, transmission of Voice, Mail, Data and Broadcasting through hand held mobile devices). The radio frequency to be used for the technology is scarce. The media interest in DoT and its decisions is on account of its being the custodian of the radio frequencies spectrum, responsible for its allocation as well as the Authority to issue licenses to operators in the Telecom sector.

03. A position paper has been prepared on the most contentious issue that is currently enjoying public attention, i.e. allocation of additional licences and 2G Spectrum to existing and new entrants. The draft of the position paper was discussed with FS and the final draft is enclosed.

04. The full Telecom Commission was scheduled to meet today. However, the meeting has now been postponed to 15th January 2008. Finance Secretary has desired that I may represent him in the meeting.

Sd/-

(Sindhushree Khullar)
Additional Secretary (EA)
09.01.2008

FS

FM

Draft (Revised 3.1.2008)

DEPARTMENT OF ECONOMIC AFFAIRS

Position Paper on Spectrum Policy

References:

(i) Letter No.10709/FS/2007 dated 22.11.2007 from FS to Secretary, Telecom.
(ii) Reply received from Secretary, Telecom – D.O.No.20-165/2007-AS-I dated 29.11.2007.
(iii) Agenda for the Cabinet dated 31st October 2003
(iv) New Telecom Policy 1999 and amendment dated 11th Nov. 2003.

Present Arrangements

01. The Statutory basis for grant of wireless license:

- The Indian Telegraph Act, 1885 (ITA, 1885) and rules made thereunder provide statutory basis for grant of licences by the Central Government for establishment, maintenance or working of wireless apparatus, equipment and appliances.

- The Indian Wireless Telegraphy Act, 1933 (IWTA 1933) and rules made thereunder, provide the Central Government with powers to grant licences for possession of such wireless apparatus, equipment and appliances.

- Wireless Planning and Coordination (WPC) Wing of Ministry of Communications & IT exercises powers of the Central Government for grant of such licences under Section 4 of the ITA, 1885 and Section 5 of IWTA 1933.

1.1 The chronology of Service Licence procedures is at **Annexure-I**.

02. In 2003, the Cabinet decided to allow licensees to provide all telecom/telegraphic services using any technology, and also approved an addendum to NTP-99 enabling

(i) Licensees to migrate to Unified Access Service (UAS) License; and
(ii) Government to issue new UAS Licences.
[*Under a UAS License, the Licensee can provide wire line and/or wireless services. The allocation of spectrum, if required, is subject to availability*]

3.1 The Cabinet also approved the GoM recommendations on release of adequate spectrum needed for the growth of the telecom sector. GoM recommended inter alia -

(1) The Department of Telecom and Ministry of Finance would discuss and finalise spectrum pricing formula, which will include incentive for efficient use of spectrum as well as disincentive for sub-optimal usages.

(2) The allotment of additional spectrum be transparent fair and equitable avoiding monopolistic situation regarding spectrum allotment/usage.

(3) The long term (5/10 years) spectrum requirements along with time frames would also be worked out by Department of Telecom.

3.2 In addition, Cabinet approved, that DoT may be authorized "to finalise the details of implementation with the approval of the Minister of Communications and IT in this regard, including the calculation of the entry fee depending upon the date of payment, based on the principles given by TRAI in its recommendations".

The Agenda Note for the Cabinet dated 31st October 2003 is at Reference (iii) (Encl.)

04. Currently, Government gets payment/revenue from Unified Access Service License (UAS) holders of both GSM and CDMA technology under three streams/routes.

(i) Entry Fee fixed on the basis of highest bid received in 2001 auction of licenses (Rs.1651 crore if operating over the entire country corresponding to circle-specific fees).

> *[Entry Fee was fixed on the basis of the highest bid received in the license auction in 2001. There were three rounds of bids in 2001. The highest bid in the first round was used as the reserve price for the second round and the higher price in the second round was used as the reserve price for the third round. The bid was finally closed in the third round. DoT states that this is not in the nature of Spectrum charges or License Fee.]*

(ii) (a) Spectrum charges fixed at 2%, 3%, 4% of Adjusted Gross Revenue (AGR) depending on the Spectrum Bandwidth. Separate criteria exist for GSM and CDMA operators. A detailed table indicating the range of spectrum charges and the allocated bandwidth is placed in **Annexure II(a)**.

(b) Start up Spectrum allocated as a part of the license linked to subscriber base. **(Annexure II(b))**.

> *[At present initial allotment is in accordance with the relevant provisions of the Service License Agreement. Clauses 43.5(i) and 43.5(ii) of the Service License*

Agreement stipulates that "initially a cumulative maximum of up to 4.4 MHz + 4.4 MHz shall be allocated in the case of TDMA based systems @ 200 KHz per carrier or 30 KHz per carrier or a maximum of 2.5 MHz + 2.5 MHz shall be allocated in the case of CDMA base systems @ 1.25 MHz per carrier, on case by case basis subject to availability".

"Additional spectrum beyond the above stipulation may also be considered for allocation after ensuring optimal and efficient utilization of the already allocated spectrum taken into account all types of traffic and guidelines/criteria prescribed from time to time"].

(iii) Revenue share as percentage of Adjusted Gross Revenue (AGR).

[*In 2001 spectrum charges for Cellular/Basic/WLL services were changed over to revenue share w.e.f 1.8.1999, the date of implementation of NTP 1999. The license fee is paid as a percentage of Adjusted Gross Revenue (AGR) earned by all operators except for Pure Value Added Service Providers, Voice Mail, E-Mail and Internet Service Providers, as defined in the License Agreement*]

4.1 The rates of License Fee (Revenue Share) for Basic/UASL and CMTS services inclusive of universal service levy are as under:

Category	**Service**	**Rate of License Fee (1.8.99 to 24.1.2001)**	**Rate of License Fee* (from 25.1.2001 to 30.3.2004)**	**Rate of License Fee* (w.e.f. 1.04.04)**
A	**Cellular/ Basic/ USAL	Provisional License Fee as revenue share @ 15% of AGR (8% for A&N islands & J&K)	12%	10%
B	Cellular/Basic/ USAL		10%	8%
C	Cellular/Basic/ USAL		8%	6%

Note:

* The License Fee includes the contribution for Universal Service Obligation Fund as USL which is 5% of AGR.

** For the first two circle cellular operators (license awarded before 1999) there is an additional relief of 2% for four years w.e.f. 1.4.2004. This is subject to a minimum of equivalent to the contribution for USO Fund and this is 5% of AGR.

<u>Source</u>:
Report of the Departmental Sub-Committee on Taxes and Levies applicable in the Telecommunication Sector, December 2007 (page 13), DoT, M/o Communications & Information Technology.

05. **Policy objectives in fixing Entry Fee, Licence Fee and Spectrum charges**

- Making telecom services accessible to all.
- Efficient allocation of a scarce good (Spectrum) owned by government
- Revenue maximization. The levies are Non-Tax revenues of government.

Options before us

06. (?) Review Entry Fee:

6.1 The entry fee regulates the number of service providers. As of July 2007 there are over 180 licensed Cellular and Unified Access Service providers in 23 telecom service areas. Six to seven million subscribers are being added on an average to the network every month. 159 licenses have been issued for providing Access Services/CMTS/UASL/Basic. The number of service providers in each service area with their market share as on quarter ending June 2007 is in **Annexure III.**

6.2 TRAI recommendations (August 2007) **do not** favour a cap to be placed on the number of Access Service providers in any service area.

6.3 Given the fact that there are reportedly over 575 applications pending with DoT (including 45 new applicants) there is a case for reviewing the entry fee fixed in 2001. This is an administratively fixed fee. Therefore any change should be governed by transparent and objective criteria applicable uniformly to all new entrants.

07. (?) Review Revenue share percentages:

7.1 There has been a persistent demand for reduction of revenue share as percentage of AGR from the Industry Associations. The Departmental Sub-Committee chaired by Member (Finance), DoT recommends that the present revenue share rates on License fee may remain. Revenue implications of revising revenue shares on alternate scenarios are at **Annexure IV.**

7.2 Revenue share as a percentage of AGR is a fee for Licence and is linked to the subscriber base. The AGR is part of the normal profits of the operator. The standard argument of the Industry is that an increase in revenue share erodes their margins forcing them to pass on the cost to the subscriber/customer thereby compromising the target of expanding coverage.

7.3 There is a strong case for revising the rates of revenue share percentages for both <u>existing</u> Licensees and <u>new</u> entrants because intense competition and aggressive subscriber acquisition by various operators will ensure that tariffs, particularly for pure telephone usage alone will be beaten down. It is a widely known fact that profit margins are mostly on value added services and not on telephone calls.

7.4 The alternative methods of revising the percentage revenue share based on AGR, for Licence Fee to be paid annually, could be:

(a) Indexed to growth of the sector; or

(b) Auction based on transparent rules. The highest/second highest bid for percentage of revenue share would be the successful bidder.

08. (?) <u>Review Spectrum Charges</u>:

8.1 The most contentious issue relates to spectrum allocation. There is no disagreement that the price charged for spectrum should be based on its scarcity value, efficient usage and that the process of allocation should be transparent and fair. The payment is for a real economic resource. It is not a fee. According to DoT it is closer to royalty charged on Coal, Crude and Natural Gas.

8.2 Additional spectrum as available has to be allocated to

(a) Existing Licensees in GSM;

(b) Existing Licensees in CDMA;

(c) New applicants for Licenses in GSM; and

(d) New applicants for Licenses in CDMA or any combination of the two technologies.

8.4 The most transparent method of allocation of spectrum would be by auction. However, there are two caveats to the auction method.

(a) The ways in which the existing licensees in GSM and CDMA would be eligible to participate in the auction vis-a-vis the new entrants; and

(b) The advantages and disadvantages of the method itself. A detailed table is placed at **Annexure** V.

The possible non-optimal outcomes can be taken care of by prescribing suitable rules of auction <u>before the bid</u> in a transparent manner applicable to all eligible bidders. Any other method for allocating spectrum, being a scarce resource, would be economically inefficient.

09. The TRAI recommendations August, 2007 suggested a Multi-disciplinary Committee to be constituted consisting of representatives from DoT/TEC, TRAI, WPC Wing, COAI and AUSPI to frame new spectrum allocation criteria.

9.1 The efficient usage of spectrum is a technical issue. It is learnt that a Departmental Committee headed by Additional Secretary (Telecom) has recently given recommendations to DoT on the technical criteria for allocation of spectrum based on TRAI recommendations, 2007. In addition, the Telecom Engineering Centre (TEC) has also made recommendations on the technical criteria for allocation of spectrum. However, the details of these recommendations are not available. Nevertheless, regardless of the allocation criteria, auction has been recommended with transparent rules as the most suitable method of allocating spectrum. The quantum of spectrum available for auction in 2G is to be decided by DoT.

9.2 The quantum available will have to be allocated through the most appropriate method accepted by the Government to existing operators as well as to the new entrants who have applied for the same until the cut off date stipulated by DoT. A decision is yet to be taken by DoT on this issue.

10. **The foregoing discussion relates only to 2G Spectrum that is the subject matter of recent petitions to MoF and Press reports ("Telecom Wars").**

---

1) **Enclosures: Annexure I to IV**

2) **Sources:**

(1) Report of the Departmental Sub-Committee on Taxes and Levies applicable in the Telecommunication Sector, December, 2007 by Department of Telecommunications (Ministry of Communications and Information Technology)

(2) TRAI recommendations on review of terms and conditions and capping of number of access providers, New Delhi, August 28, 2007.

(3) TRAI recommendations on Spectrum related issues May 13, 2005.

(4) Paper on allocation of additional spectrum to Mobile Operators, July 2005 (MoF files)

(5) Advantages and Disadvantages of spectrum auction – TRAI Consultation paper.

Chronology of Service Licence Procedure

I) The Licensing of Cellular Services was initially done in phases. In first phase, two Cellular Mobile Telephone Services (CMTS) Licences were awarded in November 1994 in each of the four Metro cities of Delhi, Mumbai, Kolkata and Chennai based on Beauty Parade and Licence fee for service licence was predetermined. Licence fee and royalty for use of spectrum were payable separately.

II) In the second phase, the two CMTS Licences were awarded in December 1995 in 18 Telecom Circles Licence Service Areas based on a bidding process (bids were for licence fee spread over 10 years licence period, this didn't include spectrum charges which was payable separately at applicable rates). In addition, right of the Government was reserved to operate the services as third operator.

III) In the year 1994 – 1995, one private Basic Service Operator (BSO) was envisaged to compete with the government operator (DOT – later BSNL/ MTNL). The BSOs were allowed to use Wireless in Local Loop (WLL).

IV) In the year 1999, NTP-99 was announced. As per the policy, the existing operators were permitted to migrate to multipoly and Revenue Sharing Regime w.e.f. 1.8.1999 for payment of licence fee and spectrum charges. MTNL and govt. operator (now BSNL) were also given CMTS Licences in 1999 – 2000. The licences were issued to 4th cellular operator in 2002 based on bidding for the entry fee for service licence.

V) It is mentioned that what was paid up-front based on the bidding process, was the entry fee for the CMTS licence and not the annual license fee and spectrum charges which are payable separately on revenue share basis at applicable rates.

VI) TRAI in its recommendation dated 27th October 2003 on Unified Licensing had, inter-alia, recommended that the existing entry fee of the fourth Cellular Operator would be the entry fee in the new Unified Access Licensing Regime. The Basic Service Operators (BSOs) would pay the difference of the fourth CMSPs existing entry fee and the entry fee paid by them.

VII) As per the Cabinet decision, the following were approved:

A) The scope of NTP-99 may be enhanced to provide for licensing of Unified Access Services for basic and cellular licence services and unified Licensing comprising all telecom services. Department of Telecommunications may be authorised to issue necessary addendum to NTP-99 to this effect.

B) The recommendations of TRAI with regard to implementation of the Unified Access Licensing Regime for basic and cellular services may be accepted. DoT may be authorised to finalise the details of implementation in this regard including the calculation of the entry fee depending on the date of payment based on the principle given by TRAI in its recommendations.

(i) Based on the Cabinet decision, an addendum to NTP-99 was notified. Guidelines for migration to UASL regime and for issue of new UAS licences were also announced. It may kindly be noted that under UAS licence, the licensee may provide wire line and/ or wireless services. The allocation of spectrum, if required, is subject to availability.

(ii) Under a transparent policy decision, the UAS licences are issued on 'First-Come-First-Served' basis without any restriction on the number of entrants.

(iii) As per UAS licence agreement, "The LICENSEE is permitted to provide, SERVICE by utilizing any type of network equipment, including circuit and/or packet switches that meet the relevant standards of the International Telecommunication Union (ITU)/ Telecommunication Engineering Center (TEC) / International standardization bodies.

The Ministry again through the Finance Secretary in November 2007 questioned the sanctity of continuing with a price determined way back in 2001 without any indexation or current valuation and sought review of the matter. DoT, conveniently quoting the 4 year old Cabinet decision of October 2003, justified to the MoF that it was authorized to calculate the entry fee for licenses depending on the date of payment, on the principles of TRAI recommendations of 2003 and that TRAI in 2007 had also not rccommended any revision.

Member (Finance) Ms Manju Madhavan of the DoT had also sought an in-depth analysis of the issue prior to taking any further action to which Secretary (DoT) also concurred. In her Note to the Secretary of the Ministry Mr. Mathur, in which she detailed the three options for sale of spectrum. One of the options was auction to which she was inclined.

But A. Raja, the MoC&IT sought to intimidate her by making disparaging remarks. He observed on the file sent to him by Secreatry Mathur:

> **Officers have neither up to date knowledge of UAS guidelines nor have bothered to carefully go through file.... These types of continuous confusions observed on the file whoever be the officer concerned does not show any legitimacy and integrity but only their vested interest ... the matter of entry fee has been deliberated in the department, several times in the light of various guidelines issued by the department and recommendations of TRAI and accordingly decision was taken that entry fee need not be revised.**

When the PAC wanted to know which alternative, out of the three alternatives suggested by her, would have been the best one in terms of transparency and revenue generation, Ms. Madhavan submitted: "As Member (Finance), I thought that auction was the best method. We had discussed this and I said auction is the most transparent and the best method that should be adopted."

It is this responsibility that the then Finance Minister P. Chidambaram wants to evade now or deny since Raja has been held by the

CBI as culpable on the price determination [CBI Chargesheet, April 3, 2011, pages 56-62]. Thus, if Raja is *prima facie* guilty so is Chidambaram.

But scrutiny reveals that when a GoM was constituted in February 2006, its Terms of Reference (ToR) were modified at the instance of the then Minister of Telecom (vide a letter written by Dayanidhi Maran as MoC&IT to PM) to keep the issue of Spectrum pricing outside its purview, and the views of the Minister prevailed in finalisation of ToR.

Though MoF had insisted for its inclusion in the ToR for the GoM, DoT maintained that 'Spectrum pricing was within the normal work carried out by them.' The MoF officials had opined then that Spectrum pricing was an issue which has far reaching consequences for the economy and needed to be debated, but this was not considered finally when Finance Minister P. Chidambaram accepted to jointly[with MoC&IT] decide the Spectrum pricing. The GoM's role, therefore, in December 2006, at the instance of the DoT, was confined to issues concerning "Spectrum vacation." It was also noted that the DoT kept the applications for UAS licence pending since March 2006 on the grounds of non-availability of Spectrum, though a decision to get the Spectrum vacated from MoD was taken way back in 2003.

The DoT admitted to the Public Accounts Committee that prior to April 2007, availability of Spectrum was not quantified and GSM Spectrum allotments to service providers/operators were made after due co-ordination with MoD on a case to case basis. Since the availability of Spectrum had not been quantified till April 2007, the basis for keeping the applications pending and seeking TRAI recommendation (April 2007) on limiting the number of Access Service Providers on the grounds of non-availability of Spectrum is inexplicable.

In this context, the Public Accounts Committee had asked DoT about the basis on which the Ministry of Finance was not associated in the discussion and finalization of the Spectrum pricing formula despite the recommendation of the GoM of 2003. In in its revealing reply, the DoT stated that based on the direction of the Cabinet in 2003 that "DoT and Ministry of Finance would discuss and finalize Spectrum pricing formula, which would include incentive for efficient use of Spectrum as well as disincentive for sub-optimal usage," it was considered appropriate to obtain the views of TRAI. Accordingly, on November 17, 2003, DoT made a reference to TRAI, requesting for their considered opinion on efficient utilization of Spectrum, Spectrum pricing and Spectrum allocation procedure. In response, vide letter dated November 19, 2003, TRAI stated as below:

> (i) In para 7.31 of TRAI recommendations, it was mentioned that while operators may be issued unified access license they should continue to provide wireless services in the already allocated/ contracted Spectrum and no additional Spectrum would be allocated only because of migration. It has been further recommended that there shall be no change in the Spectrum allocation procedure as part of migration process. Thus, the principle is that the prevailing Spectrum allocation procedure should continue till fresh guidelines on this matter are issued by the DoT. *This principle can be applied in the interim period for the new entrants also.*
>
> (ii) Thus, in the interim period before the TRAI recommendations on efficient utilization of Spectrum etc become available, if the licensor has to issue any unified access license to new applicants, the TRAI feels that Spectrum to these licensees may be given as per the existing terms and conditions relating to Spectrum in the respective licence agreement. This implies that even though unified access license is service and technology neutral, Spectrum under the new unified licence for offering mobile services may be allocated in the interim period on the technology used for offering these services. For example, if a new Unified Access provider is offering wireless mobile service using GSM technology then the allocation/contracted Spectrum in existing cellular mobile license may be provided and for those using CDMA technology, Spectrum allocation as per the provisions of basic service operators licence can be considered.
>
> (iii) Regarding entry fee to new Unified Access licensees, the matter has already been clarified *vide* Chairman TRAI's DO letter dated November 14, 2003.

Separately, on the issue of Terms of Reference (TOR) of the Group of Ministers (GOM) on 'vacation of Spectrum and raising of resources for the purpose' the following tabular statement of correspondence between and DoT and Ministry of Finance is of relevance.

S. No.	Date	Item
1.	07.12.2006	Cabinet Secretariat issued TOR for the GoM on vacation of Spectrum etc.
2.	28.03.200	Finance Secretary wrote to Secretary (DoT) for inclusion of 'Spectrum pricing' in the TOR of the GoM.
3.	02.04.200	Secretary (DoT) wrote to Finance Secretary clarifying DoT's stand and informing about the letter of Hon'ble MOC&IT to Hon'ble Prime Minister.
4.	19.04.2007	Finance Secretary wrote to Cabinet Secretary for inclusion of 'Spectrum pricing' in the TOR of the GoM.
5.	06.06.2007	Finance Secretary wrote to Secretary (DoT) for reconsideration of inclusion of the issue of 'Spectrum pricing' in the TOR of the GoM.
6.	15.06.2007	DoT informed the Ministry of Finance that the issue of Spectrum pricing and charges for the use of Spectrum is a dynamic issue. It depends, inter-alia, on the region, type of telecom services, band of Spectrum used. It is to be considered from time to time in consultation with TRAI.

The DoT also confirmed to the PAC that in the MoF letter dated November 22, 2007, the Finance Secretary had, **inter-alia, stated that it is not clear how the rate of Rs.1600 crore determined as far back as in 2001 has been applied for a licence given in 2007 without any indexation, let alone current valuation.**

In response, Secretary (DoT) on November 29, 2007, *inter-alia,* informed the Ministry of Finance that TRAI, in its recommendations dated August 28, 2007, had recommended no changes in entry fee/annual license fee and hence no changes were considered in the existing policy.

Thereafter, there was no further communication received from the Ministry of Finance in the matter [till Chidambaram and Raja met together and finalized the Spectrum price at the 2001 level].

The TRAI incidentally had suggested no change in the entry fee for a licence *on the assumption* that the spectrum price would be separated and determined by market conditions [Para 2.55 of the 2007 TRAI recommendations]. This Chidambaram and Raja inexplicably forgot to do, flouted the TRAI recommendation and fixed a combined price for entry and spectrum thereby causing the nation a huge loss.

FIRST-COME FIRST-SERVED CRITERION

The First-Come-First-Served (FCFS) basis for the issue of Licences and Allocation of Spectrum has been followed by the Department on the argument that the announced UASL guidelines have made it open for new licences to be issued on continuous basis. The Delhi High Court in 1993 had already held quoting a US Supreme Court decision with approval that where a scarce public resource like airwaves or spectrum is to be distributed amongst a large number of customers, FCFS policy is arbitrary, unreasonable and biased. Only competitive bidding such as in an auction is reasonable and fair. As an advocate Kapil Sibal had argued in favour of this very point for the petitioner but as Minister he is nowadays arguing the exact opposite! Justice Mukul Mudgal of the Delhi High Court in 2008 had observed in another case that was aborted, that "spectrum cannot be sold like cinema tickets." Cinema tickets are sold on FCFS basis.

The Public Accounts Committee's scrutiny of the records reveal that in the Basic Service Licences guidelines, there is a reference to FCFS *but nowhere in the UASL guidelines the term FCFS has found a mention* implying thereby it has no sanctity. In fact, on November 24, 2003, the then Minister of Communications and IT had approved the Department's proposal to give licence Spectrum on FCFS basis, but it was not codified in the UASL guidelines. But Parliament was duly informed during Question Hours in Rajya Sabha Unshared Question No. 1803 on December 2007.

Thus, there has been no such legally established principle as 'FCFS,' at best it can be termed as one prescription to be followed for grant of licence/Spectrum. This prescription was adopted and applied inconsistently and in deviation of the avowed objective of the NTP-99 for providing a level playing field to the prospective applicants/players.

The greatest demerit of the FCFS criterion is that there is every possibility of exclusion of the best applicant's offer. And that was what exactly happened in the grant of UAS licences in 2007-08. It was used as a tool to favour certain non-serious applicants ignoring the request of the serious and established players. The CVC observations and the Justice Shivraj Patil findings have substantiated this fact and the CBI investigation is now reinforcing it.

As mentioned elsewhere in this study a number of complaints were received in the Central Vigilance Commission regarding the First-Come-First-Served (FCFS) policy adopted by the Department in the issuance of UAS licences in January, 2008. On that basis, the CVC conducted a direct inquiry on the matter and found that there was no mention of the First-Come-First-Served policy in the guidelines issued by the DoT on November 11, 2003 and even the guidelines issued by the Department on its website did not contain anything about the FCFS policy.

Telecom expert and former VSNL Chairman Bijendra K. Syngal apprised the Public Accounts Committee that there were no basis and bases for the FCFS policy. It was a figment of imagination of the Babus at the DoT to suit the few beneficiaries of the largesse doled out by the Government. He further stated that the FCFS only served the greed of the speculators as had been proved beyond doubt by the sale of the equity by some companies at multiples of six or seven times of the price they paid in January 2008.

In the above context, the Committee desired to know from the DoT about the Sanctity of the FCFS policy. In reply, the DoT stated that the term "First-Come-First-Served" (FCFS) did not appear in the UAS licence guidelines dated December 14, 2005. However, para 11 of the guidelines states that, "Licences shall be issued without any restriction on the number of entrants for provision of Unified Access Services in a Service Area." Further the decision for grant of UAS licence on FCFS basis was taken on November 24, 2003 when first time after introduction of UAS Licensing Regime on November 11, 2003, the issue of Letter of Intent for grant of UAS licences was being decided. It was, inter-alia, decided by the then

Hon'ble MOC&IT to grant UAS licences on First-Come-First-Served basis as the announced guidelines had made it open for new licences to be issued on continuous basis at any time and spectrum was to be allotted subject to availability. This was also stated therein that "this in effect would imply that an applicant who comes first will be granted the spectrum first so it will result in grant of licence on First-Come First-Served basis."

The One Man Committee (OMC) under Justice Shivraj V Patil on examination of appropriateness of procedures followed by DoT in issuance of licenses and allocation of spectrum during the period 2001-2009, has in its report dated January 31, 2011, has observed that

> The FCFS procedure adopted and applied, that too without consistency, was clearly without any nexus with the objective of the selection of UAS licencees pursuant to NTP 1999. By applying FCFS, the best eligible applicant's offer could stand excluded. This was opposed to the principles 98 of level playing field amongst prospective applicants. The criteria of FCFS as adopted by the DoT was neither contemplated nor was it consistent with the NTP 1999, recommendations of TRAI and the Cabinet decision. Added to this, the basis of reckoning, to apply FCFS was not consistently followed. Prior to January 7, 2008, the date of receipt of applications in DoT was reckoned for the purposes of FCFS and after January 7, 2008 the date of compliance of LoI was reckoned for purposes of FCFS. This was also not in tune with extant policy.

The Public Accounts Committee asked the Department to furnish them the file notings of November 24, 2003 wherein the then Ministry of Communications and Information Technology had reportedly decided to grant UAS licences on FCFS basis. The DoT furnished the complete file notings.

A perusal of the said notings revealed that nowhere the then Minister of Communications and Information Technology had himself minuted the FCFS policy. However, he approved the file wherein there had been mention of the FCFS policy in the following two contexts:

GOVERNMENT OF INDIA
MINISTRY OF COMMUNICATIONS AND INFORMATION TECHNOLOGY
DEPARTMENT OF TELECOMMUNICATIONS

RAJYA SABHA
UNSTARRED QUESTION NO. 1803
TO BE ANSWERED ON 6TH DECEMBER, 2007

LICENSES TO NEW SERVICE PROVIDERS

1803. SHRI RAJEEV CHANDRASEKHAR :

Will the Minister of COMMUNICATIONS AND INFORMATION TECHNOLOGY be pleased to state:

(a) the process at present being followed for awarding licenses to new service providers on first come first serve basis; and

(b) when was this policy formed?

ANSWER

THE MINISTER OF STATE IN THE MINISTRY OF COMMUNICATIONS AND INFORMATION TECHNOLOGY (DR. SHAKEEL AHMAD)

(a) & (b) The process at present being followed for awarding new Unified Access Services (UAS) Licences, on first come first serve basis, is as per the UAS Licence guidelines dated 14.12.2005.

****

(i) It is also presumed that such new licence in the category of UASL would be on a first-come first-served basis on the basis of application.

(ii) As regards the point raised about grant of new licences of first-come-first-served basis, the announced guidelines have made it open for new licences to be issued on continuous basis at any time. however, the Spectrum is to be allotted subject to availability. this in effect would imply that an applicant who comes first will be granted the Spectrum first so it will result in grant of licence on first-come-first served basis.

Asked to furnish the complete details indicating inter-alia since when the FCFS policy had been adopted the level at which it was approved etc., the DoT replied that during the reign of the NDA government, on November 24, 2003, the Hon'ble MOC&IT approved the approach of granting of UAS licences on First-Come First-Served basis as the announced guidelines had made it open for new licences to be issued on continuous basis at any time and spectrum was to be allotted subject to availability.

This in effect implied that an applicant who comes first will be granted the spectrum first so it had resulted in grant of licence on First-Come First-Served basis. Prior to January 2008, UAS licences were being issued on First-Come First-Served basis as per the date of application for grant of UAS licence in that particular service area. Even though, in some service areas, LoIs were issued simultaneously in 2004 but finally the UAS licences were issued based on the date of application for grant of UAS licence. In one case in 2004, on two applications of different dates in a service area, LoIs were issued simultaneously but the UAS licence was signed first with the later applicant as the earlier applicant sought time for fulfilling the conditions of the LoI.

When the Public Accounts Committee asked Shri Nripendra Misra, former Chairman, TRAI to depose on the FCFS policy, he submitted in evidence:

... there is no such principle. It is more like what one could say as prescription. What was the practice in DoT was that if the application came, and I am now talking of 2004-2005-2006-2007 period, the applications were registered date-wise. Based on the date, they were kept on record. They were kept on record for years also because the reference was sent to the TRAI on capping of Licence issue.

But in the files of the DoT the first-come first-served reference comes, if my memory is right that comes from the Spectrum. The procedure is, if a licence is granted a letter of intent is issued. Once you issue a letter of intent, you give 15 days' time that in 15 days' time the formalities including the deposit money etc. So, all those who get LoI, they do not reshuffle the order of priority. If somebody deposits money one day, somebody deposits on third day or sixth day, because everybody has been given time to complete the formality in 15 days; after having completed the formality, and after having signed the agreement, then the letter of intent is converted into a licence; once the licence is converted, then you submit the design and drawings of frequency coordination of the Wireless Planning Cell (WPC) WPC that a question was raised that all those who have got the licence, what should be the method for Spectrum allocation and how. And there, on file, it was decided that those who have completed the formality and those who have now also completed the designs and drawings, and now have come to the WPC, there is WPC administratively it will be on a first-come first-served basis. So there is no rule as such which was there.

Meanwhile, CAG Audit scrutiny of the subject revealed that the First-Come First-Served (FCFS) policy earlier internally adopted in DoT for allocation of Spectrum, was then extended for issue of new UAS licences. Under this policy, all applications are registered in the Central Registry Section of DoT where date of receipt and serial numbers are posted on it. Priority of applications is determined based on this date of receipt in the Central Registry.

In a communication dated November 2, 2007, the Hon'ble MoC&IT had even confirmed to the Hon'ble Prime Minister that the processing of applications was to be on the FCFS basis. However, CAG audit found that DoT deviated even from the FCFS policy in letter and spirit later. Thus, the applications submitted between March 2006 and September 25, 2007 were issued the LoIs simultaneously on a single day, viz. January 10, 2008.

A notice was issued through a press release giving less than an hour to collect the same. This decision to issue LoIs simultaneously to all applicants was taken at the level of the Minister. As per the FCFS policy being followed those who were issued LoIs were given 15 days to fulfill the conditions. This included submission of a Performance Bank Guarantee (PBG) and a Financial Bank Guarantee (FBG).

By changing the FCFS criteria, some licensees, who could proactively anticipate such procedural changes were ready with the Demand Drafts drawn on dates prior to the notification of cut off date by DoT and could avail the benefit of first right to allocation of spectrum, having jumped the queue. The entire process followed lacked transparency and objectivity and has eroded the credibility of DoT.

In the light of the above findings of the C&AG, the Public Accounts Committee queried about the claim of the DoT that they had been following the FCFS policy in letter and spirit, its sanctity notwithstanding, in view of the fact that the applications submitted between March 2007 and September 25, 2007 were issued LOIs simultaneously on a single date viz. January 10, 2008.

In reply, the DoT stated that after the reference dated April 13, 2007 of DoT to TRAI, several UASL applications received in the meantime got accumulated awaiting TRAI's recommendations and decision of Government thereof. It was decided that the LoIs to all the eligible applicants who had applied upto September 25, 2007 will be issued simultaneously and an applicant who fulfils the conditions of LOI first will be granted license first.

A press releases were on January 10, 2008 issued stating that DOT has been implementing a policy of First-cum-First-Served for grant of UAS licences under which initially an application which is received first will be processed first and thereafter if found eligible will be granted LOI and then whosoever complies with the conditions of LOI first will be granted UAS licence.

Another press release was also issued on January 10, 2008 where the applicant companies who have submitted applications to DoT for grant of UAS licences in various service areas on or before September 25, 2007 were requested to depute their Authorized signatory/Company Secretary/

authorized representative with authority letter to collect response(s) of DOT.

Similarly, the companies who had applied for usage of dual technology spectrum were also requested to collect the DOT's response. All were requested to assemble at 3:30 P.M. on January 10, 2008 at Committee Room, 2nd Floor, Sanchar Bhawan, New Delhi. It was also mentioned that the companies which fail to report before 4.30 P.M. on January 10, 2008, the responses of DOT will be dispatched by post. All eligible LoI [Letter of Intent] holders for UASL were to submit compliance to DoT to the terms of LoIs within the prescribed period (15 days from the date of issue of LoI) during the office hours i.e. 9.00 A.M. to 5.30 P.M. on working days.

All the eligible applicants who applied till September 25, 2007 assembled at 3:30 pm on January 10, 2008 at Committee Room, Sanchar Bhavan where all the LoIs were issued simultaneously on First-come first-served basis. All the applicants who applied till September 25, 2007 knew that their applications were being processed by the Department for grant to licence as clarifications on their applications upto September 25, 2007 only, were sought by the Department on December 10, 2007. Most of the companies complied with the condition of LoIs on the January 10, 2008 and rest submitted compliance on the next day.

Thereafter, service area wise UAS licences were granted as per the date and time of compliance of LOIs. However, date and time of compliance of LOIs and subsequently date of signing of Licence Agreements did not in any manner pre-judice their right as allocation of available spectrum to all of them in most of the service areas were made on same day.

Asked by the PAC to furnish the reasons for issue of 122 UAS licences on a single date, the DoT replied that in a communication dated December 26, 2007 from the Ministry of Communications and Information Technology to the Prime Minister, the reasons to act without further delay were brought out as it was indicated therein that a large number of LOIs were proposed to be issued simultaneously.

D. S. Mathur, then Secretary DoT while tendering evidence before the Public Accounts Committee, submitted that the FCFS policy had been in vogue in the Department. He further stated:

Press Release

In the light of Unified Access Services Licence (UASL) guidelines issued on 14th December 2005 by the department regarding number of Licences in a Service Area, a reference was made to TRAI on 13-4-2007. The TRAI on 28-08-2007 recommended that No cap be placed on the number of access service providers in any service area. The government accepted this recommendation of TRAI. Hon'ble Prime Minister also emphasized on increased competition while inaugurating India Telecom 2007. Accordingly, DOT has decided to issue LOI to all the eligible applicants on the date of application who applied up-to 25-9-2007.

UAS licence authorises licencee to rollout telecom access services using any digital technology which includes wire-line and/or wireless (GSM and/or CDMA) services. They can also provide Internet Telephony, Internet Services and Broadband services. UAS licence in broader terms is an umbrella licence and does not automatically authorize UAS licencees usage of spectrum to rollout Mobile (GSM and/or CDMA) services. For this, UAS licencee has to obtain another licence, i.e. Wireless Operating Licence which is granted on first-come-first-serve basis subject to availability of spectrum in particular service area.

DOT has been implementing a policy of First-cum-First Served for grant of UAS licences under which initially an application which is received first will be processed first and thereafter if found eligible will be granted LOI and then who so ever complies with the conditions of LOI first will be granted UAS licence.

Department of Telecom
(AS cell)

10.01.2008

The above Press release has approval of Hon'ble MOC&.
and may kindly be released immediately.

To,
Director (M&C), PIB, Patel Bhawan, New Delhi.

उप महानिदेशक (ए. एस.)
Dy. Director General (AS)
विभाग आगम संचार

Press Release

In the light of Unified Access Services Licence (UASL) guidelines issued on 14th December 2005 by the department regarding number of Licences in a Service Area, a reference was made to TRAI on 13-4-2007. The TRAI on 28-08-2007 recommended that No cap be placed on the number of access service providers in any service area. The government accepted this recommendation of TRAI. Hon'ble Prime Minister also emphasized on increased competition while inaugurating India Telecom 2007. Accordingly, DOT has decided to issue LOI to all the eligible applicants who applied up-to 25-9-2007.

UAS licence authorises licencee to rollout telecom access services using any digital technology which includes wire-line and/or wireless (GSM and/or CDMA) services. They can also provide Internet Telephony, Internet Services and Broadband services. UAS licence in broader terms is an umbrella licence and does not automatically authorize UAS licencees usage of spectrum to rollout Mobile (GSM and/or CDMA) services. For this, UAS licencee has to obtain another licence, i.e. Wireless Operating Licence which is granted on first-come-first-serve basis subject to availability of spectrum in particular service area.

DOT has been implementing a policy of First-cum-First Served for grant of UAS licences under which initially an application which is received first will be processed first and thereafter if found eligible will be granted LOI and then who so ever complies with the conditions of LOI first will be granted UAS licence.

However, if more then one applicant complies with LOI condition on the same date, the inter-se seniority would be decided by the date of application. 'X'

'X' is not necessary as it is new stipulation

7/1

Department of Telecommunications

Press Release

Date : 10th January 2008

Sub : UASL applicants to depute their authorised representative to collect responses of DOT on 10.1.2008.

The applicant companies who have submitted applications to DOT for grant of UAS licences in various service areas on or before 25.9.2007 are requested to depute their Authorised signatory/Company Secretary/ authorised representative with authority letter to collect response(s) of DOT. They are requested to bring the company's rubber stamp for receiving these documents to collect letters from DOT in response to their UASL applications. Only one representative of the Company/group Company will be allowed. Similarly, the companies who have applied for usage of dual technology spectrum are also requested to collect the DOT's response.

All above are requested to assemble at 3:30 pm on 10.1.2008 at Committee Room, 2nd Floor, Sanchar Bhawan, New Delhi. The companies which fail to report before 4.30 P.M. on 10.01.2008, the responses of DOT will be dispatched by post.

All eligible LOI holders for UASL may submit compliance to DOT to the terms of LOIs within the prescribed period during the office hours i.e. 9.00 A.M. to 5.30 P.M. on working days.

File No.20-100/2007-AS-I

Dated 10.1.2008

10/1/2008

(A.K. Srivastava)
DDG(AS)
Dept. of Telecom

DDG(C&A): The above Press Release may kindly be uploaded on DOT website immediately.

> ... the issue rose as to what should be the first-come-first-served policy. The Department has been dealing with the applications as they were coming in even from earlier. So, the applications when they came in were recorded at the Central Registry and numbered and they were handled one after the other in sequential order. so, this was one issue whether this should be followed in the same manner or there should be a change in it.
>
> Sir, I did tell the office, given the background that I have just submitted, that since there are certain major issues that had to be first sorted out before we could really process the applications that were pending, because if you do not know how to take up applications in a sequence, if you do not know how to grant a licence, how do you process the applications, therefore, I had instructed the office that while these matters are under considerations and a decision is likely to be taken, till such time these applications should not be processed.

Asked to state whether the FCFS policy, as had been in vogue in the Department, was applied properly in the allocation of UAS licences/2G spectrum in 2008, Mr. Mathur replied that it was not permitted to be used.

When the Public Accounts Committee asked Nripendera Misra, the former Chairman, TRAI, as to what should constitute the appropriate adherence to the FCFS policy, he submitted:

> ... But my understanding is that if the letter of intent says that please complete the formality within 15 days, then all those who completed the formalities within 15 days, they remain in the same order as they got the application date. And it is only after the 15th day that any other determination can take place.

Siddhartha Behura, former Secretary, DoT (since charge-sheeted and in prison), testified before the PAC that inter-se seniority should be determined by the date of application, a condition which he had inserted in the draft Press Note of January 10, 2008 *which was deleted by the Minister* and thus overruling the Department's views. On the same issue, Siddhartha Behura, the former Secretary, DOT, deposed in evidence:

> My observation was that if they have fulfilled the condition the date of seniority shall be determined by the date of application. this is the paragraph I added to the Press Note which was presented before me. it went to the Minister because there was a discussion, since he had already decided and the matter stand decided. I said that this is the only thing which came up before me for my consideration as far as the issue of licence is concerned and that as far as this issue is concerned, I will not be able to agree to the fact that somebody who has applied first will get relegated. So, naturally, the Minister decided to overrule. I have recorded it in the note sheet.

Asked to elaborate the stance taken by him to evolve the appropriate implementation of the FCFS policy, Behura further submitted:

> There was a Press Note which came for my consideration. the first thing which came for my consideration regarding 2G was a Press Note which outlined that so many applications are pending and we shall, in the first instance, consider applications received upto September 25, 2007 and it also said that we shall, in the first instance, issue a Letter of Intent and this Letter of Intent shall be issued simultaneously to all and whoever completes the formalities regarding LoI shall be granted a licence first and he can queue up for Spectrum separately.
>
> It basically meant that somebody who has applied first meant he gets Spectrum first because licence and Spectrum as far as Telecom Department is concerned, unfortunately, continues till today to be bundles. If licence were on and Spectrum were to be treated differently perhaps it would have been different. But licence always meant a 4.4 MHz of Spectrum. So, a licence in effect meant Spectrum. So, actually if somebody comes first or second and he does not stand in the queue and gets relegated, I feel that he has not been served on the first come first serve basis. The fact that everybody was going to be issued letter simultaneously meant they were to come and fulfill the conditions first naturally because if they do not fulfill they stand to be relegated.

So, without knowing much about telecom, this exactly did not fall within the realm of telecom, I added a simple line to the Press Note saying that, however, if more than one applicant fulfils the conditions of an LoI on the same day – because the general felling around was that everybody was going to fulfill the conditions on the same day, somebody may come at 10th or 7th, just because he is coming on 7th he is not going to get relegated because somebody has come on 10th and he has come six months before, I said interse seniority shall be determined by the date of application.

This is the Press Note which was submitted to the Hon'ble Minister. Actually, the Minister had taken this decision that it shall be otherwise.

In the above context, the Public Accounts Committee asked DoT as to whether all the applicants who completed the formalities within 15 days as per the conditions of the LoI should have not received in the same order as they were on the applications date. In reply, the DoT stated that The draft Press release dated January 10, 2008 was amended by the then Hon'ble MOC & IT by deleting the sentence that "however, if more than one applicant complies with LoI conditions on the same date, the inter-se seniority would be decided by the date of application."

Accordingly, in the year 2008, UAS licences were issued based on the date and time of compliances of the conditions of the LoIs. However, the One-Man Committee (OMC) under Justice Shivraj V Patil on examination of appropriateness of procedures followed by DoT in issuance of licenses and allocation of spectrum during the period 2001-2009, has in its report dated January 31, 2011, has observed that:

After decision of the Minister for grant of UASLs to all applicants who had applied upto September 25, 2007 and to recur priority from the date of compliance with LoI, first Press Note dated January 10, 2008 137 were issued at about 1.47 P.M. notifying the same. It was further notified that DoT has been implementing FCFS basis for grant of UASLs under which initially an application, which is received first will be processed first and thereafter, if found, eligible applicant will be granted LoI and then whosoever complies with the conditions of LoI first will be granted UASL. The said Press Note though for the first notified the decision of DoT to accord priority to applicants, who complied with LoI first, wrongly mentioned that DoT has been implementing such a policy though in the past such practice was never adopted. Further, the first Press Note dated January 10, 2008 was published on the websites of DoT and PIB only. The first Press Note dated January 10, 2008 contained critical information as to drastic change in procedure followed by DoT hitherto as the priority already acquired by applicants by virtue of date of submission of applications was to change. The said press Note affected the rights of applicants inter-se. The publication on the websites without publications in newspapers and without individual communications to all the applicants was opposed to the requirements of transparency and fairness.

The LoI for grant of UASL issued on January 10, 2008 stipulated fifteen days as the period within which the terms of LoI had to be complied with by an applicant. Having stipulated the period for compliance, there was no justification in granting priority to an applicant, who complied with LoI earlier to fifteen days and also earlier to other applicants comparatively, rendering it unfair.

Justice Shivraj V Patil has further observed that:

The FCFS procedure adopted and applied, that too without consistency, was clearly without any nexus with the objective of the selection of UAS licencees pursuant to NTP 1999. By applying FCFS, the best eligible applicant's offer could stand excluded. This was opposed to the principles 98 of level playing field amongst prospective applicants. The criteria of FCFS as adopted by the DoT was neither contemplated nor was it consistent with the NTP 1999, recommendations of TRAI and the Cabinet decision. Added to this, the basis of reckoning, to apply FCFS was not consistently followed. Prior to January 7, 2008, the date of receipt of applications in DoT was reckoned for the purposes of FCFS and after January 7, 2008 the date of compliance of LoI was reckoned for purposes of FCFS. This was also not in tune with extant policy.

But, the PAC was, as was the whole country, shocked how by devising a capricious and opaque procedure, the applications submitted between March 2006 and September 25, 2007 were issued the LoIs simultaneously on a single day on January 10, 2008 and asked to fulfil the conditions including a Demand Draft of Rs. 1,659 crores, and to collect the licence within less than an hour within a 45 minutes from the publication in the Ministry website at 2.45 PM on January 10, 2008 under the orders of MOC & IT as against the prescribed period of 15 days under the procedure followed hitherto.

Evidently, the chosen companies had foreknowledge of such novel method with the result they were able to fulfil the conditions of PBG, FBG and Demand Drafts drawn on dates prior to the cut-off date by the DoT.

ARBITRARY ADVANCEMENT OF THE CUT-OFF DATE

In August 2007, TRAI had recommended that there be "no cap" on the number of licences in any service area and the recommendations was accepted by the Ministry of Communication and Information Technology after an Expert Committee of the Ministry had considered the recommendations for a month and half from September 5, 2007 onwards Government on October 17, 2007. But, the TRAI recommendation was brazenly circumvented. Bypassing its own decision of the acceptance of the recommendation, the DoT capriciously for no valid reasons, put an artificial cap even as the Expert Committee of the DoT was examining the recommendation through its Press Release dated September 24, 2007 fixing October 1, 2007 as cut-off date.

The Department reasoned that at the time of reference to TRAI in April, 2007, only 53 applications were pending but after TRAI's recommendation in August, 2007 there was a sudden spurt in the number of applications and hence the Department decided to stop receiving further applications keeping in view the likely availability of Spectrum. The Department's reasoning is unacceptable because TRAI's August, 2007 recommendation was accepted by the DoT in October 17, 2007 by which time there must have been some indications of the number of applications that would be coming. Moreover, under the statute of TRAI

Act the Authority has to be consulted on its recommendations that are not acceptable nor the issue was placed before the Telecom Commission, and yet a cut-off date was announced. Astonishingly, nobody in the DoT even thought of it as is corroborated from the fact that no material on record was available with the Department to show any initiative in this regard.

What is worse is that the cut-off date of October 1, 2007 was advanced after to September 25, 2007 through a Press Release dated January 10, 2008 in a dubious supposedly confidential decision taken by the Minister as far back as on November 2, 2007. Some of the applicant Telecom companies were privy to this decision, as Etisalat DB confessed in its counter affidavit in my Writ Petition in the Supreme Court seeking cancellation of the spectrum licenses granted. Such a decision was taken without the approval of the full Telecom Commission which was scheduled to meet on January 9, 2008 to discuss the full agenda on spectrum allocation but the meeting was deliberately postponed to January 15, 2008 anticipating objections.

What is more important is that it was so done despite the advice of the Prime Minister contained in his letter dated November 2, 2007 emphasizing allocation of spectrum and revision of entry fee in a fair and transparent manner. The CBI records show that the office of Telecom Minister was personally monitoring the receipt of applications and in fact only after ascertaining the receipt of certain companies by September 24, 2007, the cut-off date was advanced. The High Court of Delhi in the S.Tel case had ruled that "there cannot be a change in the rule after the game has begun" and that the DoT "cannot be allowed to arbitrarily change the cut-off date and that too without any justifiable reasons."

On this question whether the cut-off date was announced on the basis of availability of spectrum, the former Secretary who has since been charge sheeted, admitted on the PAC hearings that there was no synchronization and no scientific analysis nor did he see any file regarding availability of spectrum. Upon the scrutiny of written and oral evidence and the perusal of the findings of the Justice Shivraj Patil Committee, records of the CBI the judgment of the High Court of Delhi and the refusal of the Supreme Court on my impleading Petition the appeal by the DoT to interfere with the orders of the High Court. The effect of this refusal is that the advancement of the cut-off date held by the Delhi High Court as arbitrary and unjustifiable has become final.

From the written reply furnished to the Public Accounts Committee, it is found that the then MOC&IT as early as on November 2, 2007 had approved the advancement of the cut-off date to September 25, 2007 on the ground of availability of only 15MHz of Spectrum, even while replying to the Prime Minister *on the same day,* he claimed that there was 60-65MHz Spectrum still available for the 2G services! When the Department was asked to explain the position, they informed that there was a typographical error in the material furnished to Public Accounts Committee!!

This in itself shows how much fudging, forgery and misinformation was being done on the then Minister Raja's behest.

Before the CAG Audit Report was laid in the Parliament, B.K. Syngal had already apprised the Committee in detail and with documentary evidences on the arbitrary decisions taken by the DoT in putting a cap on the number of applications for the UAS licences.

Audit scrutiny revealed that the TRAI Report of August 2007 had recommended "no cap" on the number of licences in any service area. Despite this recommendation of TRAI, the DoT issued a Press Release on September 24, 2007 stating that applications for issue of licences would be accepted only upto October 1, 2007. This action, in effect, conveyed fixation of an artificial cap in the number of licenses to be awarded. However, in its response (July 2010) to the report issued to the Ministry (July 2010), the Ministry has stated that it accepted the recommendation of 'no cap' by the TRAI in October 2007. It seems that the Ministry, by issuing the press release in advance in September 2007 had, in effect, circumvented the recommendation of TRAI by taking an action counter to the recommendation and its acceptance by DoT in October 2007. To further compound the earlier decision, of restricting consideration of applications received up to October 1, 2007, the DoT further advanced this date to restrict issuance of Letters of Intent (LoIs) only to applications received up to September 25, 2007. This was ostensibly to avoid legal implications in view of the shortage of spectrum for GSM services.

PRESS NOTE

24th September, 2007

Cut-off Date for Applications for Unified Access Services Licences

It has been decided that new applications for Unified (Telecom) Access Services (UAS) Licences will not be accepted by Department of Telecommunications (DoT) after 01.10.2007 till further orders.

F.No.20-100/2007-AS-I(pt)

Department of Telecommunications
(AS Cell)

Subject : Cut off date for receiving applications for UAS Licences

As per amendment dated 11.11.2003 to New Telecom Policy-1999(NTP-99), the existing CMTS and Basic Service Licensees were permitted on 25.11.2003, migration to Unified Access Service Licensing regime. Also new Access Service Licenses were to be granted for UASL service only. The window for submission of applications for UASL was opened on continuous basis in terms of guidelines issued by DOT and put on the website. A policy of first come- first served for grant of UAS License was being followed based on decision of Hon'ble MOC&IT. However, in view of increasing demand on spectrum in a substantial manner, recommendation of TRAI was sought on 13.4.2007 on limit of number of Access Service Providers and on other terms and conditions of UAS Licences. It was also decided separately by Hon'ble MOC&IT that new UASL applications are to be processed only after receipt of TRAI recommendations and LOI is to be granted after receiving comments of WA on availability of spectrum.

The recommendations of TRAI has since been received by DOT on 29.8.2007. TRAI has, interalia, recommended no cap on number of Access Service Providers in any service area among other recommendations on terms of UAS Licences. In the meantime, the new UASL applications are pouring in and till date 167 applications from 12 companies for 22 service areas have been received. It is felt that it may be difficult to handle such large number of applications at any point of time. Therefore, it is proposed that we may announce a cut-off for receipt of UASL applications such that no new applications will be received after cut-off date till further orders. We may give a reasonable time to all who wish to submit new UASL applications so that the decision may not be challenged. The reasonable period may be, say, 15 days. Therefore, we may announce 10.10.2007 to be the cut-off date for receipt of new UASL applications till further orders.

DFA please.

24/9/07
(A.K. Srivastava)
DDG(AS)
24th September 2007

Member(T)

Secretary(T)

Hon'ble MOC&IT

In view of large number of applications pending and to discourage speculative players, we may close receiving applications on 1.10.2007 i.e. one month from the date of Trai's recommendations

A chronology of event from September 24, 2007 to January 25, 2008 is as follows:

Date	Procedural Details
24/09/2007	Hon'ble MoC&IT conveyed through press release that no application under UAS will be accepted after 01/10/2007.
18/10/2007	Ministry accepted the Recommendations of TRAI. LoIs were issued to the Reliance Communications Ltd and two others for dual technology.
19/10/2007	A Press release was issued stating that the TRAI's recommendations have been accepted by the DoT. Policy for the dual technology was also announced.
26/10/2007	Ministry of Law and Justice (MLJ) was requested to communicate the opinion of the Ld Attorney General of India/Solicitor General of India on the procedure to be followed.
1/11/2007	Opinion of the Hon'ble MLJ was received by DoT.
02/11/2007	DoT decided that only the applications received up to 25/09/2007 shall be processed which were 232 in number.
02/11/2007	The PM wrote to the MoC&IT to consider auctioning of spectrum and revision of entry fee in a fair and transparent manner.
02/11/2007	The MoC&IT wrote to the PM that sufficient 2G spectrum available to cater to the requirement of few new operators and more no. of operator will increase teledensity and bring down the tariff.
02/11/2007	The MoC&IT again wrote to the PM justifying the decision of amendment of cut off date and termed the suggestion of Ministry of Law and Justice for GOM as 'out of context.'
26/12/2007	The MoC&IT again wrote to the PM regarding the personal discussion with Hon'ble PM and External Affairs Minister on various issues including issue of dual technology and issue of new licences.
31/12/2007	The Secretary DoT and Member (Finance) DoT retired.
03/01/2008	The PM acknowledged the letter dated 26/12/2007 sent by the MoC&IT.

09/01/2008	A meeting of full Telecom Commission was scheduled for 09.01.2008 to discuss issues of new licences and allocation of spectrum to existing as well as new players by auctions postponed to 15.01.2008.
10/01/2008	Decision regarding cut off date being 25/09/2007 was conveyed through a Press Release in the afternoon of 10 January 2008.
10/01/2008	Through a press release, companies who had submitted applications on or before 25 September 2007 were advised to depute their authorized representative at 3.30 PM on 10 January 2008 to collect response(s).
10/01/2008	Out of 232 applications received up to cut off date 121 LoIs were issued to applicants found eligible.
10/01/2008	All applicants communicated their acceptance.78 applicants complied with terms and conditions including submission of entry fee, PBG and FBG.
11/01/2008	Remaining 43 applicants complied with terms and conditions.
25/01/2008	All UAS licenses were issued to be effective from 25 January 2008.

In the above context, the Committee asked the DoT whether the DoT had not put an artificial cap on the number of licences to be issued by fixing a cut-off date for receipt of the applications and whether in the process TRAI's recommendation of 'no cap' was not circumvented. In reply, the DoT stated that they had been issuing UAS licences in various service areas on continuous basis since introduction of UASL regime in 2003 subject to availability of spectrum. At the time of reference to TRAI on April 13, 2007, 53 application were pending.

After the receipt of "No Cap" recommendations dated August 28, 2007 from the TRAI, there was a sudden spurt in the applications for UAS Licenses. Keeping in view likely availability of spectrum it was decided in the department to stop receiving further applications till further orders. Therefore, on September 24, 2007, a Press release was issued which appeared in the newspapers on September 25, 2007, stating that the new applications for Unified (Telecom) Access Services (UAS) Licences will not be accepted by Department of Telecommunications (DoT) after October 1, 2007 **till further orders.**

Asked by the PAC to state whether TRAI was even consulted on the matter of receipt of large number of application after their 'no cap' recommendation and whether the matter was placed before the Telecom Commission, the DoT replies that they did not consult the TRAI on the matter nor the issue was placed before the Telecom Commission and there was no material on record as to why the Authority and Telecommunications were not consulted/apprised of the issue.

The Public Accounts Committee then pointed out that on one hand the Prime Minister was apprised by the then Telecom Minister that if more number of players were allowed, there would be greater completion resulting in lower tariff and better tele-density. On the other hand, the number of applicants were arbitrarily restricted by the DoT disregarding TRAI's recommendations.

In this regard, the Public Accounts Committee enquired whether there was not an apparent contradiction in the stance of the Department. The PAC also wanted to know whether giving just seven days time, i.e. between the issue of Press Release and the cut-off date be considered as reasonable.

In reply, the Department stated that in view of the increasing demand on spectrum in a substantial manner, recommendation of TRAI was sought on April 13, 2007 on limit of number of Access Service Providers and on other terms and conditions of UAS licences. The recommendations of TRAI were received by DoT on August 29, 2007. TRAI had, inter-alia, recommended no cap on number of Access Service Providers in any service area among other recommendations on terms of UAS licence.

In the meantime, the new UASL applications were poring in and till September 24, 2007, 167 applications from 12 companies for 22 service areas had been received. It was therein felt in DoT that it may be difficult to handle such large number of applications at any point of time. Therefore, it was proposed to announce a cut-off for receipt of UASL applications such that no new applications would be received after cut-off date till further orders. It was also proposed that a reasonable time to all who wish to submit new UASL applications may be given so that the decision is not challenged. Time period of 15 days, i.e up to October 10, 2007 was proposed. On September 24, 2007, the then Hon'ble MOC&IT who while approving the file minuted that "in view of large number of applications pending and to discourage speculative players, we may close receiving applications on October 1, 2007 i.e. one month from the date of TRAI's recommendations."

However, the One Man Committee (OMC) under Justice Shivraj V Patil on examination of propriateness of procedures followed by DoT in issuance of licenses and allocation of spectrum during the period 2001-2009, has in its report dated January 31, 2011, has observed that:

> Procedure formulated whereby the processing of applications for grant of UASLs was restricted to only such applications which were received upto September 25, 2007 when the last date for receiving an application was stipulated as October 1, 2007, is not traceable either to the power vested in terms of any procedure laid out or satisfies the requisites of law in particular the principles of objectivity, fairness and transparency.
>
> Report of the One-Man Commission (OMC) is under examination.

The Public Accounts Committee again asked on what precise and pressing circumstances the cut-off date of October 1, 2007 was advanced to September 25, 2007 and whether it did not compound the alleged arbitrariness and favoritism reply, the DoT stated that To decide the number of LOIs to be issued in each service area, a note dated November 2, 2007, was submitted to Hon'ble MOC&IT, *inter-alia* mentioning that:

> In view of TRAI recommendation of no cap on number of operators, large number of applications were being received in the DOT. Therefore it was decided that no more applications shall be received after October 1, 2007 till further orders. Till the cut-off date for receipt of UASL application, 575 applications were received from 46 companies for 22 service areas. The list of these applications along

with date of receipt, company wise and service area wise are placed at p.10/c and 11/c respectively. In order to avoid any legal implications of cut off date, all the applications received till the announcement of cut off date in the press i.e. September 25, 2007 may be processed as per the existing policy and decision on remaining applications may be taken subsequently.

WPC has indicated (in the linked file) an availability of circle wise spectrum based on the internal exercise and likely availability once M/o Defence vacates the spectrum being used by them. Since 75 MHz has been earmarked for 2G in 1,800 band of which a maximum of about 15 MHz is left unused so far which could be utilized for new licences and additional requirement of existing operators. Since the availability of spectrum is not immediately guaranteed in all the service areas as it needs to be vacated by the Defence, a clause may be inserted in the LOI that spectrum allocation is not guaranteed and shall be subject to availability.

In view of above, a decision may be taken on the number of LOI's to be issued in each circle.

On the above note, Hon'ble MOC&IT, on November 2, 2007, decided that "LOI may be issued to the applicants received upto September 25, 2007.

The PAC then queried about the basis on which the DoT suggested to the then Minister for processing only those applications which were received up to September 25, 2007 and the specific impediment that the Department faced in processing all the 575 applications received up to October 1, 2007. In reply, the DoT stated that a copy of the file noting 1/N to 20/N of file No.20-100/2007-AS-I/Pt.C where the such proposal was processed and subsequent discussions/deliberation took place along with approval of the Hon'ble MOC&IT is enclosed at **Annexure-XXXXVII.**

The Justice Shivraj V Patil Committee on examination of appropriateness of procedures followed by DoT in issuance of licenses and allocation of spectrum during the period 2001-2009, has in its report dated January 31, 2011, has observed that:

> However based on the note ... on November 2, 2007 the Minister took the view that the opinion of Minister of Law and Justice was out of context and decided that procedure for grant of new UASLs formulated earlier be continued, consequently the issue whether existing procedure was inconsistent with the extant policies/directions appears to have been ignored. On November 2, 2007, a further decision was taken to grant of Lois to those applicants for UASLs who had applied till September 25, 2007 which decision also did not satisfy the requisites of law in particular the principles of objectivity, fairness and transparency.

A perusal of the above file noting revealed that it was mainly on the basis of the availability of Spectrum that it was decided to process the applications received up to September 25, 2007.

In this context, the Committee asked Shri Siddharth Behura, the former Secretary to confirm whether the cut off date of September 25, 2007 was announced on the basis of the availability of Spectrum. He submitted: "No Sir, I do not think this was linked to the availability of Spectrum at all. Since 2003, I think on the issue of licences and availability of Spectrum, there has been no synchronization, no proper scientific analysis whether we are going to give two licences, four licences or five licences because there is Spectrum. I do not think that kind of a rational thing has ever been done in the Ministry."

He further stated: "The approach has not been taken. I have not been in any of the files that we have so much of Spectrum and therefore, we need to give so many licences. This has never happened."

Referring to the above file-notings of the DoT, which were furnished alongwith the written replies, the Committee desired to know whether it was not ironical that the then MOC&IT on November 2, 2007 approved the advancement of the cut-off date to September 25, 2007 on the ground of availability of only 15MHz of Spectrum but while replying to the Prime Minister on the same day, he claimed that there was 60-65 MHz Spectrum still available for the 2G services.

In reply, the DoT stated that Extracts of the file notings on file 20-1000/2007-AS-I/Part 'C' (where decision by the Hon'ble MoC & IT took the decision to issue LoIs to the applicants received up to September 25, 2007:

> Para 4. WPC has indicated (in the linked file) on availability of circle wise spectrum based on the internal exercise and likely availability once M/O Defence vacates the spectrum being used by them. Since 75 MHz has been earmarked for 2G in 1800 band of which a maximum of about 15 MHz has been released. Therefore, approximately 60 MHz is left unused so far which could be utilized for new licences and additional requirement of existing operators. Since the availability of spectrum is not immediately guaranteed in all the service areas as it needs to be vacated by the Defence, a clause may be inserted in the LoI that spectrum allocation is not guaranteed and shall be subject to availability.

However, while providing reply to the question 15 (a) and (b) of the Questionnaire dated November 26, 2010 of Hon'ble PAC, in para 2 (page 26) of the Answer, while reproducing the above text, the portion underlined above was inadvertently omitted. The typographical error is deeply regretted. Actual file noting referred to above may be seen at 6/N of Annexure-10.

Extracts from letter No.20-1000/2007-AS.I dated November 2, 2007 written by Hon'ble MoC & IT to Hon'ble PM.

> Para 3. I would like to bring it to your notice that DoT has earmarked totally 100 MHz in 900 MHz and 1,800 MHz bands for 2G mobile services. Out of this, so far maximum of about 35 to 40 MHz per Circle has been allotted to different operators and being used by them. The remaining 60 to 65 MHz, including spectrum likely to be vacated by Defence Services, is still available for 2G services.

It may, therefore, be seen that as on November 11, 2007, DoT had already allotted spectrum of about 35 to 40 MHz in both 900 and 1,800 MHz bands. This allotted spectrum included the 15 MHz of spectrum already released by Defence by then. A GoM was constituted for vacation of spectrum by Defence Services. It was expected that after the decision of GoM, Defence would release the balance spectrum of 60 to 65 MHz in different service areas.

The Committee then pointed out that the above said file notings of the Department had not mentioned anything about the availability of Spectrum in the 900 band and desired to know the basis on which the then Minister apprised the Prime Minister of the availability of Spectrum in the 900 band. In reply the DoT stated that extracts of D.O. letter No. 20-1000/2007—AS-Idated November 2, 2007 written by the then Hon'ble MoC&IT to Hon'ble PM pertaining to availability to Spectrum is reproduced below:

> PARA 2 of point 3. I would like to bring it to your kind notice that DoT has earmarked totally 100 MHz in 900 MHz and 1800 MHz bands for 2G mobile services. Out of this, so far a maximum of about 35 to 40 MHz, per circle has been allotted to different operators and being used by them. The remaining 60 to 65 MHz, including Spectrum likely to be vacated by Defence Services, is still available for 2G services.

As on November 2, 2007, DoT had already allotted Spectrum of about 35 to 40 MHz in both 900 and 1800 MHz bands. This allotted Spectrum included 15 MHz of Spectrum already released by Defence in 1,800 MHz by then. The Spectrum of 35 to 40 MHz allotted include 20 to 25 MHz in 900 MHz band and 15 MHz in 1,800 MHz band A Group of Minister (GoM) was constituted for vacation of Spectrum by Defence services. It was expected that after the decision of GoM, Defence would release the balance Spectrum of 60 to 65 MHz in different service areas.

Asked to furnish the file notings indicating inter-alia the original draft of the then Minister's letters to the Prime Minister their approval etc., the Department replied that no such file had been found on record in the DoT.

In response to another specific query, the Department stated that neither the cut-off date of October 1, 2007 for receiving the applications was proponed nor were the applications for grant of UAS licences which were received after September 25, 2007 rejected.

The Committee, then asked whether all the remaining 343 applications had been processed and licences/Spectrum allotted after January, 2008. In reply, the DoT stated that the remaining 343 applications received from September 26, 2007 to October 1, 2007 are still pending with the Department. Hon'ble TDSAT, in para 116 of its judgement dated March 31, 2009, in Petition No. 286 of 2007 in the matter of COAI & Othrs. Vs. UOI & Othrs, has observed that "... Already, as indicated by TRAI itself, there are 6 to 9 operators in each service area and there is demand for additional spectrum. It is therefore puzzling as to why TRAI recommended a no cap policy on the number of service providers. In our view, DOT would be well advised to review this policy keeping in view the various relevant parameters and take an appropriate decision."

Accordingly, on July 22, 2009, DoT sought recommendation of TRAI, inter-alia, on the policy of 'no capping' on the number of Access Service Providers in each service area. On May 11, 2010, TRAI in its recommendations on "Spectrum Management and Licensing Framework" has, inter-alia, recommended that:

> (i) Keeping in view the scarcity of spectrum and the need to provide the contracted spectrum to the existing licensees, the Authority recommends that no more UAS licence linked with spectrum should be awarded. (Para 2.51).
>
> (ii) The Authority would like the Government to note that the recommendation made by the Authority in para 2.51 above is subject to the court decisions in this regard. The applicants will however be free to apply for or opt for a Unified licence, which is being recommended for future licences separately. (Para 2.52)
>
> (iii) All future licences should be unified licences and that spectrum be delinked from the licence. (Para 2.62)
>
> (iv) The Authority has already recommended that in so far as future licensing is concerned, spectrum should be delinked from UAS licence. Accordingly, there is no need for any cap on the number of

access service providers. This recommendation of no cap is only if the future licences are delinked from spectrum. Otherwise, the Authority's specific recommendation is that no more licences should be given. (Para 2.71)

The PAC also asked the Cabinet Secretariat to furnish the Original ToRs of the GoM of 2006 and to state the reasons for limiting the ToRs of the GoM to only vacation of Spectrum as against the Planning Commission's suggestions to consider a transition path for cellular mobile services, Spectrum pricings etc. In reply, the Cabinet Secretariat stated that the original ToRs of the GoM of 2006 as approved by the Prime Minister were as follows:

(i) Determine the quantum of additional minimum and optimum requirement and identify frequency bands for major users, viz.,

(a) Cellular –mobile services, and

(b) Defence and paramilitary forces, for both (i) short term (i.e., less than once year) and (ii) medium term (i.e., less than five years)

(ii) Based on current occupation of Spectrum, clearly delineate a transition path for enabling users like defence and paramilitary forces to migrate to the more appropriate Spectrum slots identified at (i) above, keeping in mind technology upgradation, nature of usage and procurement procedures. The transition path should clearly lay down phasing and sequencing of steps and a feasible time-frame to enable step-by-step monitoring. It would be desirable that this exercise leads to the delineation of an exclusive band for Government/Defence purposes.

(iii) Correspondingly, suggest a transition path for cellular and mobile services to step into the Spectrum bands vacated by security forces and allocated to them.

(iv) Estimate quantum of funds and resources required to enable security forces to procure state-of-the-art equipment, technologically appropriate for the assigned Spectrum. Estimate year wise fund flow requirements, to bring about a smooth transition.

(v) Suggest a Spectrum Pricing Policy and examine the possibility of creation of a Spectrum Relocation Fund. Indicate likely source and quantum of resources so generated and guidelines for the operation of the fund. Spectrum Pricing Policy may, as far as possible, aim at revenues fully offsetting the cost of vacation of Spectrum.

(vi) Suggest guidelines to encourage and incentivize introduction of Spectrum efficient technologies.

The Cabinet Secretariat further stated that the Groups of Ministers (GoMs) are appointed by the Cabinet, the Standing Committees of the Cabinet, or the Prime Minister for investigating and reporting to the Cabinet on such matters as may be specified. When any of the aforesaid authorities take a decisions to constitute a GoM, the Cabinet Secretariat issues the requisite orders.

In the present case, the Prime Minister's Office (PMO) *vide* ID dated February 15, 2006 communicated the decision of the Prime Minister to constitute a Group of Ministers (GoM) on "Vacation of Spectrum and raising resources for the purpose." The backdrop of the constitution of the GoM was the "need for high level priority intervention to resolve various issues concerning vacation of Spectrum and upgrading the technology and equipment of existing udders like defence and funding such upgradation" the composition of the GoM, as approved by the Prime Minister (PM), was as follows: (i) Pranab Mukherjee, the then Raksha Mantri; (ii) Shivraj V. Patil, the then Home Minister; (iii) P. Chidambaram, the then Finance Minister; (iv) Priyaranjan Dasmunshi, the then Minister of Information and Broadcasting; (v) Shri Dayanidhi Maran, the then Minister of Communications and Information Technology; and (vi) Dr. Montek Singh Ahluwalia, Deputy Chairman, Planning Commission.

The order constituting the GoM on the above lines was issued by the Cabinet Secretariat on February, 23, 2006. Vide PMO ID dated November 27, 2006, the Cabinet Secretariat was informed that the PM had approved the following revised ToRs in respect of this GoM:

(i) To recommend measures for vacation of adequate additional Spectrum by the existing large users such as Defence, Space, Para-military, etc, in a time bound manner for the growth of mobile telephony and broadband sectors in the country, in the overall national interest;

(ii) To recommend alternate frequency bands/media for migration of such existing users, keeping in mind the nature of technology urgradation;

(iii) To estimate and identify the resources required by the concerned Ministries and their phasing, for putting in place necessary alternate systems by such users to enable migration;

(iv) To suggest measures for early introduction of Spectrum efficiently digital terrestrial broadcasting for vacation of Spectrum for other services in line with international practices.

The Cabinet Secretariat further stated that the necessary modifications to the ToRs of the GoM were brought about by Cabinet Secretariat memorandum dated December 7, 2006. It was further stated that the suggestions made by the Planning Commission regarding ToRs of the GoM are not available with the Cabinet Secretariat.

But in response to a specific query of the PAC, the PMO replied that the then Minister of Communications and IT [Dayanidhi Maran] addressed three letters to the Prime Minister in 2006, on January 11, 2006, February 28, 2006 and November 16, 2006. These letters dealt with the terms of reference of a Group of Ministers set up for vacation of Spectrum.

The letter of January 11, 2006 suggested draft terms of reference and the same draft was received again with the letter of February 28, 2006, in which the Minister also conveyed his feeling that some of the terms of reference of the Group of Ministers as constituted impinge upon the work normally to be carried out by the Ministry itself, and requested for modification of the terms of reference. The letter dated November 16, 2006 also requested for changing the terms of reference as attached with the letter.

The Prime Minister accepted this position. The terms of reference were accordingly revised to focus on the original goal behind setting up of the GoM, *viz.*, vacation of Spectrum and leaving out spectrum pricing from the purview of the GoM.

This however does not answer the question as to why the Prime Minister failed to set up an empowered GoM for the whole issue as asked for by at least two Cabinet Ministers: Commerce and Law and Justice while contesting the view that the MoC&IT and Minister of Finance could decide the issue of spectrum pricing.. This was mandatory under the Transaction of Business Rules for Ministries.

The then Minister of Commerce and Industry, Shri Kamal Nath had addressed a letter dated November 3, 2007 to the Prime Minister, expressing "concern on the sudden and alarming developments in the telecom sector" and adding that "several prominent international strategy and financial investors have made serious commitments in the telecom sector in India and it is important that the policies that our Government follows continue to support the growth in telecom sector and remain fair to all players." He further stated that the balance is vital for the image of India across the globe. Against this background, he suggested that it may be advisable to have comprehensive look at the issues facing the telecom sector and that he would advise setting up of a Group of Ministers.

Meanwhile, Cabinet Secretariat received a letter dated March, 28, 2007 from the then Finance Secretary reiterating that technology neutrality and Spectrum pricing should be included with the ToRs of the GoM. Finance Secretary had in his letter stated that the methodology for allocation of Spectrum and its pricing are issues that impinge on revenues as well as the ultimate price paid by the consumer; hence, these issues would have to be discussed in the GoM.

On being asked by the PAC of the Cabinet Secretariat for comments on this issue, DoT forwarded a copy of the letter dated April 2, 2007, of then Secretary, DoT to the then Finance Secretary, wherein, it was *inter-alia* stated that Spectrum pricing is within "the normal work" carried out by DoT.

MoF interestingly did not agree with the contention of DoT that these issues are within their normal work allocation, on the ground that these issues have economic and financial ramifications and need to be discussed in the GoM. Hence he sent another letter dated April 19, 2007 which was not replied to.

Cabinet Secretariat advised both the Department of Economic Affairs (DEA) and DoT on May 17, 2007 to discuss and resolve the matter at the level of Secretaries and thereafter advise the Cabinet Secretariat about the decisions taken. Nothing further was heard from DEA on this issue thereafter till November 22, 2007 and now we know why. A chronological summary of the events is given below:

Issues relating to the ToRs of the GoM

Sl. No.	Date	Item
1.	February 23, 2006	Cabinet Secretariat issues a notification for constitution of GoM on vacation of Spectrum etc. (including the issue of 'Spectrum pricing')
2.	April 3, 2006	Letter of the then Secretary, DoT intimating that further directions in the matter are awaited pursuant to the letter dated February 28, 2006 of the then MoCIT to PM.
3.	December 7, 2006	Cabinet Secretariat issues revised ToRs, deleting the issue of 'Spectrum pricing'.
4.	March 28, 2007	Finance Secretary writes to Secretary (DoT) for inclusion of "Spectrum pricing" in the ToRs of the GoM, with a copy to Cabinet Secretariat.
5.	April 2, 2007	Secretary (DoT) writes to Finance Secretary stating that Spectrum pricing is within the normal work carried out by his Ministry and ToRs have been amended following the then Minister's letter to the Prime Minister. A copy of the letter is endorsed to the Cabinet Secretariat.
6.	April 19, 2007	Finance Secretary writes to Cabinet Secretary for inclusion of 'Spectrum pricing' in the ToRs of the GoM.

The role and function of the Cabinet Secretariat was to notify the decisions taken at the level of the Prime Minister in regard to the aforesaid GoM. Since DEA had raised certain issues with regard to the notification of December 7, 2006 (which was notified based on the communication received from the PMO), Cabinet Secretariat asked both the Ministries to resolve their differences, before taking further steps in the matter.

This position was held consistent with the decision of the Union Cabinet, dated October 31, 2003, which had *inter-alia* mandated that Spectrum pricing formula would be discussed and finalized between DoT and Ministry of Finance. But the fact that at least two Ministers, of Law and Commerce of the Cabinet rank had wanted an Empowered GoM to go into the entire question, the question remained why the Cabinet Secretariat did not take the step as required and laid down in the Transaction of Business Rules framed under the Constitution, to constitute a E-GOM.

Article 77(3) of the Constitution of India provides that the President shall make rules for the more convenient transaction of the business of the Government of India, and for the allocation among Ministers of the said business. The Government of India (Allocation of Business) Rules, 1961 and the Government of India (Transaction of Business) Rules, 1961 have both been made in exercise of the power conferred under the said Article.

Further, under Rule 3 of the Transaction of Business (ToB) Rules, subject to the provisions in these rules regarding consultation with other Departments and submission of cases to the Prime Minister, the Cabinet and its Committees and the President, disposal of all business allotted to a Department is to be done by, or under the general or special directions of, the Minister-in-charge.

Thus, the responsibility of ensuring compliance with the directions of Cabinet or its Committees rests with the concerned Ministry/Department (in this case, the Department of Telecommunications (DoT). Rules make it clear that there is a disagreement between two Ministers, and either or both want a GoM, it is required to set it up.

On October 26, 2007, the Member (Technology) DoT wrote a letter to the Secretary, Department of Legal Affairs on the matter so as to enable the DoT to handle such unprecedented situation in a fair and equitable manner which would be legally tenable. He wrote that the DoT wanted the opinion of the Attorney(AG)/Solicitor General(SG). It was based on an intra DoT Note of Member(Finance) Ms. Manju Madhavan and which Note was approved by the Secretary DoT, Mr. Mathur, and put up to Minister Raja He, the Member(Technolgy) also enclosed a Statement of Cases wherein four alternatives were suggested by Ms. Madhavan to deal with the 575 applicants for the grant of UAS licence and allotment of spectrum.

The Law Secretary accordingly mooted a note on November 1, 2007 for the consideration of the Minister of Law and Justice highlighting that the legal opinion sought for from the Attorney General/Solicitor General appeared to be too broad and the issues would have to be refined further.

The Union Law Minister agreeing with views of the Law Secretary recorded on the note that "In view of the importance of the case, it is necessary that the whole issue is first considered by an Empowered Group of Ministers and in that process legal opinion of the Attorney General can be obtained."

In response to the above observation of the Minister of Law and Justice, the Minister of Communications and IT Raja wrote to the Prime Minister on November 2, 2007 *inter-alia* apprising him that "Ministry of Law and Justice, instead of examining the legal tenability of these alternative procedures, suggested referring the matter to empowered Group of Ministers. Since, generally new major policy decisions of a Department or Inter-departmental issues are referred to GoM, and, needless to say that the present issue relates to procedures, the suggestion of Law Ministry is totally out of context."

Interestingly, the Prime Minister's Office was queried by the PAC about the reasons for not constituting a GoM despite request from the Minister of Law and Justice and Minister of Commerce and Industry.

In reply, surprisingly, the PMO stated that no formal request was received from the Minister of Law and Justice for setting up a Group of Ministers. However, it may be recalled as stated above that the then Minister of Communications and IT addressed a letter dated November 2, 2007 to the Prime Minister, apprising that the Department of Telecommunications had wanted to examine the possibility of any other procedure, in addition to the current procedure of allotment of licences, and that the Ministry of Law and Justice was requested by the Department of Telecommunications to examine the legal tenability of the alternatives.

On this, the Law Minister suggested referring the matter to an Empowered Group of Ministers. The Minister of Communications and IT arrogantly stated in his letter to the Prime Minister that this suggestion of the Union Law&Justice Minister "was totally out of context" and that the Department has decided to continue with the First-Come-First-Served basis for processing of applications.

The Public Accounts Committee asked the DoT to explain the rationale on the basis of which the advice of the Ministry of Law and Justice, and that too at the Minister's level, was overlooked and whether by doing so the Department did not deprive themselves of the benefit of the discussion on important telecom issues in an inter-Ministerial forum.

In reply the DoT explained that the need for forming a EGoM arises when a new policy is being framed. Whereas, in this particular issue, no new policy for grant of UAS licences was being framed and the reference to the Ministry of Law was limited to arrange the opinion of Attorney General/Solicitor General on various possible options to deal with the large number of applications to enable DoT to handle such an unprecedented situation in a fair and equitable manner which would be legally tenable. However, the Ministry of Law, instead of arranging the opinion of Attorney General/Solicitor General in the matter, gave its own opinion which was termed as out of context.

Not satisfied with the Department's explanation, the PAC asked whether requesting for legal opinion to handle the unprecedented number of applications in a fair and transparent manner was not akin to seeking suggestions for grant of licence and allocation of spectrum in a fair and transparent manner and in that case whether it was appropriate to term the Minister of Law and Justice's advice out of context, more so when the DoT had sought the legal opinion on its own volition.

In reply, the Department stated that the reference dated October 26, 2007 of DoT to Ministry of Law and Justice with regard to issuance of LOIs was made in the background of larger number of applications. It was proposed to seek the opinion of the Attorney General of India/Solicitor General of India on the various suggested options to deal with the large number of applications to enable DoT to handle such an unprecedented situation in a fair and equitable manner which would be legally tenable.

However, the Ministry of Law, instead of arranging the opinion of Attorney General/Solicitor General in the matter, gave its own opinion which was termed as out of context by the then Hon'ble MOC&IT. The reasons indicated by the then Hon'ble MOC&IT are contained in his

MINISTRY OF LAW & JUSTICE

(Department of Legal Affairs)

The matter relates to the grant of new Unified Access Service (UAS) Licences and approval for use of Dual Technology Spectrum by UAS licencees.

The Ministry of Communications & Information Technology (Department of Telecommunications) have outlined 4 alternatives to deal with the 575 applicants for the grant of UAS and allotment of spectrum to various categories of spectrum. In that connection the Administrative Ministry have sought the views of the Ld Attorney General /Solicitor General on the different alternatives.

The questions posed for the opinion of Attorney General / Solicitor General appear to be too broad and the issue of disposal of the application s for UAS appears to be mixed up with the allotment of Spectrum. Before the request for seeking the views of the Ld Attorney General /Solicitor General the issues will have to be refined further.

MLJ may see for directions.

T.K.Viswanathan
Law Secretary
1/11/07

MLJ

MLJ I agree. In view of the importance of the case and the statement of various options indicated in the whole of the case it is necessary that an empowered view is first considered by an empowered group of Ministers & in that process legal opinion of A.G can be obtained.

1.11.07

Dy. No. 1046/07
Date 01/11/07

Law Secy: MLJ's minute above may be seen. [illegible]

1/11/07

letter dated November 2, 2007 to Hon'ble Prime Minister as reproduced below:

(i) After the announcement of TRAI Recommendations on Review of Licence Terms and Condition for (Telecom) Access Service Providers on August 28, 2007, and unprecedented number of applications were being received by the Department due to Recommendation of TRAI recommending "No Cap" on number of Licenses in a Service Area.

(ii) As unprecedented number of applications were being received, a cut-off date of October 1, 2007 was announced by the Department on September 24, 2007 and a Press Release was given. In all 575 applications for 22 Service Areas were received.

(iii) The Department wanted to examine the possibility of any other procedure in addition to the current procedure of allotment of Licenses to process the huge number of applications. A few alternative procedures as debated in the Department and also opined by few legal experts were suggested by the Department of Telecom to Ministry of Law and Justice to examine its legal tenability to avoid future legal complications, if any. Ministry of Law and Justice, instead of examining the legal tenability of these alternative procedures, suggested referring the matter to empowered Group of Ministers. Since, generally new major policy decisions of a Department of Inter-departmental issues are referred to GOM, and, needless to say that the present issue relates to procedures, the suggestion of Law Ministry is totally out of context.

However, the One Man Committee (OMC) under Justice Shivraj V. Patil on examination of appropriateness of procedures followed by DoT in issuance of licences and allocation of spectrum during the period 2001-2009, has in its report dated January 31, 2011, has observed that "relating to important Government contracts Ministry of Law and Justice is required to be consulted. The DoT itself having sought opinion as to procedure to be followed for grant of UASLs, ignored the opinion of

Ministry of Law and Justice in this regard, which required consideration of the matter by a Group of Ministers, turning it as out of context."

The Committee, then, asked whether the legal opinion on the matter was finally obtained from the Attorney General/Solicitor General, as proposed in the Member(Technology) DoT's note dated October 26, 2007. In reply, the DoT stated that in the letter dated December 26, 2007 from MOC&IT to PM it was stated that:

> Since the cases filed by Cellular Operators Association of India (COAI) on these issues before Telecom Disputes Settlement & Appellate Tribunal (TDSAT) and Delhi High Court are being represented by Solicitor General of India, he was also called for the discussions to explain the legal position.
>
> ... In these circumstances, the discussions with the External Affairs Minister and Solicitor General of India have further enlightened me to take a pre-emptive and pro-active decision on these issues as per the guidelines and rules framed there under to avoid any further confusions and delay. The issue wise details and my decisions are given in the enclosed annexure.

The enclosed annexure to the said letter dated December 12, 2007 mentioned that:

> ... Issue of Licence: The First-cum-First Served policy is also applicable for grant of licence on compliance of LOI conditions. Therefore, any applicant who complies with the conditions of LOI first will be granted UAS licence first. This issue never arose in the past as at one point of time only one application was processed and LOI was granted and enough time was given to him for compliance of conditions of LOI.
>
> However, since the Government has adopted a policy of "No Cap" on number of UAS Licence, a large number of LOI's are proposed to be issued simultaneously. In these circumstances, an applicant who fulfils the conditions of LOI first will be granted licence

first, although several applicants will be issued LOI simultaneously. The same has been concurred by the Solicitor General of India during the discussions.

Further, before issue of first Press Release dated 10.01.2008 regarding grant of UAS licences, on January 7, 2008, the opinion of the Solicitor General was obtained directly by-passing the Law Ministry. Surprisingly, the then SG, and now AG, Vahanvati agreed to violate the terms and conditions of the Service Rules for Law Officers, and gave his opinion which suited Raja. The Copy of the same is at **Annexure-**

Referring to the above letter of the Minister of Communication and IT to the Prime Minister, the Committee asked for the copies of the file noting from the DoT to find out the opinion given by the Solicitor General on the matter of issuance of the letter of Intends in January, 2008. The Department furnished the relevant file noting. A perusal of the same has revealed that the Solicitor General has given the following remarks: "I have seen the notes. The issues regarding new LoIs are not before any court. What is proposed is fair and reasonable. The Press Release makes for transparency. This seems to be in order."

When the PAC asked the Law Secretary in evidence whether any Ministry/Department could seek direct legal opinion from any Law Officer bypassing the Ministry of Law and Justice, he replied in the negative.

In the same context, the now Attorney General Vahanvati stated in a written reply as under:

> In my opinion, the Minister should not make references to any Law Officer directly. I took over as Solicitor General in 2004. Initially, Ministers used to make references to me directly. I consistently re-routed them through the Ministry of Law. Even when urgent opinions were sought I have insisted that they should be referred through the Ministry of Law. However, I would like to explain that the bulk of the work that a Law Officer does is in relation to litigation. In the course of the conduct of litigation it becomes necessary for a Law Officer to take decisions in relation to stand to be taken in the court

and affidavits to be filed. The settled practice in this behalf is that such decisions are taken with reference to the concerned Ministry without reference to the Law Ministry. In litigation, matters cannot be referred to the Law Ministry at every stage. Once a Law Officer is engaged with the approval of the Law Ministry it is his duty and responsibility to conduct the case. During such engagement it is not the practice, nor is it practical, to make a reference to the Ministry of Law and Justice with regard to the presentation and conduct of the case.

The PAC, therefore, took note of the Minister of Communications and IT's information to the PM in his letter dated December 26, 2007 that his discussion with the External Affairs Minister had enlightened him to take a pre-emptive and pro-active decisions on the issues concerned. And asked the office of the Minister of Finance (the then External Affairs Minister) to furnish a factual note on the claims of the Minister of Communication and IT.

In response, the Private Secretary to the Finance Minister in his letter dated March 25, 2011 furnished the factual comments based on the Finance Minister's recollection, which are as under:

In November, 2007, Hon'ble Prime Minister had asked Shri Pranab Mukherjee, the then External Affairs Minister, to apprise himself of the issues raised by COAI with Shri A. Raja, the then Minister of Communications & IT, and Shri G.E. Vahanvati, the then Solicitor General (SG), in the context of proceedings pending in the TDSAT.

In this context, Shri Pranab Mukherjee held a meeting with MoCIT and SG in the first week of December, 2007. SG explained that the existing operators were insisting on the allocation of additional GSM spectrum on the basis of March, 2006 guidelines which they contended were adequate. There was no substance in this contention in view of the TRAI recommended revised criteria which was stricter and was under further consideration.

SG explained that as per the directions of the TDSAT, an affidavit had been filed in November, 2007 indicating the way forward. Shri Pranab Mukherjee briefly discussed the merits of the case and enquired whether any order had been passed by TDSAT. He was informed that there was no adverse order at that state.

The meeting lasted for about 15 minutes.

On April 7, 2011 the Private Secretary to the Finance Minister wrote another letter wherein he stated that subsequent to his letter dated March 25, 2011 to the PAC, the Finance Ministry had received copies of some papers sent by the PMO to the PAC.

In the said papers, there was a reference to a "Top Secret" note dated December 26, 2007 on the subject of telecom licence and spectrum issues addressed by Shri Pranab Mukherjee, the then External Affairs Minister to the Prime Minister. As no copy of the note was retained in Shri Pranab Mukherjee's office, the said note alongwith the enclosures was obtained from the PMO and sent to the PAC.

A perusal of the then External Affairs Minister's note revealed that the Minister had *inter-alia* unambiguously opined that "while it is the prerogative of the Government to frame, revise and change the policy, it is also the responsibility of the Government to do so in a transparent manner and then follow the stated policy both in letter and spirit." He also recorded that "while under the existing policy, the Government may keep on issuing new licences, the criteria for the grant of licences may be strengthened and put in public domain at the earliest."

BEGINNING OF AUTHOR'S PUBLIC INTEREST LITIGATION IN SUPREME COURT

The grant of 122 UAS licences on January 10, 2008 out of the remaining 232 applications received given in a hush hush manner including the presence of "bouncers" and thugs in Sanchar Bhavan caused a national uproar in the country. The sequence of decisions leading to awarding of spectrum was as follows: On September 4, 2007, the DoT announced that 2G licences would be granted without a cap from that date.

On September 24, 2007, a Press Release was issued to the effect that new applications for UAS licences would not be accepted by the DoT after October 1, 2007 "till further orders." On September 24, 2007, a Press

Release was issued to the effect that new applications for UAS licences would not be accepted by the DoT after October 1, 2007 till further orders. The Press Release appeared in the Newspapers on September 25, 2007. There were 232 applications pending till September 25, 2007 and 343 more applications were received between September 25, 2007 and October 1, 2007. Thus, 575 applications for UAS licences were received as of this cut-off date. Thus in effect, the first violation of the TRAI recommendation took place by capping of applications beyond October 1, 2007

A series of illegal and controversial actions/decisions then followed by which 122 UAS licences were issued on the basis of the January 10, 2008 two Press Releases, to nine companies after drawing a new cut-off date of September 25, 2007 after all the receipt of applications stood closed as of October 1, 2007. The 343 applications made between September 26 and October 1 thus were made *post hoc* ineligible for immediate spectrum licences.

A series of illegal and controversial actions/decisions then followed by which 122 UAS licences were issued on the basis of January 10, 2008 two Press Releases, to nine companies after drawing a new cut-off date of September 25, 2007 after all the receipt of applications stood closed as of October 1, 2007. The 343 applications made between September 26 and October 1 thus were made *post hoc* ineligible for immediate spectrum licences.

The grant of these licences along with the 35 Dual Technology licences in October, 2007 and the allotment of additional spectrum to the CMSPs raised many concerns. There were allegations from many quarters on the irregularities committed in the issue of UAS licences and allotment of 2G spectrum in 2007-2008 in an arbitrary manner by advancing the cut-off date to September 25, 2007, manipulating the FCFS policy, cherry picking the TRAI recommendations, side tracking the Ministry of Finance officials, ignoring the Law Minister's advice etc. What was most scandalous was the grant of licences in 2008 at a price determined in 2001 which was about one-tenth the competitive price in 2008 to favour certain companies.

There were Lok Sabha debates on December 4 and 5, 2007 on the issue of allocation of additional 2G spectrum to the GSM operators, free of

ए. राजा
ए. राजा
A. RAJA

मंत्री
संचार एवं सूचना प्रौद्योगिकी
भारत सरकार,
इलैक्ट्रॉनिक्स निकेतन, 6, सी.जी.ओ. काम्प्लेक्स,
नई दिल्ली-110 003
MINISTER
COMMUNICATIONS & INFORMATION TECHNOLOGY,
GOVERNMENT OF INDIA,
ELECTRONICS NIKETAN, 6, C.G.O. COMPLEX,
NEW DELHI-110 003

D.O. No.20-100/2007-AS.I
Dated 2nd November 2007.

Respected Sir,

After the announcement of TRAI Recommendations on Review of Licence Terms and Conditions for (Telecom) Access Service Providers on 28th August, 2007, an unprecedented number of applications were being received by the Department due to Recommendation of TRAI recommending " No Cap" on number of Licences in a Service Area.

2. As unprecedented number of applications were being received, a cut-off date of 1st October, 2007 was announced by the Department on 24th September, 2007 and a Press Release was given. In all 575 applications for 22 Service Areas were received.

3. The Department wanted to examine the possibility of any other procedure in addition to the current procedure of allotment of Licences to process the huge number of applications. A few alternative procedures as debated in the Department and also opined by few legal experts were suggested by the Department of Telecom to Ministry of Law & Justice to examine its legal tenability to avoid future legal complications, if any. Ministry of Law and Justice, instead of examining the legal tenability of these alternative procedures, suggested referring the matter to empowered Group of Ministers. Since, generally new major policy decisions of a Department or inter-departmental issues are referred to GOM, and, needless to say that the present issue relates to procedures, the suggestion of Law Ministry is totally out of context.

4. Now, the Department has decided to continue with the existing policy (first-cum-first-served) for processing of applications received up to 25th September 2007, i. e. the date when the news-item on announcement of cut-off date appeared in the newspapers. The procedure for processing the remaining applications will be decided at a later date, if any spectrum is left available after processing the applications received up to 25th September 2007.

4. As the Department is not deviating from the existing procedure, I hope this will satisfy the Industry.

5. You will appreciate that I am writing this letter to apprise you about the latest developments in the Department.

I take this occasion to extend my warm Diwali Greetings.

With regards,

Yours sincerely,

(A. RAJA)

Dr. Manmohan Singh,
Prime Minister of India,
New Delhi.

प्रधान मंत्री

Prime Minister

New Delhi
2 November, 2007

Dear Shri Raja,

A number of issues relating to allocation of spectrum have been raised by telecom sector companies as well as in sections of the media. Broadly, the issues relate to enhancement of subscriber linked spectrum allocation criteria, permission to CDMA service providers to also provide services on the GSM standard and be eligible for spectrum in the GSM service band, and the processing of a large number of applications received for fresh licenses against the backdrop of inadequate spectrum to cater to overall demand. Besides these, there are some other issues recommended by TRAI that require early decision. The key issues are summarized in the annexed note.

I would request you to give urgent consideration to the issues being raised with a view to ensuring fairness and transparency and let me know of the position before you take any further action in this regard.

With regards,

Yours sincerely,

(Manmohan Singh)

Shri A. Raja
Minister of Communications and IT
New Delhi

<u>Annexure</u>

Enhancement of subscriber linked spectrum allocation criteria

In August 2007, the TRAI has recommended interim enhancement of subscriber linked spectrum allocation criteria. Service providers have objected to these recommendations, alleging errors in estimation / assumptions as well as due procedure not having been followed by the TRAI while arriving at the recommendations.

2. **Permission to CDMA service providers to also provide services on the GSM standard and be eligible for spectrum in the GSM service band**

Based on media reports, it is understood that the DoT has allowed 'cross technology' provision of services by CDMA service providers and three such companies have already paid the license fee. With the deposit of the fee, they would be eligible for GSM spectrum, for which old incumbent operators have been waiting since last several years. The Cellular Operators Association of India (COAI), being the association of GSM service providers, has represented against this. It is understood that the COAI has also approached the TDSAT against this.

3. **Processing of a large number of applications received for fresh licenses against the backdrop of inadequate spectrum to cater to overall demand**

The DoT has received a large number of applications for new licenses in various telecom circles. Since spectrum is very limited, even in the next several years all these licensees may never be able to get spectrum. The Telecom Policy that had been approved by the Union Cabinet in 1999 specifically stated that new licenses would be given subject to availability of spectrum.

4. **In order that spectrum use efficiency gets directly linked with correct pricing of spectrum, consider (i) introduction of a transparent methodology of auction, wherever legally and technically feasible, and (ii) revision of entry fee, which is currently benchmarked on old spectrum auction figures**

5. **Early decision on issues like rural telephony, infrastructure sharing, 3G, Broadband, Number Portability and Broadband Wireless Access, on which the TRAI has already given recommendations.**

ஆ. இராசா
ए. राजा
A. RAJA

मंत्री
संचार एवं सूचना प्रौद्योगिकी
भारत सरकार,
इलैक्ट्रानिक्स निकेतन, 6, सी.जी.ओ. कॉम्प्लेक्स,
नई दिल्ली-110 003
MINISTER
COMMUNICATIONS & INFORMATION TECHNOLOGY,
GOVERNMENT OF INDIA,
ELECTRONICS NIKETAN, 6, C.G.O. COMPLEX,
NEW DELHI-110 003

D.O. No. 20-100/2007-AS.I
2nd November, 2007.

Respected Sir, Vanakkam.

Kindly refer to your letter dated 2.11.2007 regarding various issues related to Telecom sector. In this regard I have already written to you a letter earlier today (copy enclosed) clarifying the position on processing of large number of applications received for fresh licences. Before giving clarifications to the averments contained in the Annexure to your letter, I would like to inform you that there was, and is, no single deviation or departure in the rules and procedures contemplated, in all the decisions taken by my Ministry and as such full transparency is being maintained by my Ministry and I further assure you the same in future also.

Clarifications with respect to other issues are as follows:

1. **Enhancement of subscriber linked spectrum allocation criteria**

TRAI had recommended in August 2007, enhancement in subscriber linked criteria for allotment of additional spectrum to existing operators in order to increase spectrum efficiency which is scarce. Independent to this, Telecom Engineering Centre (TEC), which is the competent body to look into such matter, was asked to examine the spectrum efficiency issues scientifically. TEC submitted its recommendations on 26.10.2007, which was in principle accepted by me. It has been placed on the website of the Ministry and therefore, anybody much less COAI is at liberty to challenge the report of TEC with scientific basis. **However, the fact still remains that no such attempts have been honestly made by them.**

2. **Permission to CDMA service providers to also provide services on the GSM standard and be eligible for spectrum in the GSM service band**

This matter was referred to TRAI for its comments on use of dual technology. TRAI, after due deliberations on the issue, recommended use of dual technology, enabling existing Universal Access Service licensees (USAL) to provide services under both (GSM and CDMA) technologies. It was examined in the Ministry and was agreed to as they will be able to rollout the network fast which will ultimately benefit the customers because of increase in teledensity and also resulting lower tariff. **These operators will get spectrum only after the allotment of spectrum to the existing operators according to their eligibility and also licence holders awaiting for initial spectrum.**

3. **Processing of a large number of applications received for fresh licenses against the backdrop of inadequate spectrum to cater to overall demand**

The issue of auction of spectrum was considered by the TRAI and the Telecom Commission and was not recommended as the existing licence holders who are already having spectrum upto 10 MHz per Circle **have got it without any spectrum charge**. It will be unfair, discriminatory, arbitrary and capricious to auction the spectrum to new applicants as it will not give them level playing field.

I would like to bring it to your notice that DoT has earmarked totally 100 MHz in 900 MHz and 1800 MHz bands for 2G mobile services. Out of this, so for a maximum of about 35 to 40 MHz per Circle has been allotted to different operators and being used by them. The remaining 60 to 65 MHz, including spectrum likely to be vacated by Defence Services, is still available for 2G services.

Therefore, there is enough scope for allotment of spectrum to few new operators even after meeting the requirements of existing operators and licensees. An increase in number of operators will certainly bring real competition which will lead to better services and increased teledensity at lower tariff. **Waiting for spectrum for long after getting licence is not unknown to the Industry and even at present Aircel, Vodafone, Idea and Dishnet are waiting for initial spectrum in some Circles since December 2006.**

I would like to bring to your kind notice that M/s Aircel and M/s Spice Telecom, who were party to the petition to the TDSAT challenging DoT orders on acceptance of TRAI recommendations, have disassociated with the petition after having clarifications from me. These operators have openly admitted that the COAI had misled them, media and the public in general.

Since assuming charge, on more than three occasions I have reviewed all the long pending TRAI recommendations **announced during the tenures of my predecessors** including Number Portability, 3G, Wimax etc. and directed my officers to process them in a transparent manner. As a result we are almost reaching to shape the modalities to auction 3G and Wimax as contemplated by TRAI. I am told that divergence of views on implementation of Number Portability have been expressed by various stakeholders and I am trying to resolve it. The final decision on all these recommendations will be taken soon.

To conclude, I would like to assure you that all my decisions and endeavours are honestly aimed at development of the telecom sector, increasing the teledensity and lowering the tariff for the benefit of the public in general and customers in particular.

With regards,

Yours sincerely,

(A.RAJA)

Dr. Manmohan Singh
Hon'ble Prime Minister of India
7, Race Course Road
New Delhi.

cost. Similarly, there was a debate in Rajya Sabha on December 16, 2008 on the alleged irregularities committed in the allocation of 2G spectrum. There were several starred and unstarred questions in both Lok Sabha and Rajya Sabha on the 2G spectrum issue. A number of Members of Parliament and presidents of political parties wrote to the Prime Minister on allocation of additional Spectrum, licences for Dual Technology, irregularities committed in the allocation of 2G spectrum in 2007-08 and related issues.

There were extensive press articles also commenting upon the gross irregularities in the issue of UAS licences/allotment of 2G spectrum in 2007-08. Several journos wrote in detail the chain of events that led to the massive loss to the exchequer on account of granting licences/spectrum in 2007-2008 at a price determined in 2001. The most prominent and probing reporting on the matter was made by J. Gopikrishnan who wrote extensively since December 2008 on the alleged 2G spectrum scam. All this made no impact on the Prime Minister.

On November 28, 2008, I wrote a letter to the Prime Minister, Dr. Manmohan Singh, to grant me sanction to prosecute under the Prevention of Corruption Act his Telecom Minister A. Raja. Despite 5 reminders to him from then to March 15, 2010, I received no reply, not even an acknowledgment. Therefore I moved the courts to seek a direction to the Prime Minister to decide whether to grant me Sanction or not.

On the basis of nationwide concerns expressed towards irregularities of grave nature in the allocation of 2G spectrum under UASL and specific complaints received by the Central Vigilance Commission (CVC) against the First Come First Served Policy (FCFS) adopted for grant of UAS licences, the Commission decided to conduct a direct inquiry on the matter on June 17, 2009.

A number of questionnaires were sent to the DoT by the CVC for clarifications on the FCFS policy. As the replies received from the DoT were not specific, on October 12, 2009 the CVC referred the matter to the Central Bureau of Investigation (CBI) for detailed investigation on the basis of the Commission's Direct Inquiry Report which highlighted serious irregularities in the grant of UAS licences/spectrum in 2008.

The CBI, accordingly, filed the First Information Report (FIR) on October 21, 2009 against "unnamed persons," and moved to investigate the matter at snail speed. The matter caught fire in the public mind when in September 2010 moved a petition in the Supreme Court for grant of Sanction to prosecute A. Raja. Thus began the unprecendent saga in the Supreme Court that won the admiration of the whole nation.

WAS THE PRIME MINISTER GUILTY OF INACTION?

The then Minister of Communication and IT in his first letter dated November 2, 2007 to the Prime Minister wrote as below:

> After the announcement of TRAI Recommendations on Review of License Terms and Condition for (Telecom) Access Service Providers on August 28, 2007, and unprecedented number of applications were being received by the Department due to Recommendation of TRAI recommending "No Cap" on number of Licenses in a Service Area.
>
> As unprecedented number of applications were being received, a cut-off date of October 1, 2007 was announced by the Department on September 24, 2007 and a Press Release was given. In all 575 applications for 22 Service Areas were received.
>
> The Department wanted to examine the possibility of any other procedure in addition to the current procedure of allotment of Licenses to process the huge number of applications. A few alternative procedures as debated in the Department and also opined by few legal experts were suggested by the Department of Telecom to Ministry of Law and Justice to examine its legal tenability to avoid future legal complications, if any. Ministry of Law and Justice, instead of examining the legal tenability of these alternative procedures, suggested referring the matter to empowered Group of Ministers. Since, generally new major policy decisions of a Department of Inter-departmental issues are referred to GOM, and, needless to say that the present issue relates to procedures, the suggestion of Law Ministry is totally out of context.
>
> Now, the Department has decided to continue with the existing policy (first-cum-first-served) for processing of applications received up to September 25, 2007, i.e. the date when the news-item on

announcement of cut-off date appeared in the newspapers. The procedure for processing the remaining applications will be decided at a later date, if any spectrum is left available after processing the applications received up to September 25, 2007.

As the Department is not deviating from the existing procedure, I hope this will satisfy the industry.

The Prime Minister sent a letter on the same day to the Minister of Communication & IT highlighting the following fact:

> A number of issues relating to allocation of spectrum have been raised by telecom sector companies as well as in sections of the media. Broadly, the issues relate to enhancement of subscriber linked spectrum allocation criteria, permission to CDMA service providers to also provide services on the GSM standard and be eligible for spectrum in the GSM service band, and the processing of a large number of applications received for fresh licenses against the backdrop of inadequate spectrum to cater to overall demand. Besides these, there are some other issues recommended by TRAI that require early decision. The key issues are summarized in the annexed note. I would request you to give urgent consideration to the issues being raised with a view to ensuring fairness and transparency and let me know of the position before you take any further action in this regard.

The Annexure to the PM's letter underlined the following important issues:

1. "Enhancement of subscriber linked spectrum allocation criteria.
2. Permission to CDMA service providers to also provide services on the GSM standard and be eligible for spectrum in the GSM service band.
3. Processing of a large number of applications received for fresh licenses against the backdrop of inadequate spectrum to cater to overall demand.

4. In order that spectrum use efficiency gets directly linked with correct pricing of spectrum, consider (i) introduction of a transparent feasible, and (ii) revision of entry fee, which is currently benchmarked on old spectrum auction figures.

5. Early decision on issues like rural telephony, infrastructure sharing, 3G, Broadband, Number Portability and Broadband Wireless Access, on which the TRAI has already given recommendations.

The Minister of Communication & IT in his second letter *also on the same day inter-alia* responded to the PM as below:

> Kindly refer to your letter dated November 11, 2007 regarding various issues related to Telecom sector. In this regard I have already written to you a letter earlier today (copy enclosed) clarifying the position on processing of large number of applications received for fresh licences. Before giving clarifications to the averments contained in the Annexure to your letter, I would like to inform you that there was, and is, no single deviation or departure in the rules and procedures contemplated, in all the decisions taken by my Ministry and as such full transparency is being maintained by my Ministry and I further assure you the same in future also.

With respect to processing of a large number of applications received for fresh licences against the backdrop of inadequate spectrum to cater to overall demand, in the said letter, it was conveyed that:

> The issue of auction of spectrum was considered by the TRAI and the Telecom Commission and was not recommended as the existing licence holders who are already having spectrum upto 10 MHz per Circle have got it without any spectrum charge. It will be unfair, discriminatory, arbitrary and capricious to auction the spectrum to new applicants as it will not give them level playing field.
>
> I would like to bring it to your notice that DoT has earmarked totally 100 MHz in 900 MHz and 1,800 MHz bands for 2G mobile

> services. Out of this, so far a maximum of about 35 to 40 MHz per Circle has been allotted to different operators and being used by them. The remaining 60 to 65 MHz, including spectrum likely to be vacated by Defence Services, is still available for 2G services.
>
> Therefore, there is enough scope for allotment of spectrum to few new operators even after meeting the requirements of existing operators and licensees. An increase in number of operators will certainly bring real competition which will lead to better services and increased teledensity at lower tariff. Waiting for spectrum for long after getting licence is not unknown to the Industry and even at present Aircel, Vodafone, Idea and Dishnet are waiting for initial spectrum in some Circles since December 2006.

On December 26, 2007, the Minister of Communication and IT wrote another letter to the PM justifying his decision and assuming *inter-alia* that "as I have already promised to you my efforts in this sector are intended to give lower tariff to the consumer and to bring higher tele-density in the country, more specifically in rural areas."

He further wrote: "Since the file for issue of LoI to all eligible applicants was approved by me on November 2, 2007, it is proposed to implement the decision without further delay and without departure from existing guidelines."

The Prime Minister acknowledged the Minister's letter on January 3, 2008.

Audit pointed out that the suggestion given and the concerns expressed by the Prime Minister in his letter dated 2nd November, 2007 was ignored by the Minister of C & IT. The Prime Minister was misled when the Minister wrote to him that the issue of auction of spectrum was considered by the Telecom Commission and was not recommended whereas as a matter of fact TRAI recommendation of August 2007 were never discussed by the full Telecom Commission between the date of submission of the TRAI's recommendation and the date of the Minister's letter, i.e. November 2, 2007.

In the above context, the Committee asked DoT as to how it would have been unfair, discriminatory, arbitrary and capricious to auction the spectrum to new applicants, as reported to the Prime Minister. In reply, the DoT stated that the issue of auctioning spectrum *vis-à-vis* level playing field between the existing and new entrant in the telecom were deliberated by TRAI in their recommendations dated August 28, 2007 as submitted below:

> 2.78 **As far as a new entrant is concerned**, the question arises whether there is any need for change in the pricing methodology for allocation of spectrum in the 800, 900 and 1,800 MHz bands. **Keeping in view the objective of growth, affordability, penetration of wireless services in semi-urban and rural areas, the Authority is not in favour of changing the spectrum fee regime for a new entrant. Opportunity for equal competition has always been one of the prime principles of the Authority in suggesting a regulatory framework in telecom services.** Any differential treatment to a new entrant vis-à-vis incumbents in the wireless sector will go against the principle of level playing field. This is specific and restricted to 2G bands only i.e. 800, 900 and 1,800 MHz. **This approach assumes more significance particularly in the context where subscriber acquisition cost for a new entrant is likely to be much higher than for the incumbent wireless operators.**
>
> 2.79 In the case of spectrum in bands other than 800, 900 and 1,800 MHz i.e. bands that are yet to be allocated, the Authority examined various possible approaches for pricing and has come to the conclusion that it would be appropriate in future for a market based price discovery systems. In response to the consultation paper, a number of stakeholders have also strongly recommended that the allocation of spectrum should be immediately de-linked from the license and the future allocation should be based on auction. The Authority in its recommendation on "Allocation and pricing of spectrum for 3G and broadband wireless access services" has also favored auction methodology for allocation of spectrum for 3G and BWA services. **It is therefore recommended that in future all Spectrum excluding the spectrum in 800, 900 and 1,800 bands**

> **should be auctioned so as to ensure efficient utilization of this scarce resource.** In the 2G bands (800 MHz/900 MHz/1800 MHz), the allocation through auction may not be possible as the service providers were allocated spectrum at different times of their license and the amount of spectrum with them varies from 2x4.4 MHz to 2x10 MHz for GSM technology and 2x2.5 MHz to 2x5 MHz in CDMA technology. Therefore, to decide the cut off after which the spectrum is auctioned will be difficult and might raise the issue of level playing field.

The Committee, then, asked whether the information to the Prime Minister that

> ... an increase in the number of operators will certainly bring real competition which will lead to better services and increase teledensity and lower tariff" was correct in view of the fact that a number of companies after getting UAS licences in 2008 did not meet their roll out obligations. In reply, the DoT stated that in December, the rural tele-density was **8.35 per cent (total rural telephone were 6,73,31,300)** and total tele-density was **23.89 per cent (total telephone were 27,28,77,406 in India)**. In January 2011, the rural tele-density has increased to **32.19 per cent (total rural telephone were 26,81,670,70, i.e. more than 20 crore phones were added in rural areas in this period)** and all-India tele-density has reached to **67.67 per cent(total telephone were 80,61,356,36 i.e. more than 53.3 crore phones were added in India in this period)**. In 2007 the local call charges were about Rs 1/minute which has now come down to ½ paise/second. In December 2007, the average revenue per user (ARPU) for GSM services was **Rs. 261** per month and for CDMA services was **Rs. 176** per month. In September 2010, the ARPU for GSM services was **Rs. 110** per month and for CDMA services was **Rs. 73** per month.

While inaugurating the India Telecom-2007 on December 12, 2007, the Prime Minister *inter-alia* stated: "at the same time, the revenue potential to the Government must not be lost sight of. After all, Government across the Globe have harnessed substantial revenue while allocating spectrum."

In the above context, when the Committee desired to know as to whether the Prime Minister's advice/concern was taken care of either by the Minister or by the DoT, it was replied that no communication had been found No communication has been found on record in DoT which was sent by the then Minister of Communications and Information Technology to the Hon'ble Prime Minister (PM) or by DoT to the Prime Minister Office (PMO) referring to the above concern/advice of the Hon'ble Prime Minister made on December 12, 2007 while inaugurating the India Telecom-2007.

The Committee asked, when the concern of the PM was not addressed whether he was not misguided when the Telecom Minister informed the PM that allotting 2G Spectrum in 2007-2008 at a price fixed in 2001 would increase tele-density and benefit the consumers, even though one applicant voluntarily offered to pay more price. In reply, the DoT just produced the extracts of the Telecom Minister's letter dated November 2, 2007.

J. Gopikrishnan, in one of his articles, wrote that a very senior Law Officer was present in A. Raja's residence on November 2, 2007 from 7 PM to 11.30 PM and he drafted all the two letters to the Prime Minister by A. Raja. One of the former Additional Private Secretaries to A. Raja confessed before the CBI that he was called to the Minister's residence to type the said letters and some other people were present there.

In the above context, the Committee asked the DoT to furnish the copies of the file notings pertaining to the drafting and approval of the said letters. In reply, DoT stated that no such records were available in the Department.

The Committee then asked the Prime Minister's Office to explain how the three letters of the former Telecom Minister to the PM was processed and examined by them. In reply, the PMO stated as follows:

> A. Raja, the then Minister of Communications and IT, addressed a letter dated November 2, 2007 to the Prime Minister, stating that the

Department of Telecommunications had wanted to examine the possibility of any other procedure, in addition to the current procedure of allotment of licences, and that the Ministry of Law and Justice was requested by the Department to examine the legal tenability of the alternatives. The Law Minister suggested referring the matter to an Empowered Group of Ministers. The Communications Minister stated that this suggestion was totally out of context and that the Department had decided to continue with the first-come-first-served basis for processing of applications.

Separately, against the background of a number of issues relating to allocation of spectrum by telecom sector companies and sections of the media, the Prime Minister, vide letter dated November 2, 2007, sent a note summarizing the key issues and requesting the Minister of Communications and IT to give urgent consideration to the issues being raised, with a view to ensuring fairness and transparency, while also asking him to let the Prime Minister know of the position before the Minister takes any further action.

The Minister replied to Prime Minister's letter dated November 2, 2007 on November 2, 2007 itself. He informed that there was, and is, no deviation or departure in the rules and procedures contemplated, in all decisions taken by his Ministry. He also stated that full transparency is being maintained by the Ministry and assured of the same in future also. On the licence processing and spectrum allocation issues, the Minister informed that auction was considered by TRAI and Telcom Commission and was not recommended. He stated that auctioning will be against level-playing-field for new applicants; that there is enough scope for allotment of spectrum to few new operators after meeting requirements of existing operators, mentioning in this connection the move for vacation of spectrum held by Defence Services; and that licensees waiting for spectrum for long after getting licence was not unknown to the industry.

Principal Secretary to PM discussed the matter with Chairman, TRAI, and Secretary, Department of Telecommunications, on November 6, 2007. It was noted that the issues emanated from the recommendations of the TRAI, made in response to a reference by the

Department of Telecommunications under section 11(1)(a) of the TRAI Act, and that TRAI's recommendations have been accepted in some cases but modified/rejected in others. It was also noted that the matter involved a difference of opinion between the Minister of Law and Justice and the Minister of Communications and IT. Rule 7 read with paragraph (1) of the Second Schedule to the Government of India (Transaction of Business) Rules provides that "cases in which a difference of opinion arises between two or more Ministers and a Cabinet decision is desired" shall be brought before the Cabinet. A note bringing out this position was submitted, along with the draft of a reply to the Minister from the Prime Minister, for consideration. The then Private Secretary to PM recorded: "PM has seen. Before proceeding with the letter, PM wants a note put up to him on whether the action proposed to be taken by the Ministry is correct or not; whether it is justified in doing what is plans to do." In response, a note was submitted stating, *inter-alia*, that Department of Telecommunications intends to ignore the advice to refer the issue of allotment of fresh licences to an Empowered Group of Ministers and intends to proceed on first-come-first-served basis which, according to the Minister, will be a continuation of the existing policy. It was submitted that this decision did not appear to be in conformity with the Transaction of Business Rules, which provide that "cases in which a difference of opinion arises between two or more Ministers and a Cabinet decision is desired, shall be brought before the Cabinet." This issue was later discussed by the Principal Secretary and the then Secretary to PM with the Prime Minister. Prime Minister desired that the Principal Secretary to PM, along with the Cabinet Secretary and Secretary, Department of Telecommunications, examine all the issues included in Prime Minister's letter dated November 2, 2007 to the Minister of Communications and IT and issues pertinent thereto, including the Minister's response and issues brought to Prime Minister's attention by various sources and issues raised in the media; assistance of technical experts may be taken as and when required. Accordingly, discussions with the Cabinet Secretary and Secretary,

Department of Telecommunications were scheduled with the Principal Secretary to PM on November 20, 2007.

As regards the third letter of December 26, 2007, the PMO explained:

The Communications Minister's letter was examined on file, along with the External Affairs Minister's note as well as an earlier note on the telecom issue, and a suggested course of action, following discussions between the then Secretary to PM and the Secretary, Department of Telecommunications, was submitted to the Prime Minister on January 7, 2008. It was conveyed by Private Secretary to PM, on January 11, 2008, on the file submitted on January 7, 2008, that the Prime Minister desired that the development concerning issue of licences also be taken into account. Accordingly, the original suggested course of action was resubmitted for the Prime Minister's consideration, with a clarificatory note dated January 15, 2008. The file was received back with Private Secretary to PM's note conveying that the Prime Minister wants this informally shared with the Department. The Secretary made a record regarding sharing informally with Secretary, Department of Telecommunications. Prime Minister acknowledged the letter on January 3, 2008.

Expressing surprise over the PM's desire to informally share the PMO's clarificatory note dated January 5, 2008 with the DoT, the Committee asked for the relevant file notings from the PMO to see the sequence of the processing of the Communication Minister's letter dated December 26, 2007. The PMO furnished the copies of the relevant file notings.

A perusal of the said notings revealed that the process of examining the Communication Minister's letter commenced from December 31, 2007 and the file was closed on January 31, 2008. One important noting on the file was made by the Private Secretary to the Prime Minister on January 23, 2008 which reads as follows:

"– PM wants this informally shared with the Department."

" – Does not want a formal communication and wants PMO to be at 'arms length'" (*sic!*).

Asked to state the action taken by the PMO on the then Finance Minister's note dated January 15, 2008 regarding pricing of additional spectrum, the PMO replied that the Prime Minister saw the Finance Minister's note and no action was formally taken by the PMO on the note. The PMO further stated that, however, the subject- matter was already under submission for the Prime Minister's consideration and, subsequently, the approach submitted after discussion with Secretary, Department of Telecommunications, was informally shared with the said Secretary. Many elements of this approach were similar to suggestions made in the Finance Minister's note.

A series of consultations took place between the Department of Telecommunications and the Finance Ministry, including a meeting of the Telecom Commission on January 15, 2008, in which the issue of spectrum usage charges was on the agenda and was discussed, and meetings between the Ministers of Finance and Communications and IT on January 30, 2008, May 29, 2008 and June 12, 2008, which were followed by the two Ministers apprising the Prime Minister in July 2008 regarding what was agreed between the two Ministries with regard to (a) raising of spectrum usage charges for 2G spectrum, (b) pricing of spectrum for 2G allocation and (c) method of allocation of 3G spectrum. The Ministers also apprised the Prime Minister that formal decision will be taken in the Telecom Commission.

It may be recalled here that in his noting dated January 15, 2008, the then Finance Minister wrote to the Prime Minister:

> Spectrum is a scare resource. The price for Spectrum should be based on its scarcity value and efficiency of usage. The most transparent method of allocating Spectrum would be through auction. The method of auction will face the least legal challenge. If Government is able to provide sufficient information on availability of Spectrum, that would minimize the risks and, consequently, fetch better prices at the auction. The design of the auction should include a reserve price.

> This leaves the question licensees who already hold Spectrum over and above the start up Spectrum. In such cases, the past may be treated as a closed Chapter and the payments made in the past for additional Spectrum (over and above the start up Spectrum) may be treated as the charges for Spectrum for that period. However, prospectively, such licensee should pay for the additional Spectrum that he holds, over and above the start up Spectrum, at the price discovered in the auction. This will place old licensees, existing licensee seeking additional Spectrum and new licensees on par so far as Spectrum charges are concerned.

Further, it bears repeating here that the Prime Minister in his interaction with the Editors of the electronic media on February 16, 2011 said:

> This was also discussed with the Finance Ministry because in terms of the Cabinet decision of 2003 the pricing and allocation of Spectrum was to be settled between the Ministry of Finance and the Telecom Department. Initially, of course, the Finance Ministry did ask for a high price of Spectrum but after many discussions, the two ministries agreed that as far as 2G is concerned, we have to live with the present system particularly with regard to the amount of Spectrum that is built and embedded into a license agreement. so this is the background why I did not proceed further with this matter of pricing of Spectrum, because if the Ministry of Finance and Ministry of Telecom both agree and they have the obligation of the Cabinet Decision of 2003 to decide on the matter and also since TRAI is an expert body and Telecom Commission has experts, if all of them are of the same view, I did not feel I was in a position to insist that auctions must be insisted.
>
> On the question of sale of Spectrum, the Prime Minister further clarified:
>
> I thought ... it was then the prevailing practice and Raja was continuing that policy, that as far as who gets licenses, the first come

> first serve policy, how it was implemented, that was never discussed with me. Licenses was not matter which got referred to me or to the Cabinet that was the decision exclusively of the telecom minister. Now subsequent events have shown that Companies sold their equity but I was told that they had not sold it to shareholders. they have sold it in a manner to dilute the equity of promoters.

In his speech in the Rajya Sabha on February 24, 2011, the Prime Minister clearly stated:

> The Government's policy of the pricing of Spectrum was taken on the basis of a Cabinet decision of 2003 which specifically left the issue to be determined by the Ministry of Finance and the Ministry of Telecommunication. Contrary to the assertion of the Leader of the Opposition, the record clearly shows that the then Minister while he initially had different view which he communicated to me on January 15, 2008, subsequently consulted the Minister, Telecommunication and the two Ministers worked an agreed formula on Spectrum charges which was reported to me in a meeting on July 4, 2008. Furthermore, this decision that was put to me by the two Ministers was in line with the recommendation of TRAI in its Report of August 2007. In that Report the TRAI had clearly stated that only 3G Spectrum should be auctioned and the policy for 2G Spectrum should continue on the same basis as hitherto.

OPPORTUNITY COST OR PRESUMPTIVE LOSS TO THE NATION

There were lots of allegations of huge losses in the allocation of UAS license/2G Spectrum in 2007-08 at a price determined in 2001. I had in my petition before the Delhi High Court in May, 2010 and later in September 2010 in the Supreme Court underlined that there was a total loss of Rs. 97,410.74 on three counts, viz. value of new 2G license, value of cross over licences and value of extra Spectrum as per the details given below:

Table 1: Value of New 2G Licenses

Sl. No.	Name	Number of Circles	Amount paid (Rs. Crore)	Market Value (Rs. Crore)	Difference (Rs. Crore)
1.	Unitech Wirelss Ltd.	22	1651	10731.5	9080.5
2.	Swan Telecom	14	1537.01	9990.565	8453.555
3.	Datacom Solutions	22	1651	10731.5	9080.5
4.	S Tel	22	1651	10731.5	9080.5
5.	Shyam Telelink	22	1651	10731.5	9080.5
6.	Loop Telecom	21	1454.91	9456.915	8002.005
7.	Spice	4	484.17	3147.105	2662.935
8.	Idea Cellular Ltd.	7	683.59	4443.335	3759.745
9.	Tata Teleservices	3	9	58.5	49.5
	Total		**10,772.68**	**70,022.42**	**59,249.74**

Note:

1. Market value is assumed 6.5 times the license fees based on sale of shared by Unitech and Swan Telecom
2. Unitech Wireless has applied for license in the names of – Unitech Infrastructures Pvt. Ltd., Unitech Builders and Estates Pvt. Ltd., Aska projects Ltd., Nahan Properties Pvt. Ltd., Hudson Properties Ltd., Volga Properties Pvt Ltd., Adonis Projects Pvt. Ltd., Azare Properties Ltd.

Table 2: Value of Crossover Licenses

Sl. No.	Name	Number of Circles	Amount paid (Rs. Crore)	Market Value (Rs. Crore)	Difference (Rs. Crore)
1.	Reliance Communications Ltd.	22	1651	10731.5	9080.5
2	Tata Teleservices Ltd.	22	1651	10731.5	9080.5
	Total		**3,302**	**21,463**	**18,161**

Table 3: Value of Extra Spectrum

Sl. No.	Name	Amount paid (Rs. Crore)	Difference (Rs. Crore)
1.	Bharti	Additional 1 per cent of Revenue	10,000
2	Vodaphone	Additional 1 per cent of Revenue	8500
3	Idea	Additional 1 per cent of Revenue	1500
	Total		**20,000**

B.K. Syngal, an expert with experience in Telecommunication while deposing before the Public Accounts Committee, submitted: "If we have to go by what we discovered in 2010, the possible loss could be even higher, but even if we are to go by the valuations at which the licences have been treated or sold, it is on an average Rs. 70,000 crore or Rs. 80,000 crore. It is now a matter of conjecture."

Asked to elaborate, Mr Syngal explained in a written note as follows:

> One has to look at various indicators to decide and arrive at the true potential of a resource, most importantly if there is an element of finiteness.' It may be of interest to the Committee that the Indian Telecom market was capitalized at around US$200 to 250 billion in 2007-08.
>
> First, the Hutch-Vodafone deal is sufficient proof of Spectrum's true economic and opportunity value discovery. Vodafone valued the company at around US$22 billion and paid a discounted price of $10.9 billion in cash for acquiring the 52 per cent stake held by Hutchison Telecom International (HTIL) in Indian mobile firm Hutch-Essar to complete a deal that gives it access to one of the fastest growing mobile markets by acquiring Hutch, when a pan-India license with Spectrum costing around Rs. 1658 crores was hawked, that is the cost of the Spectrum and assets. The questions posed were that an auction would cause end consumer tariff to go up and deferred revenue share is more beneficial than upfront payments of Spectrum etc. The counter question I posed is "have the tariffs gone up post this deal?" the answer is resounding NO. We must not use sale of assets for revenue generation etc.
>
> Second, in US the government earned US $ 34 billion by sale of Spectrum in 2006-08. The proceeds were to be used for re-farming of Spectrum from old technologies to new technologies to accrue digital dividends.
>
> Third, please also note that the telecom bell weather Bharti was quoted at around rupees 50 per share in 2002 and was at around 1,000 share in 2008, 20 times, whilst entry fee for a license with Spectrum was at around rupees 1,700 crores then (see attached). Should not the

price of license, not have moved with the share price of the company, as was also demonstrated by the Vodafone deal?

Fourth, should not have the government applies the least cumbersome method of indexation of the price discovery in 2001 by just using the Prime Lending Rate (PLR) or inflation index of say 12 per cent? This in itself would have resulted in a price of Rs. 3,665 crore and at 15 per cent 4410 crore, as also suggested by then Finance Secretary Dr. D. Subbarao (page 93 Para 2 of his letter), adding further to stay the process.

Fifth, the number of total subscribers was around 5 million at end March 2001 and 261 million at end March 2008 (attach 4). The cost of Spectrum per sub, at Rs. 1,658 crore per license, in 2001 at simple Mortgage calculation would result in Rupees 34 subscriber vis-à-vis Paise 65 when Spectrum was doled at 2001 in 2008. However, if the total cost for 4 licenses is taken, the figures would be Rs. 136 and Rs. 2.60 sub respectively.

Sixth, as late as May this year the TRAI has recommended linkage of excess 2G Spectrum to the 3G price discovery in their latest recommendations of May 11, 2010 (clauses 6.55 and 6.56 of Chapter VI, attach 5). Earlier to that a duly constituted committee of the DoT, called the Subodh Kumar Committee, l was asked to look into the Spectrum pricing of the 2G Spectrum beyond 6.2 MHz for the old licensees (2001) and beyond 4.4 MHz for the new licenses (2008). The Committee recommended that Spectrum beyond these limits will be linked to the 3G price discovery.

When the Public Accounts Committee asked as to whether the loss to the Government was presumptive or there was any basis of the loss to the Government, Mr Syngal submitted in evidence:

I have given four or five indicators. One was the Hutch-Vodafone deal which was valued at 22 billion dollars and Vodafone paid 11 billion dollars for 52 or 57 per cent depending upon which way it is counted, for entering the Indian market. The market size is of relevance. It was five millions when the cost of the spectrum and license was Rs.1,658 crore. Now if we take the cost of the spectrum for the delivery of the service at that time, it is not a first-mover advantage; it is a first-mover disadvantage to create awareness in the market of the service and also to have picked spectrum at an expensive cost in 2001. That is the rationale of saying as to whether the late entrant benefits or does not.

Let me also now explain it a little bit further. Today, the additions are about 12 million to 15 million customers per month, which means the cost of the spectrum is getting amortised and it is getting amortised at a much lower rate because you have distributed the spectrum at Rs.1,658 core only. As a matter of fact, in my calculation, I have also given that if we multiply Rs.1,658 crore with 4, the cost comes to Rs.7,000 core and the number of customers then was 5 millions only – I am aware of that fact- and today one is giving out licences at the same Rs.7,000 crore when additions are what the market was in 2001. So, the question was whether there are any economic indicators in 2007 which should have created awareness within the Government that what is being done is right or wrong according to a market economy.

The PAC, then, desired to know from the Ministry of Finance as to whether they had made any assessment of the loss. In reply, the Finance Secretary *surprisingly* stated in evidence:

On the point that you mentioned whether there is any loss which has accrued to the exchequer in allocating spectrum in the manner in which it has been allocated, we have not made any assessment of the notional or alleged loss of revenue. The view is that it is difficult to assess this on account of various reasons. One is that the spectrum allocated for 3G services is in 2.1 GHz band. We are told by the technology people that the two sets of bands are dissimilar in propagation characteristics and value parameters.

Secondly, the respective contexts in which the allocations were made for 2G and 3G bands are also perhaps different. The initial allocations of spectrum in the 2G bands were made at various points in time starting from 1994 and therefore the issue of historical legacy is perhaps an issue which comes in when there is fresh allocation in these bands.

We are also told that the volume of un-allocated spectrum available in these bands is relatively very thin and therefore there could be a problem of efficiency in price signaling and discovery. As compared to this, the auction for 3G which has just concluded and which has given the kind of revenues which I referred to has taken place on a clean slate without any such previous historical sweep and consideration.

Apart from this, our Department is largely connected with the policy formulation aspects relating to allocation of spectrum and the broad approach, as I mentioned in the beginning of my statement, has been that we are all for allocating spectrum in a rational manner, in a manner which discovers the price clearly and openly. But I do not have, at this stage, any assessment of the notional loss because it is difficult to work it out.

Asked to state categorically whether there was any loss to the Government or not, the Finance Secretary submitted to the PAC: "Sir, what I said in my statement before the hon'ble Committee is that it is difficult to draw a backward conclusion from 3G Spectrum. But a scare resource, as the market expands, always commands a premium."

The CBI, in its FIR registered on October 21, 2009 estimated a loss of Rs.22,000 crore to the exchequer on account of UAS licences given in 2008 at a price determined in 2001. In this context, when the Committee desired to know the basis on which the CBI had arrived at the figure of Rs.22,000 crore, the Investigating Agency replied that the figure of Rs.22,000 crore loss reflected in the CBI FIR no.RC DAI 2009 A 0045 dated October 21, 2009 was based on source information. This figure was arrived at based on the following premises:

(i) That M/s. Swan Telecom got 13 licences for Rs.1,537 Crores and sold it in entirety for Rs.4,200 Crores, thus making a profit of Rs. 2,663 Crores.

(ii) That M/s. Unitech got 22 licences for Rs.1,658 Crores and sold it for Rs.6,100 Crores, thus making a profit of Rs.4,442 Crores.

(iii) Both companies taken together made a profit of Rs.7,105 Crores for 35 licences.

(iv) This was taken to calculate average profit for each licence i.e. 7105 / 35 = 203 Crores. This was multiplied by 122 (total of licences issued in Jan, 2008) to calculate profit to companies which got licences in Jan. 2008, giving a figure of Rs.24,766 Crores. However, the source information referred to several smaller value circles (about 14-15) licences as well, thereby reducing margin of profit to Rs.22,000 Crores. It is to thrust the point that there was very little information at the time of registration of the case and the figure of Rs.22,000 Crores profit to applicant companies and corresponding loss to the public exchequer is based on source information with little access to records.

The Public Accounts Committee asked the CBI about the reasons for subsequent upward revision of the loss by the CBI to an amount of Rs.50,000 cr. The Director, CBI, submitted in evidence:

> We had asked the TRAI, who have set up an expert Committee to give us what should have been the correct prices for 2008. They have not done that but they have come out with the prices for 2010, what the price for spectrum for 2010 should have been which they have calculated was six times what it was sold for in 2008. That means, Rs.1,568 crore multiplied by six. So we are calculating that even if it was five times, because six was in 2010, so if it was five times in 2008, we come to a figure of Rs.50,000 crore roughly. This was the basis of our calculation.

The CAG Audit in their Report adopting various criteria and indicators, viz. the voluntary offer made by S. Tel, the price generated through 3G Auction and sale of equity by Unitech and Swan determined the presumptive loss to the exchequer in the category of issue of 122 UAS licences in 2008, 35 Dual Technology licences given in 2007-08 and Spectrum beyond contracted amount of 6.2 MHz, as under:

Category	Criteria for working out potential loss to exchequer (Value Rs. in crores)			
	S. Tel rate	Rates on the basis of 3G Auction	Sale of equity by the new licensees Unitech	Swan
New Licences	38,950	10,2498	40,442	33,230
Dual Technology	14,573	37,154	15,132	12,433
Beyond contracted quantity of 6.2 MHz	13,841	36,993	14,052	12,003
Total	**67,364**	**176,645**	**69,626**	**57,666**

The CAG Audit Report substantiated the above shown presumptive loss in the following manner:

> On November 5, 2007 through a letter addressed to the Hon'ble Prime Minister, S Tel limited who was a prospective licencee, having applied for UAS licences in July/September 2007, had offered to pay a higher price in the shape of additional revenue share for next ten years. The offer was enhanced by the firm with a stipulation to further revise it upwards, in case of any counter bid. At the prices offered by the Company, value of 122 new licenses and 35 Dual Technology licenses after discounting for the receivables in future years works out to Rs. 65,909 crores as against Rs. 12,386 crores actually received.
>
> Auction of 3G spectrum was recommended by TRAI in its Report submitted to Government in September 2006. In its Report of 2010, they have observed that it was fair to compare 2G with 3G and recommended 3G prices to be adopted as current price of 2G spectrum in 1800 Mhz band. If these recommendations, which have not so far been accepted by the Government are taken into account, then the value of 2G spectrum allotted to the 122 new licensees and 35 Dual Technology licences would be much higher at about Rs. 1,52,038 crores as against the amount actually received.

Many of the new UAS licensees of 2008 have been able to attract substantial amount of Foreign Direct Investment (FDI). Value of a new company with no experience in the Telecom sector can primarily be taken as that of the license and access to spectrum. This would have been the prime consideration for foreign companies while infusing large amount of capital in the form of equity in these companies shortly after award of license. Based on this indicator, value of a pan India license works out between Rs. 7,758 crores and Rs. 9,100 crores as against Rs. 1,658 crores priced by DoT. The total value for 122 new licences and 35 Dual Technology licences would be between Rs. 58,000 to Rs. 68,000 crores as against the actual revenue of Rs.12,386 crores realized. Thus, on the values determined through various indicators, the presumptive value of 2G spectrum on account of grant of 157 licenses in different circles during 2007-08 would be in the range of approximately Rs. 58,000 crores to Rs. 1,52,038 crores.

Spectrum was allotted by DoT to the existing operators beyond the contracted limits without imposing any upfront charge for such allotment. The value of spectrum held by 13 operators for 51 circles based on the 2001 rates worked out to Rs. 2561 crores. Based on the above indicators, value would be in the range of Rs. 12,000 crores and Rs. 37,000 crores. TRAI's recommendation (2010) for charging this additional quantity of spectrum has not been accepted by the Government so far.

While determining the loss, Audit made it explicitly clear that **"Any loss ascertained while attempting to value the 2G spectrum allocated to 122 licencees in 2008 can only be "presumptive,"** given the fact that there are varied determinants like its scarcity value, the nature of competition, business plans envisaged, number of operators, growth of sector etc. which, depending upon the market situation, would throw up the price that it commands at a given point of time. Instead of attempting to come to a specific value of 2G spectrum which could have been possible only through an efficient market discovery process, we have looked at the various indicators to assess a possible (presumptive) value, from the records made available to Audit rather than going for any mathematical/econometric models.

On December 27, 2010, while interacting with the Committee, the C&AG of India stated: "So, we have made it very clear that we are doing it only by hindsight. Now, the issue is, why is it done? It is done only as a guiding phenomenon for future, if similar process has to be undergone in future, then we have the benefit of hindsight for the future as to how should we formulate policies. This is how it is done worldwide."

Explaining in detail the Audit calculation of the presumptive loss, the C&AG further stated:

> We spent a considerable amount of time on it. I do not have the benefit of being a lawyer myself but I do have a claim to having studied economics at some point of time. Any attempt to ascertain an economic loss will have to be based on certain econometric or mathematical methods. There is just no other way of doing that. Any model is hypothetical. It is based on certain assumptions and we tried different econometric models. We have the benefit of economic advisors in the Department. We thought of those also but unfortunately no assumption on any econometric model holds true in real life and that is why if we had used any of those models I think all the hon. Members would have found fault with us for assuming 'x,' 'y' or 'z' or conditions which do not necessarily hold true in a real market situation. So, it was after considerable amount of deliberation that we decided not to use the economic model. We ascertained from other also. The view point that merged, and I have the benefit of a lot of Chartered Accountants also who helped us in this, was that we have to peg any loss of revenue to Government through certain existing market events which are real life situations, recorded situations, because those cannot be faulted. Of course, these can also be debated. There are always two sides to an argument but those were the best available under the situation.
>
> The term normally used in economics would "opportunity cost" but in this we have used the word "presumptive." Why we have used the word "presumptive"? Members have asked the question as to whether we have the parallels anywhere else in our Reports of CAG where this loss has been assessed and it has been accepted. My answer

> is a very clear yes and it happens on all our reports of revenue department where we say that the Department of Revenue, Department of Central Excise, Customs or Income Tax Department has under assessed and then they debate it also. They also call it a presumptive loss but in a large number of cases, there are at least about 40 per cent of our Reports accepting that loss and have taken measures to issue revised notices to the assessee and recorded that loss.

Responding to some related queries of the Committee, the C&AG emphatically remarked:

> I represent a Department which unlike the Finance Secretary does not have it. Hon. Member, had the Finance Secretary been present today he would accept my view point that we have the professional expertise and we are doing it every day. We have taken the opinions of the experts. We have the TRAI indicating in three different Reports that 2G and 3G are comparable; saying 2G is more or less 2.75 in the Report of 2010. This, of course, is by hindsight. So, we are also saying that 2G and 3G are comparable. Let me also make another assertion. Accountability has been fixed on the Government officers only by hindsight and much later after such investigations have been done on purported loss to Government where you can differ.
>
> Sir, we have been very honest in our Report. Let me take you to Page 58 where in conclusion we have said specifically – I am reading the last sentence – "The entire process of allocation of 2G spectrum raises serious concern about the system of governance in the Department of Telecommunications which need to be thoroughly reviewed and revamped.

The fact that there has been loss to the national exchequer in the allocation of 2G spectrum cannot be denied. However the amount of loss can be debated "That is what we are doing just now." To ensure that such losses do not occur in any Ministry or Department of the Government, there is an imperative need to fix responsibility and enforce accountability for the lapses highlighted in the Audit Report. So, you can say that the loss is Rs.66,000 core, you can say that the loss is Rs.1,76,000 core, viewpoints can differ."

On January 17, 2011, Kapil Sibal, the Minister of Communications and IT while addressing a Press Conference had *inter-alia* made the following remarks:

> The figure of Rs.1,76,000 core, with the greatest respect to the C&AG is so utterly erroneous that I would have thought that a complicated and complex issue like this should not have led to the conclusions of presumptive loss of this magnitude. It has embarrassed the Government; it has embarrassed the nation and once. I place the facts before you, you will realize that will embarrass the opposition.

The Minister also said as under:

> We are also extremely pained at the methodology adopted by the C&AG in coming to some figures which have no basis whatsoever. We believe it is human to err and to err is human and so though we respect the exercise of that constitutional authority's power, we do believe that, that exercise is fraught with very serious errors which have resulted in the kind of sensationalism which has allowed the opposition to spread utter falsehood to the people of this country.

Taking strong exception to the Minister's statement which raised several issues regarding parliamentary propriety and preserving and respecting the independence of the C&AG – an institution established by the constitution – the Chairman, PAC Dr. M. M.Joshi wrote a letter to the Hon'ble Speaker on January 19, 2011 beseeching her to take prompt steps to prevent the recurrence of such constitutional impropriety on the part of the Minister. The Speaker replied vide letter February 3, 2011.

On the issue of presumptive loss to the exchequer as revealed by the Audit, the Committee desired to know from the DoT about their own presumption/calculation of the potential loss on account of grant of 157 licences (122 UAS plus 35 Dual Technology Licences) in 2007-08. In reply, the DoT stated that in view of the policies and various decisions taken by the Department since 2003 regarding issue of UAS licences and allocation of 2G Spectrum, *no exercise had been undertaken by them to estimate/calculate the loss to the exchequer.*

The Committee then asked when the Department themselves had not carried out any exercise to estimate/calculate the loss, the basis on which the methodologies adopted by the Audit to calculate the presumptive loss was being termed as erroneous.

In reply, the DoT stated that their comments on various indicators adopted in the C&AG Report were as follows:

Offer of S. Tel Limited:

(i) M/s. S Tel Ltd. submitted its voluntary offer for allocation of spectrum vide their letter dated November 5, 2007 and December 27, 2007. In their letter dated November 5, 2007, the Company offered voluntarily to pay additional revenue share to the extent of Rs. 6,000 crores to the DoT, over and above the spectrum charges revenue share payable as per the existing policy, over a period of 10 years from the date of the spectrum allotment. In their letter dated December 27, 2007 the Company, while referring to their earlier letter dated November 5, 2007 has increased the offer to Rs.13,752 crores over a period of ten years on a scaled up payment schedule. **While the company had sought the spectrum upfront, the amount it had offered, was spread over a period of 10 years, with major revenues being back-loaded and only Rs. 250 crore each was proposed in 1st and 2nd year. The Company has also stated that, this amount shall become payable after allotment of 6.2MHz GSM spectrum in 900MHz frequency band for all the 22 circles and allowing sharing of active network and infrastructure.** UASL provides allotment of initial GSM spectrum of only 4.4+4.4MHz subject to availability. **Spectrum in 900 MHz band had already been allotted to various operators in the past and the Government almost had no spectrum in this Band. From the 4th CMTS licences (issued in year 2001) onwards, the start up spectrum is being allocated in 1800 MHz band.** In spite of being fully aware of the situation, the Company made this conditional offer to mislead the Government. Further,

Spectrum is allocated to license holders consequent to receipt of service license and on fulfillment of prescribed criteria. **There is no provision in the license conditions to allot spectrum on demand and allow sharing of spectrum, as was made out in the S Tel offer.** Therefore, this conditional offer of the Company did not have any merit for consideration.

(ii) Moreover, the company in their counter reply affidavit to SLP No.33406 of 2009 before Hon'ble Supreme Court in the matter of "Union of India Vs. S. Tel Ltd.," stated that they have withdrawn their offer made to DoT vide letter dated December 27, 2007 at the argument stage before the Division Bench of the Hon'ble High Court of Delhi in LPA No.388 of 2009 in the matter of "Union of India Vs. S. Tel Ltd."

Rate on the basis of 3G option:

(i) The Report has selectively relied on the recommendations dated May 11, 2010 of TRAI on "Spectrum Management and Licensing Framework." The Audit has not considered the recommendations of TRAI that Spectrum in the 800, 900 and 1,800 MHz bands (presently used as 2G spectrum) should not be subject to auction. Spectrum in 800 and 900 MHz bands shall however may be subject to auction as and when it is refarmed for 3G and other future technologies. Further, the recommendations of TRAI for charging 3G price was for spectrum beyond 6.2 MHz and not for initial spectrum.

(ii) There was a legacy methodology for allocation of 2G spectrum while the 3G spectrum was allocated first time. TRAI, in its recommendations dated 28.08.2007, recommended that "As far as a new entrant is concerned, the question arises whether there is any need for change in the pricing methodology for allocation of spectrum in the 800, 900 and 1,800 MHz bands. **Keeping in view the objective of growth, affordability, penetration of wireless services in semi-urban and rural areas, the Authority is not in favour of changing the spectrum fee regime for a new entrant.** Opportunity for equal competition has always been one of the prime principles of the Authority in suggesting a regulatory framework in telecom services.

Any differential treatment to a new entrant vis-à-vis incumbents in the wireless sector will go against the principle of level playing field. This is specific and restricted to 2G bands only i.e. 800, 900 and 1,800 MHz. This approach assumes more significance particularly in the context where subscriber acquisition cost for a new entrant is likely to be much higher than for the incumbent wireless operators." Therefore, it is not appropriate to compare the pricing of 2G spectrum with the 3G spectrum.

Sale of Equity by M/s Swan & M/s Unitech:

(i) M/s Swan Telecom Pvt. Ltd. and M/s Unitech Wireless Companies were awarded Licenses for Unified Access Services for 13 and 22 service areas respectively in February-March 2008. These companies have informed that they have made strategic partnership for investment in the company as per the Companies Act and have entered into agreement with foreign companies namely, Etisalat Mauritius Limited and Telenor Asia Private limited, Singapore respectively for infusion of equity capital into the company by issuing fresh equity for rolling out the Telecom network in the licensed service areas.

(ii) The valuation of a company is a complex exercise and depends on a number of factors including the business case over the period of license. The investment brought in by strategic foreign partners of these companies would be utilized for rolling out the services and even this would enhance their capital base keeping the absolute share holding of the promoters intact. In the above cases, as per the licensee companies, they have issued additional equity for bringing in foreign investment and as they have not transferred promoters' equity shares, promoters' equity has not been diluted. Foreign investment brings in capital as well as technology. It is a normal practice in the corporate world to bring investment into the company for rolling out or expansion of business. On earlier occasions also, FDI has been infused in licensee companies as per FDI policy of the Government. Government has been encouraging FDI in the country since

> beginning. As per Foreign Direct Investment (FDI) policy applicable in Telecom sector, FDI (both direct and indirect) allowed for Unified Access Service License is 74 per cent. FDI up to 49 per cent is under the automatic route. FDI in the licensee company/Indian promoters/investment companies including their holding companies shall require approval of the Foreign Investment Promotion Board (FIPB) if it has a bearing on the overall ceiling of 74 per cent."

Asked by the PAC to state specifically whether there would be a notional loss if a scarce resource like Spectrum was given at a price discovered few years earlier, the Department replied that the premium placed on a scarce resource from the perspective of a producer need not necessarily translate into a loss when seen from the viewpoint of the consumer and public welfare. Government policy is formulated with a view to maximize public welfare, and not merely to maximize Government revenues. The pricing of different natural resources is often done in a manner that meets this objective. The rationale of the pricing decision in the case of 2G Spectrum may be seen in the background of the telecom policy as it evolved over the years. The terms and conditions of licenses which were originally awarded through a bidding process, after the National Telecom Policy 1994 introduced private participation in the telecom sector, changed under the New Telecom Policy 1999. The new policy recognized the need to bring greater competition in the telecom sector in both urban and rural areas and to provide a level playing field. With the implementation of the 'migration package' with effect from August 1, 1999, the policy evolved to replace a high one time entry fee with annual recurring license fee and spectrum usage charges in the form of a revenue share. The vision of the X Five Year Plan that "revenue generation should not be a major determinant of the macro policy governing the sector ..." and that "spectrum policy needs to be promotional in nature; revenue considerations playing a secondary role" also guided the telecom sector policy in this regard. The various measures taken pursuant to the policy helped in increasing teledensity and in reducing the prices of mobile services.

> The provision of telecom services involves large investments. If the government charges a very high entry fee, it would reduce the resources available to the service providers to create infrastructure. This would eventually impact the prices charged by the service providers and thereby limit services to those who can afford higher priced services. Therefore, the concept of a notional loss when spectrum is given at a price discovered few years earlier has to be balanced with the gains accruing to the consumers and the general improvement in public welfare in the form of faster economic growth, etc.

The Public Accounts Committee asked the CBI as to whether they agreed with the calculations of the C&AG. In reply, the Director, CBI submitted in evidence: "We are not experts on that subject. So, we have asked TRAI to set up a Committee and then give us the exact loss figures ... we have calculated roughly between Rs. 40,000 crore and Rs. 50,000 crore. That is our rough figure."

The PAC then desired to know from the TRAI, the status of the request made by the CBI to the Authority to set up a Committee and calculate the exact loss. The TRAI in its reply stated that the CBI vide its letter dated January 19, 2011 had informed TRAI that in view of the directions of Hon'ble Supreme Court of India for investigation with emphasis on loss caused to public exchequer, it is necessary that price of the CMTS/Basic/UAS License which comes bundled with a spectrum of 4.4 MHz + 1.8 MHz be calculated on technical and commercial parameters for all telecom circles for various years from 2001 to 2008 on yearly basis. Further, they requested TRAI that the expert committee appointed by it may also be asked to work upon such prices for all telecom circles for various years from 2001 to 2008 on yearly basis.

Accordingly, TRAI vide its letter dated January 27, 2011 requested the Experts to calculate the price of spectrum of 4.4. MHz + 1.8 MHz, based the technical and commercial parameters for the years 2001 to 2008 on yearly basis."

The Authority further stated that earlier TRAI had requested these Experts to study the issues involved and provide the value of spectrum in

1800 MHz band duly taking into consideration the inputs from the service providers. The Experts submitted their report titled "The 2010 value of spectrum in 1,800 MHz band" dated January 30, 2011. This I produced during the Supreme Court hearing of my Writ Petition for cancellation of licences awarded for 2G Spectrum allocation in 2008.

On February 8, 2011, TRAI recommended to be DOT that the price given by the experts be adopted as the best available figure.

A perusal of the TRAI's recommendations on "the 2010 value of Spectrum in the 1,800 MHz band" revealed that the Expert Committee's report makes an assessment of the value of the 1,800 MHz band spectrum from the technical as well as the commercial points of view. Having done so, the report determines the value of 1,800 MHz spectrum in two tranches – price of contracted spectrum, i.e. up to 6.2 MHz and price of incremental spectrum, i.e. beyond 6.2 MHz.

TRAI further stated that the experts not only relied on the data relating to various LSAs but also on certain assumptions, some of which, though inherent in an exercise of this nature, are nevertheless significant. The various assumptions made by them have been clearly brought out in the report. In the light of this, the Authority feels that while the figures given by the experts may be adopted, it should be done with the full realization that these are estimated figures and may or may not always match the exact market price.

A copy of the TRAI's evaluation of and comments on the said report is at. Whatever the national loss, the loss being from Rs.50,000 crores to Rs.2,00,000 crores, it is staggering. About 30 per cent of this loss (hence gain to the licencees), may be taken as the pay-offs or bribe.

Hence, there is today the nation-wide public shock and indignation over the gross irregularities in the allotment of 2G spectrum and the colossal fiduciary loss caused to the public exchequer. The loss figure has eleven zeroes! Well before the C&AG report was tabled in Parliament, in my petition to the Supreme Court, to give an authoritative figure on the loss I had calculated a net loss of Rs.97,410.74 crore which did not include crossover losses and from Wimax. The C&AG, based on a set of parameters, pegged the presumptive loss or opportunity cost to the nation at Rs.1,76,645 crores.

The CBI calculated the bribe roughly between Rs. 40,000 crore to Rs. 50,000 crore based on the premise of the profits made by Swan and Unitech by sale of equity. The CBI, however, clarified that they were concentrating the investigation on criminal conspiracy and the money trail.

The nation was further shocked to note that pending the PAC examination of the C&AG Report, the Minister of Communications and Information Technology addressed a press conference on January 17, 2011 to describe the presumptive loss calculated by the C&AG as "utterly erroneous and embarrassing to the Govt." He described the calculation methodology adopted by the C&AG "without basis and a serious error on the part of the constitutional authority" and charged that the sensation thus caused "allowed the Opposition to spread utter falsehood."

The whole country disapproved of the public criticism of the institution of the C&AG and Parliament itself. More so, the frontal attack was made by the Minister, who obviously forgot his law education in his sychophancy of the principal beneficiary from the scam, and whose Ministry and his predecessor were under scanner, especially at a time when the matter was under examination in the PAC, obviously with an intent to confound and mislead.

It is even more surprising that the Ministry of Finance responsible for macro management of the economy and mobilization of resources for development, *has made no assessment of the loss on the ostensible ground that it is difficult to work it out* except conceding that spectrum is a scarce resource and that the spectrum commands premium as the market expands! Intriguingly, neither the DoT nor the TRAI has quantified the precise loss.

> Unfortunately, the DoT instead of admitting an unconscionable act, advanced the plea that theoretical exercises based on economic modelling are fraught with simplistic assumptions and that no methodology can be suggested by them to calculate the loss. Thereby attempting to defend the indefensible even as the findings of the experts engaged by the TRAI, who found that the value of 2G spectrum is higher than 3G in rural segments, the unexpectedly high

earnings from 3G revenue not to mention the written advise of our hapless PM for auction of 2G spectrum in "a fair and transparent manner."

On the presumptive loss of Rs.1.76 lakh crores, the C&AG had himself explained to the Public Accounts Committee that the calculation was based on certain econometric or mathematical methods after trying different econometric models and consultation with CAs and thus the loss of revenue to the Government calculated on real market situations cannot be faulted but may be debated. The C&AG has further explained that accountability is fixed in the Government after the events are investigated and drew the attention of the PAC to the C&AG report which says the entire process of allocation of 2G spectrum raises serious concern about the system of governance in the DoT which need to be thoroughly renewed and revamped.

The PAC censured the DoT for giving dual technology licence to the CDMA operators and new UAS licences in 2007-08 at a price determined in 2001 as not only imprudent but also one that smacks of a sinister design. Ignoring the voluntary offer of a Company to pay much more than the 2001 price even without auction did not persuade the Government to realize the true market price of spectrum.

Revenue generation from the auction of 3G & BWA Spectrum in 2009 unquestionably established the true value of Spectrum was more than ten times the 2001 level. Arguments in some quarters that the 3G price cannot be compared with the 2G price are untenable simply because two different means were adopted for the allocation of 2G&3G Spectrum.

Also a thorough technical analysis done by Dr. Rohit Prasad and published as "Value of 2G Spectrum in India" in *Economic and Political Weekly* January 23, 2010, vol. XLV, No.4 reveals that the market price of spectrum calculated on widely varying assumptions significance exceeds the upfront fees charged from the operators especially Swan Telecom Pvt. Ltd. and Unitech Wireless Ltd.

In other words, had the allocation of 2G Spectrum made through a fair and transparent method like auction as recommended by the TRAI and even DoT officials like Manju Madhavan as also advised by the Prime

Minister himself, no accusation would have been raised against a fair and transparent procedure regardless of the revenue realized. Since that was not done and 2G Spectrum was arbitrarily, unreasonably and *mala fide* given at a throwaway price while the 3G auction gave revenue five times more than the base price.

Therefore, as the PAC concluded, it is imperative and incumbent upon the government to calculate the exact loss caused to the exchequer instead of washing off their hands on the simplistic plea that it is difficult to estimate the loss. The PAC further recommended that the Government must recover the unlawful gains made by all those responsible for the staggering national loss. *This can of course be done only by cancellation of the 2008 2G spectrum allotments and licences at Raja's behest.* The Supreme Court heard my arguments extensively as also those of the Government and the Telecom Companies and has reserved its orders. The judgment is awaited.

ISSUE OF LICENCES TO INELIGIBLE COMPANIES

CAG Audit's examination on the allocation of 2G Spectrum revealed that the allegedly favoured Companies were: (i) Unitech Infrastructure Pvt. Ltd. (Brand name Uninor); (ii) Unitech Builders and Estates Pvt. Ltd. (Brand name Uninor); (iii) Azare Properties Ltd (Brand name Uninor); (iv) Hudson Properties Pvt. Ltd. (Brand name Uninor); (v) Nahan Properties Pvt. Ltd. (Brand name Uninor); (vi) Adonis Projects Pvt. Ltd. (Brand name Uninor); (vii) Aska Projects Ltd. (Brand name Uninor); (viii) Volga Properties Pvt. Ltd. (Brand name Uninor); (ix) Shipping Stop Dot Com (India) Private Limited (Now Loop Telecom Pvt. Ltd); (x) Allianz Infratech (P) Ltd. (merged with Etisalat DB); (xi) Datacom Solutions Pvt. Ltd. (Changed to Videocon Telecommunications Ltd.); (xii) S Tel Ltd.; and (xiii) Swan Telecom Private Limited (Now Etisalat DB Telecom India Private Limited).

According to audit observations, out of the above 13 companies, six newly incorporated applicant companies namely Unitech Builders and Estates Pvt. Ltd, Hudson Properties Pvt. Ltd, Nahan Properties Pvt. Ltd, Aska Projects Ltd, Volga Properties Pvt. Ltd and Adonis Projects Pvt. Ltd which belonged to Unitech Group having Brand name as Uninor had declared the business activity in the main object clause of Memorandum of Association (MOA) as real estate instead of telecom as the resolution effecting the alteration was not yet registered as on the date of application.

Further Shipping Stop DoT Com (India) Pvt. Ltd. which later on changed to Loop Telecom Pvt. Ltd. had declared its business activity as to design develop, sell, maintain computer software and programmes.

The following major deficiencies in the Applications for UAS Licensees were pointed out by Audit.

Sr. No.	Name of Applicant Company/Changed name	Date of Incorporation the Company	Date of application	No. of licenses issued	Major shortcomings observed
1.	Unitech Infrastructure Pvt. Ltd. (Brand name Uninor)	10.8.2007	24.9.2007	1	The business activity in the main object clause of MOA was real estate instead of telecom as the resolution effecting the alteration was not yet registered as on the date of application; Suppressed the non – registration of alteration in the main object clause of MOA by ROC; Authorised share capital was only Rs. 5 lakh against the requirement of Rs. 10 crore; Deposited the stamp duties for increase in the authorised share capital on October 3, 2007; Registration of the resolution effecting the increase in the authorised share capital was done on October 11, 2007; Submitted false certificate from Company Secretary in respect of Paid up capital;
2.	Unitech Builders and Estates Pvt. Ltd. (Brand name Uninor)	10.8.2007	24.09.2007	1	The business activity in the main object clause of MOA was real estate

					instead of telecom as the condition prescribed by ROC while doing the registration of resolution was not yet met; Suppressed the conditional registration of alteration in the main object clause of MOA by ROC; Authorised share capital was only Rs. 5 lakh against the requirement of Rs. 10 crore; Deposited the stamp duties for increase in the authorised share capital on October 3, 2007; Registration of the resolution effecting increase in the authorised share capital was done on October 8, 2007; Submitted false certificate from Company Secretary in respect of Paid up capital;
3.	Azare Properties Ltd (Brand name Uninor)	1.8.2007	24.09.2007	1	The business activity in the main object clause of MOA was real estate instead of telecom as the resolution effecting the alteration was not yet registered as on the date of application; Suppressed the non – registration of alteration in the main object clause of MOA; Authorised share capital was only Rs. 5 lakh against the requirement of Rs. 10 crore; Deposited the stamp duties for increase in the authorised share capital on October 3, 2007; Registration of the resolution effecting increase in the authorised share capital was done on

					October 8, 2007; Submitted false certificate from Company Secretary in respect of Paid up capital;
4.	Hudson Properties Pvt. Ltd. (Brand name Uninor)	1.8.2007	24.09.2007	1	The business activity in the main object clause of MOA was real estate instead of telecom as the condition prescribed by ROC while doing the registration of resolution was not yet met; Suppressed the conditional registration of alteration in the main object clause of MOA by ROC; Authorised share capital was only Rs. 5 lakh against the requirement of Rs. 10 crore; Deposited the stamp duties for increase in the authorised share capital on October 3, 2007; Registration of resolution effecting increase in the authorised share capital was done on October 8, 2007; Submitted false certificate from Company Secretary in respect of Paid up capital;
5.	Nahan Properties Pvt. Ltd. (Brand name Uninor)	16.8.2007	24.09.2007	6	The business activity in the main object clause of MOA was real estate instead of telecom as the condition prescribed by ROC while doing the registration of resolution was not yet met; Suppressed the conditional registration of alteration in the main object clause of MOA by ROC; Authorised share capital was only Rs. 5 lakh against

					Rs. 22 crore; Deposited the stamp duties for increase in the authorised share capital on October 3, 2007; Registration of the resolution effecting increase in the authorised share capital was done on October 8, 2007; Submitted false certificate from Company Secretary in respect of Paid up capital;
6.	Adonis Projects Pvt. Ltd. (Brand name Uninor)	28.8.2007	24.09.2007	6	The business activity in the main object clause of MOA was real estate instead of telecom as the condition prescribed by ROC while doing the registration of resolution was not yet met; Suppressed the conditional registration of alteration in the main object clause of MOA by ROC; Authorised share capital was only Rs. 5 lakh against the requirement of Rs. 26 crore; Deposited the stamp duties for increase in the authorised share capital on October 3, 2007; Registration of the resolution effecting increase in the authorised share capital was done on October 8, 2007; Submitted false certificate from Company Secretary in respect of Paid up capital;
7.	Aska Projects Ltd. (Brand name Uninor)	16.8.2007	24.09.2007	3	The business activity in the main object clause of MOA was real estate instead of telecom as the condition prescribed by

					ROC while doing the registration of resolution was not yet met; Suppressed the conditional registration of alteration in the main object clause of MOA by ROC; Authorised share capital was only Rs. 5 lakh against the requirement of Rs. 25 crore; Deposited the stamp duties for increase in the authorised share capital on October 3, 2007; Registration of the resolution effecting increase in the authorised share capital was done on October 8, 2007; Submitted false certificate from Company Secretary in respect of Paid up capital;
8.	Volga Properties Pvt. Ltd. (Brand name Uninor)	1.9.2007	24.09.2007	3	The business activity in the main object clause of MOA was real estate instead of telecom as the condition prescribed by ROC while doing the registration of resolution was not yet met; Suppressed the conditional registration of alteration in the main object clause of MOA by ROC; Authorised share capital was only Rs. 5 lakh against the requirement of Rs. 25 crore; Deposited the stamp duties for increase in the authorised share capital on October 3, 2007; Registration of the resolution effecting increase in the authorised share capital was done on

					October 8, 2007 Submitted false certificate from Company Secretary in respect of Paid up capital;
9.	Shipping Stop Dot Com (India) Private Limited (Now Loop Telecom Pvt. Ltd)	12.3.1997	03/09/2007	21	The business activity in the main object clause of MOA was to design, develop, sell, maintain computer software and programmes as the resolution effecting the alteration was not yet registered as on the date of application; The resolution effecting the alterations in main object clause of the MOA to include the telecom sector was registered by the ROC on September 28, 2007 only; Suppressed the non-registration of alteration in the main object clause of MOA by ROC; Authorised share capital was only Rs. 5.20 crore against the requirement of Rs. 128 crore; Deposited the stamp duties for increase in the authorised share capital on September 25, 2007; Request for Registration of increase in the authorised share capital was submitted on October 24, 2007; Submitted false certificate from Company Secretary re. Paid up capital;
10.	Allianz Infratech (P) Ltd. (merged with Etisalat DB)	21.12.2006	5/09/2007	2	The business activity in the main object clause of MOA was real estate instead of telecom as the resolution effecting the alteration was not yet registered as on the date of

					application; Suppressed the non-registration of alteration in the main object clause of MOA by ROC; Authorised share capital was only Rs. 5 lakh against the requirement of Rs. 8 crore; Deposited the stamp duties for increase in the authorised share capital on December 24, 2007; Form No 5 along with other papers to increase the authorised share capital was submitted in ROC on December 27, 2007 Submitted false certificate from Company Secretary re. Paid up capital;
11.	Datacom Solutions Pvt. Ltd. (Changed to Videocon Telecommunications Ltd.)	7.6.2007	28.08.2007	21	Suppressed the non-registration of the resolution effecting alteration in the MOA effecting increase in the authorised share capital by ROC; Authorised share capital was only Rs. 1 lakh against the requirement of Rs. 138 crore; Increased authorised share capital on the day preceding the date of submission of application through a resolution; Submitted false certificate re. Paid up capital though the resolution effecting the increase in the authorised share capital and alterations in the MOA/AOA was not yet registered by ROC;
12.	S Tel Ltd.	19.6.2007	07.07.2007	6	Suppressed the non-registration of alteration in the MOA/AOA regarding increase in the authorised share capital Authorised

					share capital was only Rs. 10 lakh against the requirement of Rs. 18 crore as on the date of application; Submitted the form for Registration of the resolution effecting the increase in the authorised share capital on August 3, 2007; Submitted false certificate from Company Secretary re. Paid up capital though the resolution effecting the increase in the authorised share capital and alterations in the MOA/AOA was not yet registered by ROC;
13.	Swan Telecom Private Limited (Now Etisalat DB Telecom Private Limited)	13.7.2006	02.03.2007	13	Suppressed the non-registration of alteration in the MOA/AOA regarding increase in the authorised share capital done on the preceding day i.e. March 1, 2007; Deposited the stamp duties and Form 5 to ROC Mumbai for registering the resolution effecting the increase in the authorised share capital on 14 March 2007; Submitted false certificate from Company Secretary re. Paid up capital; Net worth of Rs. 314.7 crore claimed on behalf of Reliance Telecom Ltd whose share was claimed to be less than 10 per cent, was not to be included while computing the net-worth of the applicant company.

Audit carried out by the CAG during the course of verification of the files of the DoT and public documents accessed from the Ministry of

Corporate Affairs, Government of India, New Delhi, found that as many as 85 Licenses out of the 122 new licenses issued to 13 Companies in 2008 were granted to those companies which did not satisfy the eligibility conditions prescribed by the DoT. All 85 licenses were given to companies which did not have the stipulated paid up capital at the time of application. Further, 45 out of these 85 licenses were issued to companies who failed to satisfy conditions of main object clause in their Memorandum of Association.

Six newly incorporated applicant companies belonging to Unitech Group had suppressed the fact of conditional nature of certification of registration done by the Registrar of Companies (ROC) on September 20, 2007 while registering the alterations in the main object clause in the MOA/AOA of these Companies. The ROC while certifying the alteration of the main object clauses of all six companies had stated that the certificate was subject to the change of name of the Company. Since in terms of Section 21 of the Companies Act 1956, the change of name of the Company could be done only with the approval of the "Central Government signified in writing," the condition of the change of name of these applicant Companies was met in May 2008 only. As a result, all these six new companies were registered afresh with the new names in May 2008 by the ROC. Hence the alteration of the MOA of these Companies became effective in May 2008 only. As a result thereof, the MOA of these companies did not permit them to operate in the telecom sector on the date of application, i.e. September 24, 2007.

Apart from this, these six companies had suppressed the fact of conditional certification of the alterations in the MOA/AOA by the ROC while submitting their applications for UAS licence on September 24, 2007. They had also misrepresented the altered MOA/AOA as the original MOA/AOA in their applications before DOT. The submission of the altered MOA/AOA of the Companies without full disclosure of the factual position of the alteration of the main object clause in the MOA/AOA and their conditional registration by the ROC was a fraudulent act of these six companies with the intentions of obtaining the UAS licenses for 20 service areas.

A few illustrations are:

(i) Azare Properties Limited and Unitech Infrastructures Private Limited (Brand name Uninor) also misrepresented the altered MOA/AOA as the original MOA/AOA along with their applications to the DoT. Further they suppressed the fact that alterations had not been registered by the ROC as yet on the date of submission of their application. The ROC while certifying the alteration of the main object clauses in the MOA/AOA of these companies on October 5 and 9, 2007 respectively had also directed that the certificate was subject to the change of name of the Company. The directive of the ROC was complied with only in May 2008 and thus the alteration of the MOA of these Companies became effective in May 2008 only. As a result thereof, the MOA of these companies did not permit them to operate in the telecom sector on the date of application i.e. September 24, 2007.

(ii) Allianz Infratech Private Limited (Merged with Etisalat DB Telecom India Private Limited), in their applications to the DoT on September 5, 2007 submitted the MOA/AOA of the company, which didn't include the telecom sector in their main object clause. Even the alteration in the main object clause of the MOA of the Company was certified by the ROC on October 26, 2007 only. Hence it rendered them ineligible for grant of UAS licence on the date of submission of their application in September 2007.

(iii) Shipping Stop DoT Com (India) Pvt. Ltd. which later on changed to Loop Telecom Pvt. Ltd. had declared its business activity as to design develop, sell, maintain computer software and programmes. They also submitted their applications for grant of UAS licenses for 21 service areas on September 3, 2007 to the DoT without disclosing the fact of non registration of alteration of the main object clauses in the MOA/AOA with the ROC as on the date of the application. The company had changed the main object clauses in their MOA/AOA so as to include the telecom sector in their MOA/AOA but these alterations were registered by the ROC on September 28, 2007 only. The altered MOA of the Company by the Loop Telecom Private Limited suppressing the fact of non registration of the alterations in the main object clause of their MOA/AOA by the ROC on the date of application was submitted.

FALSE AND FICTITIOUS CLAIMS OF HIGHER PAID UP CAPITAL BY 13 COMPANIES

DoT (December 2005) had prescribed that the applicant company shall have a minimum paid up equity capital of Rs. 3-10 crore depending on the Service Area(s) (Service Areas A – Rs.10 crore, B- Rs. 5 crore and C – Rs.3 crore) as on the date of the application and shall submit a certificate to this effect by the applicant's Company Secretary along with application.

13 Applicant Companies, which had applied for 123 UAS licenses and were granted 85 UAS licenses, did not have the requisite authorized share capital on the date of submission of the applications. Of these, eight applicants belonging to Unitech Group (Brand name Uninor) had been incorporated in August-September 2007 with an authorised share capital of Rs. 5 lakh each. All these eight companies passed the special resolutions for increase in the authorized share capital between 2 PM to 5 PM on September 20, 2007 in the extra-ordinary general meetings of the respective companies and deposited the requisite stamp duties on October 3, 2007 for increase in the authorized share capital. After they submitted the requisite applications along with the proof of payment of stamp duties on October 5, 2007, the certificate of the registration of the increase in the authorized share capital was issued by the ROC only on October 8/11, 2007. Table I gives these details of the applications of these companies.

The Committee during its scrutiny of issue of Licenses to ineligible Companies found that certain Companies which had declared real estate as their business activity in their main object clause of MoA had been awarded licences; certain Companies which did not have authorized share capital/paid up capital on the date of applying for UAS Licenses were given the same; the Department of Telecommunications (DoT) failed in cross verifying the status of Companies with the Ministry of Corporate Affairs; there was gross violation of rules & regulations to favour M/s Swan & Unitech; S-Tel having won cases on the issue of arbitrariness in cut-off date was forced to withdraw its case in the Supreme Court owing to DoT raising false Security concerns; and apart from subverting rules and regulations, in case of M/s Swan, BSNL was made to sign an MoU for providing intra-circle Roaming Arrangement.

An independent expert with vast experience of Telecom Sector testified before the Committee that "all pseudo methods" and "dirty tricks" were used by these companies to get into the telecom market at the cost of tax payers' money.

The Committee found that as many as 85 Licenses out of the 122 new licenses issued to 13 Companies in 2008 were granted to those Companies which did not satisfy the eligibility conditions prescribed by the DoT. All 85 Licenses were given to Companies which did not have the stipulated paid up capital at the time of application. The Committee found that in order to increase the authorized share capital Extraordinary General Meetings were held and resolutions passed to the said effect. The enabling provisions of the Companies Act, 1956 allows Companies to increase their authorized share capital by way of passing resolutions through General Body Meetings and also by way of application to the said effect to the ROC within 30 days or beyond that with a payment of fine.

The Public Accounts Committee Draft Report noted that, these Companies had declared real estate as the business activity in the main object clause of MOA instead of telecom sector as on the date of application. However, the subsequent resolutions altering the main object clause of MOA had not been registered as on the date of application. The Committee found that the UAS guidelines of December 14, 2005 did not stipulate that the telecom sector be the declared activity of the Companies applying for grant of licences.

The Economic Times dated January 9, 2008 had published an article titled "6 fail to cross DoTted line" in which the Companies that were to be awarded Licences had been named. The article had clearly stated that "DoT to Issue LOIs to 10 Companies" and naming them as "Lucky 10," it stated that Unitech, Datacom, Stel, HFCL Infotel, BPL, Shyam Tele, Swan Communications, Idea, Tata Tele and Reliance Communications were those Companies. The article further stated that DoT would begin issuing the LOIs from Wednesday and try to complete the process by that weekend.

In order to have clarity on the issue that certain companies were privy to the information about the time when the LOIs were to be issued, the Public Accounts Committee cross examined the representatives of M/s

Etisalat DB Telecom Pvt. Ltd. (formerly known as M/s Swan Telecom Pvt. Ltd.). The PAC asked the representatives as to how on January 10, 2008, when LOIs were issued and 45 minutes time between 2.45 pm and 3.30 pm was given to fulfil the requirement of submitting the drafts, a Demand Draft for Rs.1651 crores drawn on Punjab National Bank of Mumbai could reach Delhi from Mumbai on the same day. The witness in their written submission have stated that most of the applicants had deposited the same on January 10, 2008. Further, regarding the clarification of the DD, it was stated that the DD was drawn on Punjab National Bank in New Delhi and a photocopy of the same was annexed. But to the dismay of the Committee they found that instead of Rs. 1,651 crores DD drawn on PNB, they were furnished with a copy of Banker's Cheque dated January 9, 2008 drawn on SBI, New Delhi for Rs.203.60 lakhs!

Thus, to favour a few companies licences had been issued to Companies which had suppressed facts, disclosed incomplete information and submitted fictitious documents to the DoT and thus used fraudulent means for getting UAS licenses and spectrum. Owners of these licenses had obtained them at unbelievably low prices and had in turn sold significant stakes in their companies to the Indian/foreign companies at high premium within a short period of time.

The premium earned by these new entrants to the telecom sector was nothing but the true value of the spectrum, which should have normally accrued to the public exchequer. The Committee, therefore, recommend that all those Companies who suppressed facts and furnished fictitious documents be sternly dealt with in accordance with the undertakings taken from them before signing the Licence agreements and the Committee apprised.

The scrutiny of the subject by the PAC further revealed that different decisions were taken in respect of M/s Loop Telecom Pvt. Ltd. and M/s Swan Telecom Pvt. Ltd. with regard to alleged violation of the substantial equity clause 8 of UAS Guidelines.

In the case of M/s Loop Telecom Pvt. Ltd. a reference was sent to Ministry of Corporate Affairs for examination but in case of M/s Swan Telecom Pvt. Ltd. the then Minister Raja had decided that the then SG Vahanavati's opinion may be directly sought as he was representing the

DoT in TDSAT and at other judicial forums including in the High Court, Delhi.

The SG in his opinion had very conveniently held that "the applicants fulfiled all the necessary conditions cannot really be faulted." However, when DoT officials again sought permission to refer the matter to the Ministry of Corporate Affairs for investigation, the Secretary (T) on April 17, 2009 held the view that "in view of the opinion of SG no such reference is required" and the Minister approved the same on April 18, 2009.

No wonder the Public Accounts Committee found that the DoT wrongly referred the case to SG directly without routing the case through Ministry of Law and Justice as required under the Service Condition Rules for AG and SG. The PAC in its as yet Draft Report, therefore, come to inescapable but firm conclusion that both the Ministry of Communications and Information Technology and the SG were equally responsible for favouring M/s Swan by circumventing the due procedure.

Since the then Secretary, DoT stands chargesheeted, the PAC has thought it fit to demand explanation of Mr. Vahanvati, as to why he prevented the DoT from referring the matter to Ministry of Corporate Affairs. The Public Accounts Committee also deplored the role of the Minister who went out of the way to ensure that certain Companies which were granted UAS Licences were disqualified or rendered ineligible had the matter been referred for the opinion of Ministry of Corporate Affairs which under the Ministership of Salman Khurshid brought disgrace to the government by his partisanship..

M/s S. Tel had challenged the legal validity of the Press Release dated January 10, 2008 as the said Press Release arbitrarily advanced the cut-off date from October 1, 2007 to September 25, 2007 three months and ten days after the deadline was over. M/s S.Tel were deprived from being granted LOIs for UAS Licences for 16 circles for which they had applied on September 27, 2007.

A single Judge and later a Division Bench ruled in S Tel's favour holding the said advancement of the cut of date as arbitrarily and illegal. The Hon'ble Supreme Court on appeal by DoT refused to interfere on my intervention with the order of the Delhi High Court. M/s S. Tel however decided not to pursue with their case as they had received a letter regarding the cancellation of the commercial launch citing security reasons by the DoT.

The Company was arm-twisted to withdraw the case despite having received favourable verdicts from the High Court. Since the impugned Press Release was quashed by the High Court of Delhi being arbitrary and unjustified, the necessary logical action to be taken is to cancel all the licences issued in 2008.

CAG Audit had observed that Swan Telecom Private Limited (changed to Etisalat DB Telecom India Private Limited) applied for grant of UAS licence in 13 service areas in March 2007. From the declaration of the Company for UAS licence, it was evident that at the time of applying for UASL, the equity stakes of Reliance Telecom Ltd in Swan Telecom Private Limited was 10.71 per cent. Since Reliance Telecom Ltd were operating in all the service areas for which Swan Telecom Limited had applied for UASL, the application of Swan Telecom Private Limited was not in conformity with the UASL Guidelines.

Further, Swan Telecom was given an opportunity to resubmit a revised stake holding pattern in December 2007 i.e. 9 months after their date of application which declared that Reliance Telecom Limited had divested their entire stakes. This was accepted by the DoT and Swan Telecom Private Limited was given the benefit of seniority from the date of their initial application i.e. March 2007.

Audit also found that the e-mail ID of the corporate as well as registered office of the Swan Telecom Private Limited in their application dated March 2, 2007 was shown as hari.nair@relianceada.com. The same e-mail ID (hari.nair@relianceada.com) also was given for the correspondence address and the authorised contact person of the applicant company. Though the Company Secretary Hari Nair had given a certificate while applying for a UAS licence for J&K Service Area in January 2007 that the Tiger Traders Private Limited held the shares of Swan (then Swan Capital private Limited) as trustees of Indian Telecom Infrastructure fund and these corporate beneficiaries are not part of Reliance ADA Group and neither Anil Ambani nor his family or Reliance ADA Group companies holds any shares in these companies, it was holding NCRPS of Rs.1 at a premium of Rs.999 by the RTL in Swan Telecom, a newly incorporated company with no fixed assets that raised doubts.

After observing these deficiencies Committee wanted to know whether the Department of Telecommunications took the help of the Company Secretaries/CAs while examining the applications and what punitive action was taken/proposed against those companies who had suppressed facts, disclosed incomplete information and submitted fictitious documents for getting UAS licences/Spectrum, the Department in their reply have submitted as under:

> For examination of the applications, DoT does not take the help of Company Secretaries/Chartered Accounts. The Unified Access Services (UAS) licences were granted in terms of the extant UAS Licence Guidelines dated 14.12.2005 and based on certain eligibility criteria specified and validated by the information/documents/certificates submitted by the applicant companies duly certified by their Company Secretary as mentioned in the Guidelines/Application Form.

Based on the *Report of Comptroller and Auditor General of India* (CAG) on "Issue of Licences and Allocation of 2G Spectrum by the Department of Telecommunications," DoT, on December 14, 2010 have issued show cause notices to 13 companies for termination of the 85 Unified Access Services (UAS) licences issued in the year 2008, who stated to be ineligible on the date of their respective applications for grant of UAS licences. The companies have submitted their replies which are presently under examination of the Department."

On the measures contemplated by DoT to make the verification process foolproof entailing due diligence, fairness and transparency it was submitted as:

> As a matter of abundant precaution, Department of Telecom (DoT) also takes an undertaking from the applicant company that "if at any time, any averments made or information furnished for obtaining the

ITEM NO.48 COURT NO.10 SECTION XIV

S U P R E M E   C O U R T   O F   I N D I A
RECORD OF PROCEEDINGS

Petition(s) for Special Leave to Appeal (Civil) No(s).33406/2009

(From the judgement and order dated 24/11/2009 in LPA No. 388/2009 of The HIGH COURT OF DELHI AT N. DELHI)

UNION OF INDIA Petitioner(s)

VERSUS

S TEL LTD. Respondent(s)

(With appln(s) for personal hearing before the court and prayer for interim relief and office report))
(For directions)

Date: 12/03/2010 This Petition was called on for hearing today.

CORAM :
HON'BLE MR. JUSTICE B. SUDERSHAN REDDY
HON'BLE MR. JUSTICE SURINDER SINGH NIJJAR

For Petitioner(s)
Mr. G.E. Vahanvati, AG
Mr. Vikas Singh, Sr.Adv.
Mr. Sanjay R. Hegde,Adv.
Mr. A. Rohen Singh, adv.
Mr. Ramesh Kumar Mishra, Adv.

For Respondent(s)
Mr. Dayan Krishnan, adv.
Mr. Gautam Narayan, Adv.
Mr. Nikhil Menon, adv.
Mr. Nikhil Nayyar,Adv.

For impleadment Dr. Subramanian (In person
Dr. Roxna Swamy, adv

UPON hearing counsel the Court made the following
O R D E R

Leave granted.

This appeal is disposed of in terms of the signed order.

In view of our order in the Civil Appeal, no further orders as such are required to be passed in the impleadment application-I.A. No. 2.

(Sukhbir Paul Kaur)
Court Master

(Vijay Dhawan)
Court Master

(Signed Order is placed on the file)

IN THE SUPREME COURT OF INDIA
CIVIL APPELLATE JURISDICTION

CIVIL APPEAL NO.2355 OF 2010
(Arising out of S.L.P.(C) No.33406 of 2009)

UNION OF INDIA ... Appellant(s)

Versus

S. TEL LTD. ... Respondent(s)

O R D E R

We have heard learned Attorney General for India and learned counsel for the respondent/writ petitioner and also Dr. Subramanian Swamy, who appears in person, in his impleadment application-I.A. No.2.

Leave granted.

Pursuant to our directions the respondent/writ-petitioner filed an additional affidavit in which it is inter alia stated :

> "It is further submitted that market conditions have changed ever since the respondent filed its applications for UASL for the said 16 Circles, primarily due to the fact that the Respondent's competitors who had applied and gotten licences in January, 2008 have already commenced or are in an advanced stage of commencing the service in the service area and a period of two and a half years has also since elapsed." (para 5)

That apart, the learned Attorney General appearing for the Union of India and learned counsel for the respondent/writ petitioner suggested the

minutes of the Order which is to the following effect :-

> "Having regard to the statements made in the additional affidavit dated 11.3.2010. the Union of India reiterates that the application made by the respondent on 28th September, 2007 has not been rejected but has been put in abeyance and that the Government will consider the pending applications including the application made by the respondent on 28th September, 2007 for 16 circles on a first-come-first-serve basis in due course as per the prevailing policy and consultation with the TRAI."

Taking the additional affidavit and the suggestions made by the learned Attorney General, this appeal is disposed of as requiring no further adjudication.

However, we make it clear that the findings recorded by the High Court with regard to the cut off date is not interfered with and disturbed by this Court in the present case.

In view of our order in the Civil Appeal, no further orders as such are required to be passed in the impleadment application-I.A. No.2.

....................J.
(B.SUDERSHAN REDDY)

......................J.
(SURINDER SINGH NIJJAR)

New Delhi,
March 12, 2010

licence was found incorrect, then their application and the licence if granted thereto on the basis of such application, shall be cancelled." If any misrepresentation of facts is brought to notice at a later date necessary action can be taken as per due procedure under the provisions of the UAS licence Guidelines/ agreement.

Commenting upon the ineligible Companies, the former CMD, VSNL while deposing before the Committee stated:

> I firmly remain convinced that it is the money which could have come to the Government ... SWAN Telecom has not rolled out services even today. Where is the question of bringing in competition? It is only the natural law which is taking the pricing down from the existing competition. It is not due to the new licences. LOOP Telecom, DATA Com. Videocon, etc. are there. Who has started the service? They have only started the service just to say that they have licence and they meet some obligations. So, where is the competition? It was only speculation because something was available and they saw the potential that they can trade in the market. Therefore, the regulation of 2007 was wrongly interpreted. The entire Council, the Prime Minister, the Finance Secretary and the Law Minister were given a go by and not heard, maybe, to benefit the few.

During the cross-examination of the representatives of M/s Etisalat DB Telecom India Pvt. Ltd. the Committee wanted to know how on 10th January, 2008 when LOI was issued and 45 minutes time between 2.45 p.m. and 3.30 p.m. was given to fulfil the requirement of submitting the drafts, a Demand Draft for Rs. 50 crore, drawn on the Punjab National Bank of Mumbai on the same day could reach Delhi from Mumbai. To this the witness replied: "About this draft, we will come back tomorrow."

In a post-evidence information M/s Etisalat DB Telecom India Pvt. Ltd. (earlier known as M/s Swan Telecom Pvt. Ltd.) *vide* their letter dated April 15, 2011 has replied as under:

> It is a matter of record that most of the applicants had the demand drafts ready and deposited the same on January 10, 2007 and in most cases much prior to the Company depositing the same.

> Further, in relation to the query as to whether the demand drafts for the license fees submitted on January 10, 2007 were drawn from Punjab National Bank in Mumbai, we have to submit that in fact the demand draft was drawn on the Punjab National Bank in New Delhi, a photocopy of the same is annexed as Annexure-7 hereto.

On the scrutiny of the said DD the Committee found that though they had questioned about Rs. 50 crore DD drawn on PNB, Mumbai they were furnished with a copy of Banker's Cheque dated January 9, 2008 drawn on SBI, New Delhi for Rs. 203.66 crore.

The deposition of former CMD, VSNL regarding the various issues about the operators *inter-alia* was as: "Sir, in the case of Swan, the rules were changed. In 2009, it is very clear that you cannot sell your equity, whether it is license or equity."

On being pointedly told that there was a difference between equity and license, the former CMD, VSNL added: "Sir, I am aware of it. In the case of Swan, the equity was sold and then the fresh equity was also issued. Then, a reference was made *post facto* whether it is right or wrong. So, the advice of the Company Law Board was taken whether the issuance of fresh equity is not selling the equity. The issuance of fresh shares is not selling the equity."

When the Committee wanted to know the number of Companies who had taken the license, sold their equity and had not sold the license and the attainment of the intended competition, the former CMD, VSNL deposed as under:

> They have sold part of the equity, which means losing some control. Then there have been issuance of fresh shares, which later on only the Government clarified that it is permissible because it is not selling the equity. However, I have given a calculation in my response that— later on because it goes into the shareholders premium account—one can get bonus shares and then one can issue those bonus shares to cash it or make profits.
>
> And also the question is that the spectrum or the competition which was supposed to have been brought in is not there. Etisalat,

> there are no customers; Loop, there are no customers; Videocon, there are I think about 30,000 customers; the only two companies which have some customers are Shyam Sistema and Unicorn, about five to six million each. Otherwise, the rest of the licensees have no customers. It is also hurting in yet another way because the spectrum charge which we get is on the AGR (Annual Gross Revenue), and then comes Adjusted Gross Revenue. It is first Annual Gross Revenue and then Adjusted Gross Revenue. Now, the Government is losing the spectrum charge, the Government is losing the licence fees, the Government which should have got service charge, the Government is losing it. There is another set of industry which is wanting that spectrum. Their revenues are far higher and the Government would have benefited. So, the Government today is losing and losing on all counts. First, you sell licence in 2007 at 2001 price despite all economic indicators saying that it is not right. Then, you lose out going forward on the revenue share, on the spectrum charge and on everything else. Then the biggest plank that yes we will bring in more competition. Where is the competition? There is no competition. It is the existing players who are really, really capturing the market.

When specifically asked by the Committee that shares of a Company could not be sold within three years as there was a lock in period and how did some companies sell within six months, the former CMD, VSNL deposed as under:

> After all this happened, in the Swan and the Unitech, these are the two classic cases, all the connected ex-post facto approvals were taken. But, yes, the lock in period, the roll out obligations, etc. were there. In the recommendations of the TRAI in 2007 and even previously, they were there. But they were all given a go-by, because selling of shares was treated differently from the issuance of fresh equity. The question is that despite so many letters, simple indexation, they did not do.

Elaborating on the above issue and clarifying about the disposal of applications the former CMD, VSNL *inter-alia* stated as under:

Some of the applications are not yet disposed. Those which were disposed were up to September 25.

The question here is, the Minister says that there was no cap but he had already applied a cap and that is the matter which was taken by the High Court and has been treated as vulnerable arbitrary application. That has also been upheld by the Supreme Court.

On November 2, 2007 the response was from the Minister that this was no cap but the cap had been applied. There are two letters and the response went to the Prime Minister the same day.

M/s Etisalat DB Telecom India Private Limited, vide letter dated November 18, 2010, to Hon'ble Prime Minister had made observations in their defence on the said CAG Report on following paras:

(a) Para no. 4.7.3 of the CAG Report regarding alteration of MOA with respect to Telecom activity as part of main object clause and amendment in MAA with respect to authorized share capital, after the date of application.

(b) Para no. 4.7.4.6 of CAG Report regarding violation of substantial equity clause by M/s Reliance Telecom Ltd., on the date of application

(c) Para no. 4.7.4.6.2 of CAG Report regarding counting of networth of M/s Reliance Telecom Ltd., for grant of UAS licenses to Swan Telecom Pvt. Ltd.

DoT sent their comments to the Public Accounts Committee when asked as under:

(a) Based on the said CAG report, show cause notices have been issued to M/s. Etisalat DB Telecom India Pvt. Ltd. for termination of the Unified Access Services (UAS) licences issued in the year 2008. Reply of the company is awaited for further action in the matter. Therefore, at this juncture, DoT is not in a position to comment on the representation of the company.

(b) The comments from Ministry of Corporate Affairs have been received in the matter *vide* their OM No. 3/92/2010/CL-II dated December 24, 2010 and December 21, 2010. [These comments, incidentally, have now been disowned, and the Minister shifted out to a relatively harmless portfolio.]

(c) As per the certificate submitted by M/s Swan Telecom Pvt. Ltd., the networth of M/s Swan Telecom Pvt. Ltd itself was (Rs. 1,100.28 crore) more than the required networth of Rs. 1,030 crore for grant of 13 UAS licences to the company. Therefore, the networth of M/s. Reliance Telecom Ltd. was not taken into consideration while granting UAS licences to the M/s. Swan Telecom Pvt. Ltd.

M/s Reliance Communication Ltd. vide letters dated November 26, 2010 had also submitted their views on the findings/observations made in the CAG Report to the PAC on following issues:

(i) Clarification on the C&AG's observations on increase in the authorized share capital of Swan Telecom Pvt. Ltd. in March 2007.

(ii) Clarification on the C&AG's observations regarding non fulfillment of the requirement of net worth by Swan Telecom Pvt. Ltd. on the date of application.

(i) Clarification on the C&AG's observations regarding holding of substantial equity by Reliance Telecom Ltd. in Swan Telecom Ltd. on the date of application.

(ii) Clarification on the C&AG's observations to term Swan Telecom Ltd., as a front company of TRL.

Commenting on this matter, the DoT told the PAC as under:

The issues raised by M/s Reliance Communications Ltd. are linked to grant of UAS licences to M/s Etisalat DB Telecom India Pvt. Ltd. (formerly Swan Telecom Pvt. Ltd.), were on the date of application (02.03.2007), since M/s. Reliance Telecom Ltd. was having some equity stake in M/s. Swan Telecom Pvt. Ltd. As stated earlier, based on the said CAG report, show cause notices have been issued to

M/s. Etisalat DB Telecom India Pvt. Ltd. for termination of the Unified Access Services (UAS) licences issued in the year 2008. Reply of M/s Etisalat DB Telecom India Pvt. Ltd. is awaited for further action in the matter. Therefore, at this juncture, DoT is not in a position to comment on the representation of M/s. Reliance Communications Ltd.

As per the certificate submitted by M/s Swan Telecom Pvt. Ltd., the networth of M/s. Swan Telecom Pvt. Ltd. itself was (Rs. 1100.28 crore) more than the required networth of Rs. 1030 crore for grant of 13 UAS licences to the company. Therefore, the networth of M/s. Reliance Telecom Ltd. was not taken into consideration while granting UAS Licences to the M/s. Swan Telecom Pvt. Ltd.

The comments from Ministry of Corporate Affairs have been received in the matter.

To a query by the PAC about the role of Reliance Communication in the formation of Swan Telecom, the Chairman, Reliance Communications Ltd. in his written submission has stated as:

With respect to the formation of Swan Telecom, it is to confirm that the company under the name Swan Capital Private Limited was incorporated only on July 13, 2006, which was changed to Swan Telecom on February 15, 2007. The shareholders on the date of incorporation of the company i.e. July 13, 2006 were as under:

Shareholder	Equity share of Rs. 10 each
Power Surfer Interactive (India) Pvt. Ltd.	4,999
Reliance Energy Management Services Pvt. Ltd	5,000
Himanshu Agarwal	1
Total	**10,000**

These shareholders sold their entire shareholding in Swan Telecom to Tiger Trustees Private Limited (formerly known as Tiger Traders Private Limited). In this manner, Tiger Trustees Private Limited became 100 per cent owner of Swan Telecom on that date. Swan Telecom also issued 30,00,000 fresh equity shares on January

22, 2007, of which 27,03,000 equity shares were issued to Tiger Trustees Privates Limited and 2,97,000 equity shares were issued to Reliance Telecom Limited.

In a post-evidence reply made to the Committee on the allegation regarding business activity in the main object clause of MOA as pointed out in the Audit Report, M/s Unitech Wireless (Tamil Nadu) Pvt. Ltd. have stated that as per the UASL guidelines there was no requirement to have telecom activity as part of the MOA at the time of applying for licence. Further, DoT letter dated December 10, 2007 for the first time stipulated submission of a certificate to the effect that telecom activity/business was a part of the objects for which the company was established according to its MOA and AOA.

On the issue of Paid-up Capital, M/s Unitech Wireless (Tamil Nadu) Pvt. Ltd. in their submission made to the Committee have stated that the ROC does not issue any certificate recording the increase in the authorized share capital and further added as: "We are not aware whether thiere is any recordal dated October 8, 2007/October 11, 2007 as alleged in the CAG Report ... increase in authorized capital is effective as soon as the shareholders' resolution is passed and that too, from the date of such resolution and it does not require an affirmation or recordal by the RoC to bring it into effect."

On being specifically asked as to how the Department proposed to fix responsibility on the Officers who failed to enforce to the basic eligibility conditions of the Companies that were granted licence/Spectrum causing huge loss to the Exchequer, it has been submitted as under: "Various agencies are investigating the matter. Any official found to have been negligent in discharging his duties or in collusion with companies in perpetrating fraud/misrepresentation by the companies, then suitable action will be taken as per rule."

The Public Accounts Committee while scrutinizing the subject found that the Ministry of Communications & Information Technology in their internal notings had raised the issue of issuance of licence to M/s Swan Telecom Pvt. Ltd. and a reference was also drawn to a stand taken in a similar case. Para 3 of the Ministry note dated February 12, 2009 states as under:

> In a similar instance where a complaint had been received by this department in respect of grant of UAS Licence to M/s. Loop Telecom Pvt. Ltd. regarding alleged violation of the substantial equity clause 8 of UAS Guidelines by M/s. Loop Telecom Pvt. Ltd. under a Corporate veil, the reference has been sent to Ministry of Corporate Affairs (*vide* letter dated August 5, 08 at 3/c) for examination wherein it is informed by the Ministry of Corporate Affairs that they are examining the matter."

Further the said note that was put up also stated as: "In view of above, Ministry of Corporate Affairs may be requested to examine the matter and comment whether the clause 8 of UASL guidelines dated December 14, 2005 regarding 'substantial equity' have been violated under any corporate veil as per DFA at 5/c please."

However, the file notings about the decision taken by the Minister shows: "Discussed with Secretary(T) with DDG (AS-I) legal advice may be obtained."

The DDG (AS-I) in his note dated 5.02.2009 had stated as under:

> The matter was discussed with Secretary(T) in the presence of Member(T) and separately in a meeting with Member(T) and LA(T). The issue of alleged violation of substantial equity clause i.e. clause 8 of UAS licence guidelines dated December 14, 2005 by M/s Swan Telecom Pvt. Ltd. as on date of their applications for grant of UAS licenses, has been raised by Dr. Arvind Gupta in his Writ Petition (Civil) No. 7815 of 2008 before Hon'ble High court of Delhi in the matter of Dr. Arvind Gupta V/s Union of India. Learned Solicitor General of India along with Shri Vikas Singh, Sr. Advocate (former ASG of India) and Shri Sanjay Hegde, Advocate are defending the case of behalf of Union of India in the High Court of Delhi. Since the matter is subjudice in the Hon'ble High Court of Delhi, it is desirable that we may seek opinion of Learned Solicitor General of India in this case for further action to be taken by DoT.

Interestingly the Secretary(T) noted in the file that: "Through the Ministry of Law we may refer the matter to SG." The Minister of Communications and Information Technology however directed: "May be sent to SG directly since the cases are represented by him before the TDST and other Judicial Forums including HC Delhi." That is not a valid reason under the Service Conditions & Rules for Law Officers. Why the fascination of Raja for the opinion of Vahanvati?

As Solicitor General of India, Vahanvati tendered his opinion dated March 24/25, 2009 concluding that the applicants fulfilled all the necessary conditions cannot really be faulted *inter-alia* as under:

> Be that as it may, by a communication dated December 12, 2007, M/s Swan Telecom Pvt. Ltd. gave all the necessary clarifications, submitting point-wise clarifications/information/supporting documents. All the documents were thereafter processed. The fact that Reliance Telecom Limited was no longer involved with the applicant was specifically noted. The consideration is quite extensive and detailed. Finally the Secretary noted, on January 9, 2008, that they fulfilled all the requisite conditions and LOI may be approved. This was approved by the Hon'ble Minister on January 9, 2008.
>
> In the circumstances, my opinion is sought as to whether this matter should be referred to the Department of Company Affairs. Whether the application as originally filed was in order or not was the subject matter of divergent opinions and a view had already been taken that if regard be given to the equity share capital in the company, the application could not be said to be in violation of Clause 8. In any case, before the company was asked to issue clarifications, on its own the applicant gave full particulars of the shareholding *vide* the said letter dated December 7, 2007. It also submitted further clarifications on December 12, 2007. The file shows that there has been a full consideration of all relevant material and the conclusion that the applicants fulfilled all the necessary conditions cannot really be faulted.

However, the DoT in their notes dated March 30, 2009 and April 1, 2009 while seeking permission to refer the matter to the Ministry of Corporate Affairs for investigation had putforth as under: "Draft at 5/c has been examined with reference to the date of submission of applications for grant of UAS Licences by M/s Swan Telecom Ltd. The applications were submitted on January 23, 2007 and March 2, 2007. The details of share holding pattern was as mentioned in the draft at 5/c. The same can be referred to Ministry of Corporate Affairs for investigation."

The DDG (AS-I) in his self-contained note dated 9.04.2009 putforth the following:

> In view of the facts detailed in para 1 above and the legal opinion of Ld. S.G. in para 2 above, vide note 9-10N, the matter was submitted for decision whether the said allegations, with regard to violation of clause 8 of UAS guidelines dated December 14, 2005 by M/s Swan Telecom Pvt. Ltd. on the date of application(s) under any corporate veil, need examination by Ministry of Corporate Affairs and consideration of DFA at 5/c. At 10/N, DDG(AS-I) noted that administrative decision on above may be taken in view of opinion of Ld. SG on 6-8/N. At 11/N, the draft at 5/c was examined by the Finance Branch wherein Member(F) noted that Draft at 5/c on the subject may be referred to Ministry of Corporate Affairs for investigation. At 11/N, Secretary(T) directed for a self contained Note based on SG's opinion for MOC.

Reproducing the opinion of Ld. SG (*vide* his notes dated March 25, 2009) in the subsequent para, the DDG(AS-I) submitted for consideration and administrative decision whether a reference was needed to be made to MoCA. To this, the Secretary (T) in his notings dated April 17, 2009 states that in view of the opinion of SG no such reference was required. The proposal was approved by the Minister on April 18, 2009.

When the Committee sought to know the opinion of Attorney General for India regarding whether the matter of alleged violation of substantial equity clause by M/s Swan should have been referred to the Department of Company Affairs, he has opined as follows:

Since the matter was subjudice and since the license had been issued over a year ago, I was of the opinion that at that stage it was not necessary to make any further reference to the Ministry of Company Affairs since according to the Department there had been full and exhaustive considerations of the facts of the case. I was not called upon to opine as to whether the application of Swan Telecom was proper or what the shareholding of Swan was. I have never "cleared" the application of Swan.

On being specifically asked as to why it was not considered appropriate to refer the case to Ministry of Company Affairs despite notes from DoT clearly brining out reasons for the same, he in his written submission has stated as: "The issue raised before me did not relate to the alleged violation of the substantial equity clause."

To a pointed query about his opinion on the eligibility of the said Company, he has submitted as under: "No. The opinion was on the aspect of future course of action in view of the pending litigation."

TRAI's Recommendations for Cancellation of Licences of Some Companies

TRAI had analysed the reports submitted by the licensees after 2008, and found that there were several companies who having got the licence had not complied with the roll out obligations at all. Many licensees had complied with the roll out obligations but with delay (including delay beyond 52 weeks from the due date of compliance).

TRAI in their letter to DoT in November, 2010 had stated that in pursuance of section 11(1)(b)(i) of the TRAI Act 1997 (as amended), TRAI had sought compliance of licence terms and conditions pertaining to roll out obligations, from all the Service Providers who had been issued licenses from December 2006 onwards. TRAI categorized them as follows:

Category	Subject	1	2
A	Licensees who complied with the roll out obligations	Satisfactory	Not Satisfactory
B	But with delay upto 52 weeks	Satisfactory	Not Satisfactory
C	But with delay involving more than 52 weeks	Satisfactory	Not Satisfactory
D	Licensees who have not complied with the roll out obligation	Period of 52 weeks from the due date of compliance had not yet expired	Period of 52 weeks from the due date of compliance has expired or service has not been started even though registration has been with the TERM cell.

TRAI quoting clause 35 of the licence conditions which provided for imposition of Liquidated Damages/Cancellation in case of delay/non-compliance of rollout obligations requested DoT to take immediate necessary action as follows:

(i) Category A2-Cancellation of licenses needs to be seriously considered in view of non-utilisation of spectrum and resultant loss of revenue to exchequer. This may however require legal examination.

(ii) Category B2-Liquidated damages may be imposed as per licence conditions. Besides, Cancellation of licenses needs to be seriously considered in view of non-utilisation of spectrum and resultant loss of revenue to exchequer. This may however require legal examination.

(iii) Categories C2 and D2-Licenses may be cancelled as per licence conditions in addition to levy of liquidated damages.

When the Committee enquired if the Department had issued show cause notices to the ineligible Companies/the Companies who failed to meet their roll out obligations, after getting UAS licenses/2G Spectrum in January, 2008, for cancellation of their licenses, the Department of Telecommunication have replied as:

> Show cause notices for termination of UAS licenses due to violation of rollout obligation conditions have been issued to M/s Etisalat DB Telecom India Private Ltd. for Delhi and Mumbai service areas and M/s Siestema Shyam for Kerala, West Bengal and Assam service areas. Four more cases are under process of approval for issuing the show cause notices to licensees who got UAS license in January 2008, for termination of licenses due to violation of rollout obligation conditions. Action in respect of other similarly placed cases is being taken on the same lines.

The Committee had sought to know why DoT on its own had not taken any action against the defaulting operators when all the operators were required to submit primary data on roll out obligations to DoT first and this information was subsequently sent to TRAI. To this DoT replied as:

> Regarding submission of information, UAS license condition number 9.1 prescribes, 'The LICENSEE shall furnish to the Licensor/TRAI, on demand in the manner and as per the time frames such documents, accounts, estimates, returns, reports or other information in accordance with the rules/orders as may be prescribed from time to time. The LICENSEE shall also submit information to TRAI as per any order or direction or regulation issued from time to time under the provisions of TRAI Act, 1997 or an amended or modified statute.' However, there is no specific provision in the UAS license agreement regarding data/ information to be submitted to DoT first or vice-versa. Action is being initiated for imposition of liquidated damages.

S-TEL'S WITHDRAWAL OF THE CASE AGAINST DOT

S-Tel had sought quashing of the Press Release dated January 10, 2008 which had deprived them from being granted LOIs for UAS Licences for 16 circles for which they had applied after September 25, 2007. On July 1, 2009 a Single Judge dismissed the case in S-Tel's favour. DoT's appeal against this judgment before a division bench in the High Court of Delhi was dismissed again in S-Tel's favour. Then DoT filed an appeal in the

Hon'ble Supreme Court. When the Committee sought to know about the developments in the matter, the Director on Board, S-Tel Pvt Ltd deposed as under:

> If I can submit, we did not withdraw our offer. What happened was that we only told the Supreme Court not to pursue with the case. As you might recollect, the case was filed by us at the High Court but the judgement was reserved for more than 9 to 10 months.
>
> Subsequently, when the judgement was given, it was the DoT which went on appeal to a Delhi High Court Bench. The High Court Bench also confirmed the original judgement of the single judge judgement. Subsequently, the Government decided to go for an appeal to the Supreme Court. So, at that time, we decided that we should not pursue with this case and, therefore, we said that we are not pursuing.

On being further queried as to why such an action was taken, the Director on Board, S-Tel Pvt. Ltd. deposed as under:

> Actually, by that time, 2½ to 3 years had already elapsed and all our assumptions had gone totally awry. The most important thing in this industry is, you should get food when you are hungry. Now the spectrum is the most important thing here. If you do not get spectrum ahead of others or at least along with others, there is no use. In the last three years all other operators have got spectrum and they have rolled out their services. The total number of subscribers attractable is limited. The time to market is a very important phenomenon. In these three years, many operators had already come in, 12 to 13 operators were in the market, most of the subscribers were already grabbed by other operators and the most important thing, the single key performance parameter in this business is Average Revenue Per User (ARPU). So, the ARPU which was supposed to be at 250 had come down to a level of 160 and today it is not even 90. So, when such a reduction took place, we found that the economic viability is to be revisited. What we said was, in our affidavit that we filed, we clearly

told the court that we want to have the flexibility to choose the circles as and when they are given to us, wherever it makes economic sense, we will enter. That is what we informed the court.

When the Committee pointed out that, the DoT approached Supreme Court through an SLP to quash the High Court verdict at which stage the Janata Party President Subramaniam Swamy requested for his impleadment and sensing danger, Raja wanted S Tel to withdraw from thc case. On March 5, 2010, Friday evening, after office hours, DoT issues an order asking S. Tel to close its operation in three States citing security reasons. The reply of S. Tel, Director was: "Yes, Sir. We received a letter regarding the cancellation of the commercial launch."

The Committee further quoted news reports as:

> There was no show cause issued to S Tel before that and later Home Ministry revealed that they never raised any security concern. Arm twisted S Tel surrendered before Raja on March 8, on Monday and declared that they have no troubles with DoT policy. Vahanvati produces S Tel's surrender letter to Supreme Court which was rejected and directed the company to file an affidavit. Due to Subramanian Swamy's presence Raja's design failed and court said that they will not interfere into the High Court order declaring the change of cut off date as illegal.

When asked if this was true, the Director replied as under: "Correct, Sir."

On being asked to explain as to what happened later, the Director, S-Tel stated as under:

> As you have correctly pointed out, we had filed the reply to the DoT. But we filed an affidavit with the Supreme Court in which we said because of changed circumstances in the business which is very much the same as what we told the DoT in our letter, we would like to have the choice to choose the circles as and when we want. Therefore we are not proceeding with this particular case.

During the course of deposition before the Committee the Director S-Tel submitted that: "We received a letter on March 5 saying that the commercial launch approval given has been withdrawn. So, we immediately ran to the DoT Secretary and then we submitted an application saying we have not done anything and we would be very happy to comply with the requirements."

Elaborating about the contents of that letter dated 5th March, 2010, the Director S-Tel stated as under: "The letter said: 'The approval for launch of commercial services under reference is hereby withdrawn till further orders in the interest of national security.'"

DoT on July 6, 2010 had sought the advice of the Ministry of Law and Justice regarding cancellation of 2G Spectrum allotment made to some telecom service providers. In this connection, the Department of Legal Affairs *inter-alia* clarifying the matter referred to them, stated as under:

> Important fact of this case is the statement made by M/s S.Tel on affidavit stating the decision of the Government for giving UASL licenses to those who applied up to September 25, 2007 was not arbitrary but based on likely availability of spectrum and administrative decisions thereon. If observations of the Supreme Court and statement made by M/s S. Tel before the said Hon'ble Court are read together it may be concluded that there was no allegation on the part of S.Tel Ltd., that the DoT has been arbitrary in granting UASL licenses and there is no substance in Dr. Subramanian Swamy's allegation that 2G allotment was arbitrary or grossly unfair.

UTILISATION OF BSNL'S INFRASTRUCTURE BY SWAN

BSNL signed a Memorandum of Understanding (MOU) with M/s Swan on October 13, 2008. The clause No. 3.2 of the MOU (Annexure-I) states "Various terms and conditions for provision of Intra-Circle Roaming arrangement to SWAN'S GSM subscribers in the BSNL's GSM network will be as per Annexure-II forming part of this MOU."

Regarding the issue of M/s Swan Telecom Pvt. Ltd. signing on MoU with BSNL on October 13, 2008 to use the infrastructure facilities of BSNL the former CMD, VSNL deposed as under:

> Any response I give relating to Swan/Etisalat could be misconstrued. BSNL has not allowed up until that point and even today roaming on their network or sharing of the infrastructure. Swan was the first company which signed a roaming agreement with BSNL because they could just create some capacity in three or four towns and they could issue any number of SIMS. When they have a roaming capability availability from BSNL, they can use their network. Up until then, BSNL did not allow any roaming on this network to any private operator. The first one was Swan.

On being asked as to why special treatment was given to Swan, he put it as: "Swan is special, Sir."

When the Committee asked DoT the circumstances that led to BSNL permitting a Private Company to share its infrastructure and the sum that the BSNL charged for the purpose the Ministry have replied as under:

> From the different clauses of the MoU including the aforesaid terms and conditions for provisioning of intra-circle roaming arrangement with SWAN (part of MoU at Annexure-II), it is clear that there were adequate provisions for charging arrangement in respect of Intra Circle roaming between BSNL and SWAN and the interest of BSNL was fully protected.
>
> BSNL did not have any free arrangement with M/s SWAN but had well defined charging arrangement like usage charges including 52 paise per minute (or part thereof) to begin with and to be reviewed as per above clauses. In addition, Inter-connection usage charge including NLD/ILD charges, termination charges, transit charges and Data Clearing House charges were to be borne and paid by the roaming Partner. Amount of additional charges towards spectrum, license fee, other taxes paid by BSNL on account of Intra-circle roaming charge revenue, one-time set up cost on actual basis was also to be borne by the Roaming Partner. Charges for other services like SMS, MMS, GPRS VAS etc., if availed by the Roaming Partner through BSNL's network, were to be determined and prescribed separately. The statement in the Pioneer is thus factually in-correct.

Further probing into the matter, the Committee sought payment details in respect of the above mentioned charges alongwith relevant Annual Gross Revenue (AGR) statements filed by Swan/Etisalat, Quarterly/Annually reflecting the same. To this, DoT in their reply dated April 18, 2011 have submitted as:

> BSNL had entered into only an MOU recognizing only general basis of cooperative and mutually beneficial working arrangements and no roaming or any other arrangement had been implemented. No LSA-wise agreement had been signed, no resources had been shared, no facility had been extended in any manner and also no payment or any financial transaction had taken place between either of the organizations on account of intra-circle roaming arrangement. It is only after the availability of shareable capacities in BSNL network in different LSAs that LSA-wise agreements were to be signed with prospective private operators in the respective LSAs where separable capacities become available and where intra-circle and other arrangements were considered feasible, mutually beneficial and in the interest of BSNL after working out complete technical and commercial details. In view of non-implementation, as stated above, no claims were applicable and no charges were levied and collected.

On being specifically asked if BSNL had entered into arrangement with any other Telecom Operators on similar conditions, DoT has replied as:

> The arrangement was entered into only with M/s Swan Telecom Limited, to start with, and it was on non-exclusive basis. There were many technical issues to be addressed, as it was for the first time that such an arrangement was being conceived. LSA-wise agreements were to be signed only after meeting various conditions like availability of separable capacities in the circles and resolving of various technical, security and commercial issues etc.

To other queries of the Committee as to whether any revision was carried out subsequent to MoU and if BSNL had reviewed the arrangement it had with Swan once it was taken over by Etisalat, DoT have replied as: "Since no LSA-wise agreement was signed, no revision was applicable. BSNL would have reviewed the arrangement at the time of signing LSA-wise agreement but as no agreement was signed, no review was needed."

FAILURE OF INSTITUTIONAL OVERSIGHT AND STATUTORY COMPLIANCE

Setting up of an independent regulatory body was considered appropriate by the Government for proper regulation of the Telecom Sector after the entry of the Private operators into the field as well as with a view to assuring the investors that the sector would be regulated in a balanced, fair and competitive manner. Accordingly, the Telecom Regulatory Authority of India (TRAI) was established by virtue of the TRAI Act, 1997, which was amended in the year 2000, with the mandate of making recommendations either *suo-moto* or on request from the licensor on the following matters:

(i) Need and timing for introduction of new service provider;

(ii) Terms and conditions of licence to a service provider;

(iii) Revocation of licence for non-compliance of terms and conditions of licence;

(iv) Measures to facilitate competition and promote efficiency in the operation of telecommunication services so as to facilitate growth in such services;

(v) Technological improvements in the services provided by the service providers;

(vi) Type of equipment to be used by the service providers after inspection of equipment used in the network;

(vii) Measures for the development of telecommunication technology and any other matter relatable to telecommunication industry in general;

(viii) Efficient management of available spectrum.

FUNCTIONS OF THE AUTHORITY

(1) Notwithstanding anything contained in the Indian Telegraph Act, 1885 (13 of 1885), the functions of the Authority shall be to:

(a) Make recommendations, either *suo-motu* or on a request from the licensor on the following matters, namely:

(i) need and timing for introduction of new service provider;
(ii) terms and conditions of licence to a service provider;
As per proviso of sub-section (1) of section 11:

Provided that the recommendations of the Authority specified in clause (a) of this sub-section shall not be binding upon the Central Government.

Provided further that the Central Government shall seek the recommendations of the Authority in respect of matters specified in sub-clauses (i) and (ii) of clause (a) of this sub-section in respect of new licence to be issued to a service provider and the Authority shall forward its recommendations within a period of sixty days from the date on which that Government sought the recommendations.

Provided also that if the Central Government having considered that recommendation of the Authority comes to a prima facie conclusion that such recommendation cannot be accepted or needs modifications, it shall, refer the recommendations back to the Authority for its reconsideration, and the Authority may within fifteen days from the date of receipt of such reference, forward to the Central Government its recommendation after considering the reference made by the Government. After receipt of further recommendation, if any, the Central Government shall take a final decision.

The recommendations of the Authority are not binding upon the Central Government. However, it is mandatory for the Central Government to seek recommendations of TRAI in respect of matters specified in (i) and (ii) above in respect of new licence to be issued to a service provider and it is required to forward its recommendations within a period of 60 days from the date on which the Government sought the recommendations19. Central Government can issue a licence to a service provider if no recommendations are issued from TRAI within said period or within such period as may be mutually agreed upon between the Central Government and TRAI.

If the Central Government, having considered that recommendations of TRAI, comes to a *prima facie* conclusion that such recommendations cannot be accepted or needs modifications, it is required to refer the recommendations back to TRAI for its reconsideration, and TRAI may within 15 days from the date of receipt of such reference, forward to Central Government, its recommendations after considering the reference made by Government. After receipt of further recommendations, if any, Central Government is required to take final decision.

TRAI also has regulatory and tariff setting functions, like ensuring compliance of terms and conditions of licence, laying standard of Quality of Service (QoS) to be provided by service providers and notifying the rates at which telecommunication has to be provided and ensuring effective compliance of USOs. It has also power to call upon any service provider at any time to furnish information or explanation, in writing, relating to its affairs. It is to ensure transparency while exercising its powers and discharging its functions. It is given powers to punish for violation of its directions. Thus, the role of TRAI in relation to services in telecom sector is vital.

In short, in the issue of licence allocation and pricing of Spectrum, expansion and provision of effective telecom service in the country, the mandate, role and responsibility of TRAI, are guided by the provision of Section of 11 of the TRAI Act 1997 (as amended).

The Committee desired to know the kind of recommendations of TRAI that were binding upon the Government and the kinds that were advisory. In reply, TRAI stated that as per the provisions of section 11(1) of the TRAI Act, the recommendations of the Authority specified in the clause (a) of sub section (1) of Section 11 were not binding upon the Central Government.

In the same context, Brijendra K. Syngal apprised the Public Accounts Committee that in terms of section 11(1) of the TRAI Act, one of the functions of TRAI shall be to levy fees and other charges at such rates and in respect of such services as may be determined by regulations, such are, port charges, charges and revenue sharing, interconnection usage charges, etc. for which TRAI has absolute powers as per the TRAI Act. On licensing and other matters TRAI has recommendatory powers. However, the Government cannot reject any recommendations outright. The government has to make a reference back to TRAI before rejecting any recommendations.

The Committee thus asked as to whether any institutional arrangement had been put in place to have consultation/discussion between TRAI and DoT in the matters of development of telecom services including the allocation of Spectrum and whether any mechanism had been developed to sort out the differences of opinion between the Regulatory Body and the DoT on a particular issue. In reply, the TRAI stated that no such arrangement/mechanism had been there except for matters specified in sub-clauses (i) & (ii) of clause (a) of sub-section (1) of section 11 where the relevant provisions are as below:

In view of the fact that TRAI could make *suo-moto* recommendations on any matter specified in clause (a) of sub section (1) of Section 11 of the TRAI Act, the Committee asked whether TRAI exercised their *suo-moto* recommendatory powers when the so called FCFS basis was adopted by the DoT in the issue of UAS Licence/allocation of 2G Spectrum. In reply, TRAI stated that issue of licences and allocation of Spectrum to the telecom service providers was being done by the DoT. The Authority also explained that the issue of FCFS criteria for award of telecom licences did not figure in the TRAI's recommendations of 2007.

On the same issue, Mr. Syngal clarified that TRAI should have exercised its *suo-motu* powers to make recommendations on the creation of the "First Come First Serve" (FCFS) basis for allocation of 2G Spectrum by the DoT. However, TRAI itself is also the reason for the creation of this FCFS as in its August 2007 recommendations, it had advocated "no auction" of 2G spectrum, but had also said "no cap" on the number of players who could apply for the 2G-UAS license. This meant that limited spectrum (finite resource) would have to be rationed amongst an unlimited number of applicants (infinite players).

Notwithstanding the FCFS aberration created, the TRAI could have released suo-motu recommendations on the issue and suggested a more appropriate methodology of allocation of spectrum via a market based methodology, which would have led to market based price discovery for the scarce resource. The clarification came too late from TRAI, after the damage was done by the Minister.

TRAI made its recommendations on allocation of Spectrum during the years 2003, 2005, 2007 and 2010. The extracts of the main recommendations in this regard are a part of the CAG and Justice Shivraj Patil Committee Reports.

The Public Accounts Committee had queried on what ground the DoT ignored the TRAI's recommendations of 2003 to introduce additional players through a multistage bidding process and continued to grant UAS Licence/2G Spectrum or a price determined in 2001. In reply, the Authority stated that in para 7.39 of TRAI's recommendation of October 2003 the Authority had stated that the induction of additional mobile service providers in various service areas can be considered if there is adequate availability of spectrum. As the existing players have to improve the efficiency of utilization of spectrum and if Government ensures availability of additional spectrum then in the existing licensing regime, they may introduce additional players through a multi-stage bidding process as was followed for 4th cellular operator. However in para 7.30, the then Authority had stated that "Efficient utilization of spectrum by all service providers is of utmost concern to TRAI especially in a country like India where wireless subscribers are growing at a very fast rate.

However, based upon the international statistics (number of cellular subscribers and allotted spectrum, please see annexure -IV), TRAI is of the opinion that existing operators need improvement in efficiency of utilization of the spectrum TRAI shall provide its recommendations on efficient utilization of spectrum, spectrum pricing, availability and spectrum allocation procedure shortly. DoT may like to issue spectrum related guidelines based on the recommendations submitted by TRAI." Subsequently in November, 2003 the then Secretary, TRAI, issued a letter DO No. 101-35/2003-MN dated November 19, 2003.

In the same context, Telecom expert Shri Syngal stated that it was unclear why the DoT might have chosen to ignore TRAI's recommendations of 2003. Quite clearly the step has led to the creation of the current situation and substantial losses to the public exchequer. It is enjoined upon DoT as well as the TRAI to have done their home work properly. DoT did not put the right questions to TRAI and TRAI chose to ignore its own recommendations; maybe behind the scene activities to do the job right. What has been stated by TRAI is that it could have created a non-level playing field for the new entrants, how has not been explained by TRAI? TRAI has just kept quiet on this subject.

What were the compulsions on the part of TRAI to make a *volte-face* in 2007? In its recommendations of 2007, the Authority in para 2.79 of its 2003 recommendation had held that in future all spectrum excluding the spectrum in 800, 900 and 1800 bands should be auctioned so as to ensure efficient utilization of this scarce resource. I

In the 2G bands (800/900/1800MHz), the TRAI held that allocation through auction may not be possible as the service providers were allocated spectrum at different times of their license and the amount of spectrum with them varies from 2x4.4 MHz to 2x10 MHz for GSM technology and 2x2.5 MHz to 2x5 MHz in CDMA technology. Therefore, to decide the cut off after which the spectrum is auctioned will be difficult and might raise the issue of level playing field.

On the same issue, Mr. Syngal opined as follows:

> Again there is no clear answer to why the TRAI has overturned its own recommendation of 2003 in which it had advocated the auctioning of new licenses. The one and only reason which comes to my mind is deliberate attempt by DoT not to have posed a question on pricing of the spectrum. The Regulator might have used the same to either keep quiet or do what he did. It could also be some instructions not to recommend more ethical process.

The August 2007 recommendation, which advocated "no auction" of 2G spectrum led to the creation of the FCFS and allocation of 2G spectrum at throwaway prices. Subsequently, some of the companies, which acquired spectrum at these throwaway prices, divested stake at multiple valuations, establishing the fact that spectrum had been short-sold leading to massive losses to the public exchequer.

When Nripendra Misra, former Chairman, TRAI, was asked to state the reasons for TRAI's overturn, he submitted in evidence: "The issue of auction was very clearly recommended in 2003 and in fact, a multi-stage auction was recommended and not only that, it was also written that it will be in a same manner as the fourth cellular licence was granted. So, the fourth cellular licence which was granted on the auction basis – the same methodology for auction was recommended."

After that, there was no reference from the Government. That is what I said, that from 2006 onwards we were writing to the Government that please take TRAI recommendation on the subject and the Government said, I read the last line of the letter from the Government "no further useful purpose will be served by entering into correspondence on this subject."

So, the Government, in their wisdom, decided that there is no need for taking recommendation of TRAI because UASL licence is the same UASL licence granted in past. What was recommended in 2007 was again a reminder that the market dynamics has changed and, therefore, Government should evolve a mechanism to capture the market features. We did not go in great detail. In case of 3G we went in great detail because the Government had said-please give us the procedure and the manner of 3G spectrum auction. So, we gave the detailed procedure of auction, how auction will take place, what will be the criterion etc. But in the reference of April, 2007 on which we were sending recommendation in 2007 on 2G, there was no reference from the Government at all on the methodology for grant of licence and the manner in which licence should be granted.

Asked to state the references made to the TRAI, Dr. J.S. Sarma, the Chairman, TRAI, stated in evidence:

> On April 13, 2007, the reference was made. At page 143 of the recommendations given on August 28, 2007 in that document, the Government have made the following reference. It says, in order to ensure policies, keep pace with the changes and developments in the telecom sector, the Government is contemplating to review the following terms and conditions in the access provider license. (1) substantial equity holding (2) transfer of license (3) guidelines on

merger and acquisitions (4) permit service providers to offer access service using combination of technologies (5) roll out obligations (6) requirement to publish printed telephone directory, etc. TRAI was requested to furnish recommendation in terms of clause 11(1)(a) of TRAI Act as amended by TRAI Amendment Act.

Nripendra Misra further apprised the Committee in evidence:

These are the only six points on which they sought our recommendation. They did not seek recommendation on grant of new licence. But since that capping point was there, we did repeat 2003 recommendation. What we recommended is in para 2.73. The allocation of spectrum is after the payment of entry fee and grant of licence. The entry fee as it exists today is in fact a result of the price discovered through a market based mechanism applicable for the grant of licence to the fourth cellular operator which is in 2002. In today's dynamism and unprecedented growth of telecom sector the entry fee determined is not be realistic price for obtaining a licence. It needs to be reassessed through a market mechanism. So, the recommendation existed in 2003, reiterated in 2007, and that is auction should be the mode for grant of licence. Now there is a very important point just now because often this is mentioned that TRAI changed its recommendations. Actually what later in the body of recommendation comes is, since spectrum is a part of licence, on the issue of grant of licence it says please find a market mechanism. On the issue of allocation of spectrum because it is part of the licence and since 900 and 1800 MHz has already been given to the incumbents, therefore, TRAI made a recommendation that as far as 900 and 1800 MHz are concerned auction perhaps may not be proper but all other spectrum bands in future should be auctioned. What it means is applicable to all 3G is not a licence. 3G is part of UASL. It is only the spectrum band which has been auctioned. 2.1 GHz has been auctioned. So, the TRAI recommendation was, leave 900 and 1800 and auction in future all other spectrums in future but as far as licence is concerned please auction before granting licence.

Dr. J.S. Sarma, Chairman, TRAI, further apprised:

> According to TRAI, every time a licence is to be provided, the recommendations of the Authority have to be sought. The Government on the other hand feels that every time a new licence is to be provided, there is a difference between a licence to every service provider and a general class of licence, this recommendation of the Authority is required only when a new licence is to be provided.

Asked to state whether any legal advice was sought and obtained on the matter, another representative of the TRAI submitted:

> As per our legal adviser also, what Chairman has said when any new applicant is given a licence though the existing licence the UAS licence, then also the Government should seek recommendation from us. The TRAI had written to the Government, at least twice which I know, that this is the case and we had requested the DoT also to take the advice of the Law Ministry if they had nay doubt.

The Committee then asked about the response of the Government on the matter. In reply, the Chairman, TRAI stated: "To be best of my recollection, in January, 2008 a letter was written by the then Chairman, TRAI but after that I am not very sure whether there was any response."

In this regard, when the Committee desired to know from Nripendra Misra as to the response of the Government to TRAI's legal opinion and his letter dated January 14, 2008 he deposed:

> The letter sent by TRAI was that please take the recommendations from TRAI on the grant of a licence and also take recommendations on the terms and conditions of the licence. There were series of letters and there was also legal opinion sent, further a request made that it was better to seek opinion of the Law Ministry on the subject. We received a reply from the Government that our legal opinion i.e. TRAI is not acceptable. Their judgment, if it is the same type of licence, that means, if it is a UASL licence and again UASL licence and again UASL

licence, it is a new licence in a circle. Therefore, the Government did not accept the recommendation of TRAI. Why I raise this point is because this must be very clear that on grant of licence, TRAI did not make recommendation because there was no such reference. It was only *suo-moto* that we said in 2007 that the market dynamics must be taken into consideration.

Mr. Misra further apprised:

We had also sent series of letters saying that please take the entire recommendation into consideration because they have got inter-linkages and let there be no, for want of any better word, I would say "cherry picking." The Government as per law are competent to accept one and not accept another part of the recommendation. But we had said that please take the entire thing in totality, otherwise, the integrity of recommendation is getting compromised. Government went ahead some time in 2007 and on their own they decided to have certain criterion, certain cut off point of the date and press notes were issued, all that is a matter of record and I have no comments on that and licences of 2G were issued. Also in 2007 reference, the Government had sought our recommendation on merger and acquisition. So, we had also given our recommendation on merger and acquisition party. It was accepted in parts and was not for acquisition accepted. But the Government was competent to take that decision and the licences were thus given and the rest which followed is known that in some of the companies, there was a foreign telecom companies making investment had come.

On the issue of legal opinion, Mr. Misra submitted:

We have a position of Advisor (Law) in TRAI. It is of the rank of the Additional Secretary. The person who was servicing this Division was Additional Secretary (Law) on deputation to TRAI. Presently, he is Secretary (Legislative matters). It was his opinion which was enclosed with our letter from TRAI saying that "please seek opinion of TRAI if

> you wish to grant any new licence." In our letter, of course, we suggested that "please take opinion of the Law Ministry on this particular opinion which is enclosed."

In response to a specific query, Mr Misra replied that his letter had not been replied on the points raised.

Asked to state specifically whether auction of Spectrum including that 800, 900 and 1800 MHz bands should be the most favored method, the Chairman, TRAI deposed: "Sir, generally auction is the correct procedure. But so far as the spectrum in 800, 900 and 1800 MHz, that is the 2G spectrum is concerned, we have clearly pointed out in our recommendations why auction is not feasible, but at the same time it does not mean that we should continue with that old price, that is why we have related it to the auction determined price which is in the 3G."

When the Committee enquired about the specific impediments that TRAI could anticipate in the auction of the Spectrum in the 800, 900 and 1800 MHz bands, the Chairman, TRAI, stated that the Authority in the context of 800, 900 and 1800 MHz bands was conscious of the legacy, the prevailing practice and the over riding consideration of the level playing field.

Asked to elaborate, the Chairman, TRAI, submitted: "In the 2G bands, allocation through auction may not be possible as service providers were allocated spectrum at different points and at different times of their licences and the amount of spectrum varies from 2.4 to 2.10 except for dual use technologies. Therefore, to decide the cut off after which the spectrum auctioned will be difficult and might raise the issue of level playing field."

The Committee then queried whether level playing field should have given an overriding consideration for not auctioning the 2G Spectrum as market forces could have determined it. In response, the Chairman, TRAI stated: "I am only reading it from the Report."

When Nripendra Misra, during whose tenure, the TRAI recommendations of 2007 were finalized, was asked to state whether TRAI's recommendation against auction of 2G Spectrum was appropriate, he submitted:

My present view—and I remain committed—is, there is no other procedure to be followed but auction. I will even go to the extent, if you ask me as to whether I would like to correct my recommendation that 900 and 1800 MHz spectrum should be auctioned, I will say that there should be auction of all the spectrum and licence should be de-linked from spectrum totally. In that way, your licence fee will come down and spectrum will be put in the marketing domain which happens all over the world.

Mr. Misra further submitted:

Sir, two points are self-evident. One is that the value of spectrum as a scarce resource more so when there was a visible shortage of spectrum. In 2007-2008, there was a shortage of spectrum unlike 2003-2004.

Secondly, the kind of exponential growth which took place, unlike 2002-03 and 2003-04, both these things clearly indicate that the price of spectrum was undervalued because even if it is licence plus spectrum auctioned in 2001, actually that is giving the price of spectrum. So, the price of spectrum not determined through market process was definitely much lower and that becomes more than established when a foreign company comes and wishes to participate in new licence company's equity. I have seen the press release of the Ministry wherein it says that whatever money has come is FDI an it will be used in infrastructure expansion. But still the truth remains that the so-called high price bid is nothing but the price of spectrum and that gets more than established in 3G."

Dr. J.S. Sarma, Chairman, TRAI, summed up by saying:

We have gone by the principle that spectrum must have its price. When we considered these recommendations between July, 2009 and May, 2010 and when we gave recommendations, it must be noted that we were already faced with the situation of fait accompli. We were dealing with the situation of ensuring a level playing field and also ensuring that the price of spectrum is properly determined. It is for beyond 6.2 MHz and beyond 20 years. We said that 6.2 is the contractual Spectrum.

In 2003, TRAI had recommended a "No Cap" principle in the number of players and reiterated the same in their 2007 recommendation. B.K. Syngal apprised the Committee that the "No Cap" on recommendation of TRAI meant that limited Spectrum (Finite source) would have to be rationed against an unlimited number of applications (infinite players).

In the above context, the Committee desired to know the basis on which TRAI recommended that there should be "No Cap" on the number of Access service providers in any circle/service area. In reply, TRAI just reproduced para Nos. 2.32, 2.34, 2.35, 2.36 and 2.37 of their August 2007 recommendations.

Asked to state categorically as to whether TRAI ascertained the availability of Spectrum in various bands, the Authority replied that as per the available records, no letter was written from TRAI to DoT to ascertain the amount of Spectrum, available in various bands while recommending "No Cap" in August, 2007.

But Nripendra Misra had a different version to share with the Committee. He deposed in evidence:

> We did write to the Government to please provide information as to how much spectrum is available. It is on record. Not only that, based on our in-house research, TRAI also wrote to the Government that as per our information, the present spectrum already allocated to the service providers and whatever now remains is annexed. Please confirm whether what we are saying is right or wrong. Even that letter was sent. the Government did not share since spectrum management is their privilege.

Asked to state whether it was within the purview of the DoT to deny such an information to TRAI, Mr Misra replied: "The Act says that the management of Spectrum is the Department's responsibility. So, legally, TRAI could not force them to give the information."

The Committee then asked TRAI whether it should be prudent to permit unlimited service providers to enter the field in view of the scarce nature of spectrum. In reply, TRAI stated that in their recent recommendations on "Spectrum Management and Licensing Framework" dated May 11, 2010, this Authority has considered this issue in para 2.51 and recommended that keeping in view the scarcity of spectrum and the need to provide the contracted spectrum to the existing licensees, no more UAS licence linked with spectrum should be awarded.

The TRAI recommendations of May 2010 advocate that all UAS licences should be allocated 6.2 MHz GSM spectrum which was beyond the contracted amount of 4.4 MHz for UAS licences granted post October 2003. In this context, the Committee desired to be apprised of the reasons for the Authority's recommendation for additional allocation of 1.8 MHz spectrum. In reply, TRAI stated that recommendations to allocate additional spectrum of 1.8 MHz has been made keeping in view the contractual obligation in the UAS License, already entered into by the Government before the issue was referred to TRAI in July 2009. The Authority has dealt with this issue at length in Para 3.105 to 3.109 of the above mentioned recommendations.

The Chairman, TRAI, further submitted in evidence: "... we have clearly indicated why it is 6.2 MHz by reference to the licensing provisions of the licences issued from 1994-95 onwards. It has been clearly demonstrated that the contracted spectrum is 6.2 MHz and therefore those who have 4.4 MHz are legally entitled to get 6.2 MHz."

Audit pointed out that 9 operators as per the details below had been allotted spectrum beyond the upper limit laid down in the UASL agreement. Thus while the DoT, on one hand, was not processing pending applications for licence due to non availability of spectrum, on the other hand it was allotting spectrum to existing operators beyond the contracted limit without any upfront charges being imposed or without determination of market price of spectrum. Based on the amount charged from CDMA operators for grant of GSM spectrum in 2007, the value of spectrum held by these operators beyond the contracted unit worked out to Rs. 2561 crore though its market value on date would be higher.

The Technical Committee appointed by Hon'ble MoC&IT for "Allocation of Access (GSM/CDMA) spectrum and pricing" recommended in May 2009, that the additional spectrum assigned beyond 6.2+6.2 MHz in a service area should attract an upfront charge equivalent to the 3G auction price from the date of assignment.

Subsequently, TRAI also recommended in May 2010 for charging the additional spectrum held by operators beyond the licensed quantity which is under consideration of the Government. In the event of these recommendations being accepted, the additional flow of revenue to the Government would come to Rs. 36,993 crore.

Name	Amount of additional spectrum (MHz)	No. of Circles
Aircel	3.6	1
Bharti	32.4	13
BPL(Mumbai)	3.8	1
BSNL	61.6	19
IDEA	12.6	6
MTNL(Delhi and Mumbai)	12.4	2
Reliance	1.8	1
Spice (Punjab)	1.6	1
Vodafone	19.6	7

In the above context, when the Committee desired to hear the views of the TRAI on the matter, the Chairman, TRAI, submitted:

> First of all, our recommendations contain not only the charging for excess spectrum, it also speaks of rationalization of spectrum charges and also reduction in Uniform Licence Fee. The total amount of money the service providers will have to pay towards the excess spectrum is not something that will cause a very heavy burden. It is true that they have to pay, but it is not something-when you see the uniform licence fee and also rationalization of spectrum charges – that is likely to be that heavy. It is a question of principle here.
>
> Secondly, as regards the point you made regarding some people not having to pay more and some people having to pay more, it is a question of how much excess spectrum one has. If somebody has

excess spectrum, they have to pay. So there is no distinction between one service provider and the other service provider.

In so far as the issue of CDMA spectrum being clubbed with GSM spectrum is concerned, this issue has already been dealt with. This recommendation has already been made by TRAI. Government have decided that they will not club the two together.

The Committee asked whether it meant that the GSM players had to cough up more money. In reply, the Chairman TRAI responded: "That is because some GSM players who have excess spectrum will have to pay more money. We have not asked them to pay from the date of allotment of spectrum which was the demand of various stake holders. We have said that they will pay only for the balance period their licences."

When the Committee desired to know from the DoT the latest position on the TRAI's recommendation for charging the additional spectrum held by the operations beyond the licenced quantity and action taken to review the allocation of excess spectrum as per the concerns expressed by several Members of Parliament, the DoT replied that the initial spectrum of 4.4 MHz/6.2 MHz is allotted to the GSM operators as per the provisions of licence conditions of their respective license agreements, subject to availability. Additional spectrum is also considered as per the criteria orders/guidelines etc.

TRAI in its recommendation made on May 11, 2010 mentioned that the subscribed linked criteria, as adopted by the Government in January 2008 be kept for six months to enable all operators who are already qualified for the additional spectrum based on the prevalent subscribed linked criteria or those who would be qualified within the next six months, to be assigned additional spectrum subject to availability and the Prescribed limit recommended as in Para below which specified that: "the limit on spectrum to be assigned to a service provider will be 2x8 MHz for all service areas other than in Delhi and Mumbai where it will be 2x10 MHz. Similarly for CDMA spectrum the Authority recommends that the limit on spectrum will be 2x5 MHz for all service areas and 2x6.25 MHz in the Metro areas for Delhi and Mumbai."

TRAI has further, on May 18, 2010, requested the Government to await its recommendations on spectrum pricing and reframing. On February 8, 2011, TRAI has made its further recommendations regarding spectrum pricing. After examining the above recommendations of TRAI, the Committee of DoT has submitted its report on February 22, 2011. Subsequently, on these recommendation of TRAI, Hon'ble MoC & IT has also had interaction with the telecom service providers on March 8, 2011. Final decision on these recommendations of TRAI will be taken in due course of time.

As regards the crossover technology issue, the DoT granted 35 Dual Technology licences in October, 2007 based on the recommendations of the TRAI. In this context, when the Committee desired to know the circumstances that led to TRAI's recommendation for crossover technology, Shri Nripendra Misra submitted in evidence:

> That, in fact, arose from one application from one of the existing service providers. It was Reliance which moved an application that they should be given spectrum for GSM technology as well, and the argument was that licence is technology neutral. Therefore, whether they use CDMA technology or they used GSM technology, they should not be constrained because of that, the option to exercise should be theirs, grant of spectrum is a privilege of the Government depending on the availability. When this application came, the phrase which was used was cross over, that is, you are having CDMA, can you also cross to GSM, that means you can offer twin technologies in the same circle.

Asked to state whether it was not the operators themselves who preferred their own technology i.e. either GSM or CDMA and whether it was prudent to permit the CDMA operators to provide GSM service also in the same circle, Mr Misra submitted:

> On the crossover technology, it said that yes it is true that the licence is technology neutral, but after having made a choice about the spectrum band – as I said, 800 MHz is for CDMA and 900 MHz and

1800 MHz for GSM- one has already decided the growth path. While there is no bar to cross over, but one must pay once more the same fee which was paid by GSM player in the same circle. Although it was not welcomed by CDMA players because they thought they are being punished twice, but finally it got implemented. Those who got the facilities of cross over, whether it was a GSM player to CDMA or CDMA player to GSM, they paid the fees as was required and they were permitted to offer services. No new licence was required for it because the same licence could grant it.

The Committee, then, asked TRAI regarding the specific studies made by the Authority before recommending grant of spectrum under combination of technology. In reply, TRAI stated that while framing its recommendations of 2007, on the issue of grant of spectrum under the combination of technologies, the then Authority studied the following documents:

- New telecom policy, 1999 (NTP'99) along with its addendum issued on 11th November, 2003
- Principle of technology neutrality underlined in the common regulatory framework for Electronic Communications Networks and Services of the European Union.
- Various clauses in the Unified Access Service License and CMTS License
- International practice in the allocation of spectrum meant for different technologies to the same service provider.

As regards delinking allotment of spectrum from issue of licences, Nripendra Misra apprised the Committee the Government did not accept TRAI's recommendation made at various points of time to separate spectrum from licence. He elaborated:

> ... The TRAI had then recommended that the licence and the spectrum should be separated. This recommendation was repeated in 2003 and in 2005 that licence is one thing and spectrum is another thing, therefore, one could put a much lower licence fee but put Spectrum in the auction mode because that is the national asset. This

> issue of spectrum separation from the licence, somehow the Government did not find acceptable and even today the licence and the spectrum are together for all types of licence. The recommendation obviously of TRAI remains but the Government has not accepted it.

The Committee then desired to know from TRAI about the percentage of the acceptance of the Authority's recommendations by the DoT. In reply, the Chairman TRAI stated in evidence: "while we normally see that a large number of our recommendations are accepted and acted upon, but at the same time, we also note that there are cases where they do not accept our recommendations."

Asked to state the main reasons for the Government's reluctance to accept the key recommendations of TRAI, the Chairman, TRAI submitted:

> The structure of the Authority in India is different from that of certain other countries where most of the licensing and spectrum related functions are actually performed by the regulator and not by the Government. That is the major difference. for instance, OFCOM in UK or FCC in USA and other regulators, German regulators, they actually do the licensing as well as the spectrum related functions whereas these are continued to be performed by the Department in India.

When the Committee queried about the measures contemplated by the Authority themselves to improve the situation, the Chairman, TRAI replied: "We are currently actually formulating certain amendments to the Act. some time back, they have been formulated and sent by the Authority and it has come back to us for a re-look. As part of that, we would be considering that issue."

ARE TRAI RECOMMENDATIONS BINDING ON THE DOT?

An impression that TRAI recommendations are binding is entirely false. TRAI Act allows DoT to reject, modify or accept recommendations subject to procedure laid down under TRAI Act, Section 11, Fifth Proviso (Page 29)

> Provided also that if the Central Government having considered that recommendation of the Authority, comes to a prime facie conclusion that such recommendation cannot be accepted or needs modifications, it shall refer the recommendation back to the Authority for its reconsideration, and the Authority may, within fifteen days from the date of receipt of such reference, forward to the Central Government its recommendation after considering the reference made by the Government. After receipt of further recommendation if any, the Central Government shall take a fifnal decision.

DoT is fully empowered to reject or modify TRAI's recommendations —and it routinely does. It has to follow the statutory process of re-reference before modification.

THE TELECOM COMMISSION

By and in terms of resolution No.15/1/87-CAB-1 dated April 11, 1989 of the Government of India, Telecommunications Commission was set up. The constitution of the Telecom Commission is as under:

(a) The Commission consists of full time and part time members;

(b) The Secretary to the Government of India in the Department of Telecommunications is the ex-officio Chairman of the Commission;

(c) The full time Members of the Commission are ex-officio Secretary to the Government of India in the Department of Telecommunications. One of these Members is Member for Finance; and

(d) The Secretary and the full time Members of the Commission are to be drawn from the best persons available, including from within the Department of Telecommunications.

There are four full-time Members of Telecom Commission. They are Member (Services), Member (Production), Member (Technology) and Member (Finance). Similarly, there are four part time Members. They are

Secretary-Department of Information Technology; Secretary-Finance, Department of Economic Affairs; Secretary-Planning Commission; and Secretary-Department of Industrial Policy and Promotion.

The Telecom Commission is responsible for the following:

(a) To formulae the policy of Department of Telecommunications for approval of the Government;

(b) To prepare the budget for the Department of Telecommunications for each financial year and getting it approved by the Government; and

(c) To implement the Government's policy in all matters concerning telecommunications.

As per the Rules of Business for Telecom Commission, 1989 all cases of the nature specified in **Annexure – A** to it shall be brought before the Commission which include *inter-alia* important matters of policy relating to telecommunications and proposals for acceptance of any rules and procedures which involve significant deviations from normal rules and procedures of the Government.

So far as the quorum for the meeting of the Telecom Commission is concerned, it is three full time Members present in person including the Chairman provided that at meetings which the Chairman considers expedient to be held in his absence, the requirement shall be deemed to have been met if the Chairman authorized another Member to place before the Telecom Commission and bring on record his views.

Audit scrutiny revealed that the recommendation of TRAI in 2007 were crucial from the perspective of the management of the Telecom sector and Spectrum management and yet they were not put up to the full Telecom Commission before the acceptance of the recommendations. Audit also pointed out that it was a fact that a meeting of the internal members of the DoT was held on October 10, 2007 to discuss the TRAI recommendations but there was nothing on record in the file to show as to why the recommendations of the TRAI were not taken to the full Telecom Commission. Neither the agenda papers nor minutes of the meeting of the internal members of the Telecom Commission held on October 10, 2007 to discuss the recommendations of TRAI were circulated among the other members of Telecom Commission i.e. Finance Secretary, Secretary Industry, Secretary IT and Secretary Planning Commission. As such, no meeting of the full Telecom Commission took place between the date of submission of the recommendations ofTRAI i.e. August 27, 2007 and the date of issue of LOI to 121 applicants i.e. January 10, 2008 to discuss the recommendations of the TRAI. Thus DoT chose to consider the recommendations without the benefit of the inputs from four important Secretaries of the Government of India on crucial issues related to the Telecom sector.

The Public Accounts Committee asked the DoT to furnish the reasons for not placing the TRAI recommendations of 2007 before the Telecom Commission for their consideration, more so when the Authority had made a clear departure from their 2003 recommendations to auction licence/Spectrum. The Committee also desired to know the reasons for not consulting the Telecom Commission before or at the time of granting 122 new UAS licences in 2008 in view of their recommendations in 2007 to discover the market mechanism for grant of new licences. In reply, the DOT stated that the matter was not placed before the "Full Telecom Commission." But the internal Telecom Commission in its meeting held on October 10, 20007 deliberated the TRAI's recommendations on "Review of licence terms and conditions and capping of number of access providers."

The Department further stated that granting of UAS licence in the year 2008 was part of a process continuing since introduction of the UAS licensing regime in November, 2003. It was also stated that 51 UAS licences had already been granted prior to the grant of 122 UAS licences in 2008. No individual case for issue of UAS licences was placed before the Telecom Commission.

In an evidence held on January 21, 2011 the Committee asked the Secretary, DOT to clarify what the Department meant by "Internal Telecom Commission" and whether there was any "External Telecom Commission" too. In reply, the Secretary DOT submitted:

> I will clarify. The Telecom Commission has full-time members and part-time members. The full-time members are the member (Finance), Member (Technology), Member (Services) and the Chairman of the Telecom Commission, which is the Secretary. These

are full-time members. The Secretary, Finance, the Planning Commission Secretary, the Secretary DIPP, Secretary DIT are part-time members in the sense that they attend the meetings of the Commission from time to time. This has been the practice.

On the same day in another evidence, the Committee asked D.S. Mathur, former Secretary, DoT, to clarify whether there was anything called 'Internal Telecom Commission' in the DoT. In reply, Mr. Mathur submitted: "No, Sir. There is a Telecom Commission, by that we generally mean that all the four Members of the Commission who are Members in the Department and the Chairman who is the Secretary next. When we think that the other four Secretaries should also be invited, then it is referred to as the Extended Telecom Commission."

In the above context, when the Committee specifically desired to know from the DoT, whether there was any reference to "internal," "extended," external or "full" Telecom Commission in the Rules of Business of the Telecom Commission, the DoT in a post-evidence reply stated that the Resolution, Rules of Business and the Rules for the Transaction of Business of the Telecom Commission did not contain any reference to Internal Telecom Commission/External Telecom Commission/Full Telecom Commission; only the term "Telecom Commission" did find a place. The first meeting of the Telecom Commission with both full time and part time members was held on July 1, 1989 and the first weekly meeting of the Telecom Commission with full time members only was held on July 10, 1989. The records indicated that initially the weekly meetings were held and over a period of time the weekly meetings of the full time members of Telecom Commission came to be termed as meetings of the internal Telecom Commission.

The Telecom Commission was set up by the Government in 1989 with the objective of formulation of the policies of the DoT for approval of the Government as well as to oversee the implementation of the policies and preparation of annual budget of the DoT. Unfortunately, an artificial and convenient division has been created by inclusion of full-time and part-time members of the Commission. The permanent members of the Commission including the Chairman are employees of the DoT and the presence of three permanent members constitutes the quorum. The other members, part-time but permanent Government servants, are Finance Secretary, Industry Secretary, Secretary IT and Secretary, Planning Commission. The Committee note that as per the Rules of Business of the Telecom Commission matters of policy relating to telecommunications and proposals for acceptance of any rules and procedures which involve significant deviations from normal rules and procedures of the Government are to be brought before the Commission. But the Committee are constrained to find that the TRAI recommendations of 2007, which were very crucial from the perspective of the management of the Telecom Sector and Spectrum Management, were never placed before the Telecom Commission. The DoT's reply that it was discussed in the internal Telecom Commission on October 10, 2007 is unacceptable in view of their own admission that the Resolution, Rules of Business and Rules for the Transaction of Business of the Telecom Commission do not contain any reference to "Internal," "External" or "Full" Telecom Commission; only the term 'Telecom Commission' finds a place. Thus, it is established that the prevalent practice has been developed in the DoT as a camouflage to take very convenient decisions through the permanent internal members of the DoT and avoid uncomfortable decisions in the entire Telecom Commission where the part-time but independent members, particularly the Finance Secretary, would be raising objections. This fact has been corroborated by one of the former Secretaries of the Department of Telecommunications. The Committee strongly disapprove such a dubious practice and impress upon them to henceforth discard distinguishing between the full time and part-time members or for that matter between internal or full Telecom Commission as the Commission is one entity.

The Telecom Commission was set up for fair and independent working of the DoT but the manner in which the Telecom Commission is operated, it has been reduced to a mere charade rendering its very integrity questionable. The Committee, therefore, recommend suitable amendments in the Business Rules so that it is made mandatory to refer all matters relating to policy and change in policy or procedure to the Telecom Commission by doing away with the procedure of internal or full commission for their approval. Further, all such policy or procedural changes once approved by the Commission must be notified after due approval of the Cabinet. The Committee observe that one of the convenient methods adopted by the Department to keep the part-time members at bay is to put in a clause in the Business Rules to consolidate the quorum with the presence of three full-time members only. The Committee exhort the Government to revisit the Transaction of the Business Rules of the Commission with a view to revising the quorum rule making the presence of the Finance Secretary, or his authorized representative not below the rank of Joint Secretary in the Department of Economic Affairs, as essential condition for constituting the quorum.

THE RADIA TAPES

The justification for examining and commenting on the "Radia Tapes" becomes imperative on the part of the Committee in view of some of the conversations between Ms Niira Radia on the one hand and some politicians/journalists/bureaucrats on the other, centering around allocation of portfolios in the Union Cabinet, payment of bribe in the allotment of 2G Spectrum etc. which has a direct bearing on the subject under examination of the Committee. In this context, the Committee find that the transcripts of the Radia Tapes were first published in the *Outlook* and the *Open* magazine. The Editor of the "Open Magazine" and the Editor-in-Chief of the *Outlook* submitted emphatically before the Committee that they published some selected transcripts of the Radia Tapes in the national and larger public interest. They have also categorically declared the authenticity of the published documents and informed the Committee that nobody whose transcripts they have printed has challenged their veracity and none of them has so far taken recourse to any legal action against either of the magazines for publishing the transcripts. The Committee commend the brave initiatives taken by the two magazines in larger public interest indischarge of their journalistic duly to reveal the truth.

Ms Niira Radia while deposing before the Committee stated that the publication of her conversations with many people in some magazines was a part of corporate conspiracy against her but did not disclose who the conspirators are. Similarly, while responding to various queries of the Committee, she gave an impression that she was predetermined not to come out with the facts. The Committee feel that her reluctance to speak the truth is somehow an indication of her guilty conscience.

A good deal of Radia Tapes contain conversations which center around the anxiety to get the Telecom Ministry portfolio allocated for the second time to A. Raja as the conversations show that Mr. Tata has had a bad chemistry with Dayanidhi Maran, as per his own admission. Ratan Tata's personal hand-written letter to Mr. Karunanidhi, the DMK President and the Chief Minister of Tamil Nadu, praising Raja's achievements, is an irrefutable testimony. The Committee are surprised that a person of Tata's stature sent a personal letter to the DMK patriarch when the latter had nothing to do with framing and implementation of policies at the central level.

The Public Accounts Committee agreed that a personal hand-written letter should not have been commented upon by them but since it was made public and shows keen interest and involvement of big Corporate Houses in the ministerial portfolio allocation, a matter which has a direct bearing on the subject under examination of the P.A. Committee. The Radia tapes only reveal the proverbial tips of the iceberg and provides glimpses of the often unreported back room deals, shady trade offs, the role of middlemen who have acquired certain hallow of respectability by assuming more fashionable and modern nomenclatures, corporate wars, quid pro quos between lobbyists and certain journalists, unsatiable greed for wealth, etc.

The disclosures made by the tapes have given a new dimension to corruption in India. Till date, no person has ever questioned the validity of the tapes. Most of the conversations are focused, from my understanding, on who should be the Telecom Minister and to some extent who should not be the Telecom Minister. With whom Ms Radia had conversation on allocation of portfolio and 2G Spectrum, there were several prominent journalists. Then there were Ratan Tata and Kanimozhi and Raja himself.

The Public Accounts Committee had wanted to know form Ratan Tata during his deposition before the Committee whether his conversation with Ms Radia as recorded in the tapes did not imply that he

BOMBAY HOUSE,
FORT, MUMBAI- 400001.

Personal & Confidential

November 13, 2007

Dear Mr. Chief Minister,

I am taking the liberty of writing to you on the subject of the telecommunications sector which has been in the news these past few weeks and where there has been much public controversy – mainly created by powerful vested interest groups within the industry.

Ever since Mr. Raja took over as Minister, there has been a rational, fair and action-oriented leadership in the ministry. On the issue of spectrum also, his stated policies, for most part, have been legally sound, rational and well-reasoned. Part of the existing controversy revolves around one approval, which is being contested in the courts. In all other cases his stated policies appear fair and he deserves everyone's support.

The telecom industry is the fastest-growing sector in the country's history and the leadership to this sector is with your party. It is essential that history praises the vision, creativity, and high growth achieved by you and your Minister. Our industry is in the viewing glass

BOMBAY HOUSE,
FORT, MUMBAI- 400001.

of the entire world, because our market is so large. If done well, the DMK can possibly claim Telecom to be its greatest achievement and most significant contribution to the nation's growth. This growth would need to come from rational and fair policies – without favourites and without pandering to vested interest groups who are only interested in serving themselves.

I have the highest regard and respect for you as a person of great equity and great vision. I would like to see you derive great kudos for the visionary growth in this sector, which I believe can be delivered under your leadership by Mr. Raja. I have therefore requested Ms. Nira Radia to personally carry this letter to you and to explain to you the public perceptions, the orchestrated misinformation and the vested interests that are seeking to de-rail the process of growth through technological and spectrum battles, rather than seeking national gain.

I hope you will take this letter in the spirit in which it has been written.

With regards,

Yours sincerely, Ratan.

Untouched: 23 UAS Licenses issued in Dec 2006 but 2G spectrum was given in Jan 2008 at 2001 rates						
Sl	Circle	Company name	Price for 3G spectrum decided in auction held in 2010			Paid to get 6.2 MHz 2G spectrum in 2008 @ 2001 rates
			per 5 MHz	per 1 MHz	per 6.2 MHz	
A	B	C	D	E = D / 5	F = E x 6.2	G
1	Assam	Vodafone Essar Spacetel Ltd	41.48	8.30	51.44	5.00
2	Bihar	Vodafone Essar Spacetel Ltd	203.46	40.69	252.29	10.00
3	HP	Vodafone Essar Spacetel Ltd	37.23	7.45	46.17	1.10
4	J&K	Vodafone Essar Spacetel Ltd	30.30	6.06	37.57	2.00
5	North East	Vodafone Essar Spacetel Ltd	42.30	8.46	52.45	2.00
6	Orissa	Vodafone Essar Spacetel Ltd	96.98	19.40	120.26	5.00
7	Mumbai	Idea Cellular Ltd	3,247.07	649.41	4,026.37	203.66
8	Karnataka	Aircel Limited	1,579.91	315.98	1,959.09	206.83
9	Maharashtra	Aircel Limited	1,257.82	251.56	1,559.70	189.00
10	Rajasthan	Aircel Limited	321.03	64.21	398.08	32.25
11	AP	Aircel Limited	1,373.14	274.63	1,702.69	103.01
12	Delhi	Aircel Limited	3,316.93	663.39	4,112.99	170.70
13	Gujarat	Aircel Limited	1,076.06	215.21	1,334.31	109.01
14	Mumbai	Aircel Limited	3,247.07	649.41	4,026.37	203.66
15	Bihar	Aditya Birla Telecom Ltd	203.46	40.69	252.29	10.00
16	MP	Dishnet Wireless Ltd	258.36	51.67	320.37	17.45
17	UP (East)	Dishnet Wireless Ltd	364.57	72.91	452.07	45.25
18	UP (West)	Dishnet Wireless Ltd	514.04	102.81	637.41	30.55
19	Haryana	Dishnet Wireless Ltd	222.58	44.52	276.00	21.46
20	Kerala	Dishnet Wireless Ltd	312.48	62.50	387.48	40.54
21	Kolkata	Dishnet Wireless Ltd	544.26	108.85	674.88	78.01
22	Punjab	Dishnet Wireless Ltd	322.01	64.40	399.29	151.75
23	MP	Vodafone Essar South Ltd	258.36	51.67	320.37	17.45
Total					**23,399.92**	**1,655.68**
Difference between Column Nos. G & H (Loss to the Government)						**21,744.24**

was advocating Shri Raja's case for becoming Telecom Minister. In reply, Mr. Tata deposed as follows:

> Let me just say two or three things. I am not questioning the authenticity of the tapes. I will say that at no stage have we done anything for Raja or in any way gratified him. I will also say that Ms Radia was not working for us alone. She had many other clients. She has been in fact a supporter of Mr. Raja in many ways. The conversations in my view do not in fact imply that we were arranging his Cabinet positions and securing anything. We had a chemistry problem with Mr. Maran in the past and certainly, between the two at that time, I would have much preferred to see Mr. Raja rather than Mr. Maran.

He further clarified:

> On Ms Radia, let me reiterate that we have not had any arrangements, dealings or any interaction with her other than what I have described. She has been our public relations person interacting with the media. She has been no different on advocacy than a CII or a FICCI in terms of endeavouring to have a level playing field. At no stage have we had a facilitator doing more than what I had indicated. We are not her only clients and she is not captive to us. I can speak for what we have done and I can hold my hand to my heart and say that we have not dithered on that at all.

Referring to his personal handwritten letter to the DMK patriarch wherein he had *inter-alia* stated that 'on the issue of Spectrum also, his (Raja's) stated policies for most part have been legally sound, rational and well-reasoned; the Committee asked whether he was not advocating for Mr. Raja's continuance as the Telecom Minister. In reply, Mr. Tata submitted:

> I have stated repeatedly and I would just say it again that if done well, the DMK can possibly claim telecom to be its greatest achievement,

> etc. for the nation's growth. This growth would need to come from rational and fair policies without favourites and without pandering to vested interested groups that are only interested in serving themselves.
>
> What I am trying to say is that if there is a controversy of what Mr. Raja is alleged to have done, it is in the implementation of the policy. The policy of creating greater number of applicants, opening the industry to more players is not an irrational policy.

The Public Accounts Committee then querried the basis of writing the letter to the Chief Minister of Tamil Nadu who had nothing to do with framing or implementation of the policies at the central level and whether in the fitness of things it would have not been more appropriate had he written to the Prime Minister. In reply, Mr. Tata stated: "Quite right but there is a context to this letter. The context was that there was a great deal of pressure on the Chief Minister at that time to remove Mr. Raja when there was no controversy."

He further stated: "I explained the context in which I wrote to the Chief Minister. There could have been many things one could have done. One might have issued a press statement saying that his policies were fair."

Chapter III

The Money Trail and CBI Investigation

As discussed above, Swan Telecom Pvt. Ltd., incorporated in July 2007, was earlier owned by Anil Ambani and known as Swan Capital Pvt. Ltd. Swan Capital applied for GSM circle licence in January, 2007. In February 13, 2007, it changed its name to Swan Telecom Pvt. Ltd. Then it was sold to two real estate entrepreneurs, viz., Shahid Balwa (Managing Director) and Vinod Kumar Goenka (Director) who have taken over the charge of the company. Swan Telecom Pvt. Ltd. bagged an allotment of licences in 13 circles worth Rs.1537 crore. However, within weeks the company sold its 45 per cent stake to Etisalat (UAE giant) worth Rs.4500 crore. Swan Telecom became known as Etisalat DB.

On December 17, 2008, began the first bribe money trail. Swan Telecom Pvt. Ltd. allotted Rs. 380 crore worth of shares to the Chennai based Genex Exim Ventures, a company floated only just 4 months before the deal by a meager capital of Rs.1 lac. According to the documents available with ROC, Chennai, Genex was incorporated on September 17, 2008 with two directors Mr. Mohammed Hassan (58) and Ahamed Shakir (41) who hail from Kilukarai, a small coastal village famous for hawala operations, in Ramanathapuram district in Tamil Nadu. Ahmed Syed Salahuddin (32) who represented the company on the board of Swan, also came from the same village.

There are more indications of a Tamil Nadu link especially when the corporate veil is pierced, and which ultimately lead to the family members of the DMK President Mr. Karunanidhi. Ahmed Syed Salahuddin, who represented the company on the board of Swan, is the younger son of Syed Mohammed Salahuddin, an NRI businessman, who heads the Dubai-based real estate conglomerate ETA Ascon Star Group. This group began its Indian operations in 2006 by floating several real estate firms across the State. Raja was then Union Environment Minister, and his party DMK had assumed power in Tamil Nadu.

ETA signed an MoU with the Tamil Nadu Government for setting up an IT Special Economic Zone worth Rs. 3,750 crore when A. Raja became Telecom Minister in May 2007. Tamil Nadu Chief Minister Mr. Karunanidhi was present at the MoU signing ceremony for the proposed project of Kancheepuram, near Chennai, on a nearly 500 acre plot.

It is mysterious that a large business group entered Swan's board through a company with a meager Rs. 1 lac paid up capital. Incidentally, Genex Exim has not filed any document with the authorities to show its source of income, even after acquiring Rs. 380 crore worth of shares from Swam Telecom.

As Telecom Minister, A. Raja, had blatantly favoured Swan Telecom. This is evident from a rather unusual deal struck between the said company and the state-owned BSNL. And discussed above. The "intra-circle roaming deal" signed between the company and BSNL on September 13, 2008, was literally silent when it comes to money.

According to the MoU, Swan could use spectrum, communication towers and the entire network of BSNL free of cost. Though the BSNL management suggested charging 52 paise per call, this clause was mysteriously absent in the MoU. BSNL was forced to sign this deal just 10 days before the sale of Swan's shares to Etisalat. It is not clear why an amount was not specified in the MoU and in the absence of a consideration what is the position of the Agreement entered into between the Company and BSNL. The arrangement helped swell Swan's coffers without the company investing a single rupee.

BSNL Chairman and Managing Director, Kuldeep Goyal, sought to quell the trouble by coining a new word for the agreement between Swan and BSNL as "Limited MoU," while they have never entered into an agreement in respect of "intra-circle roaming deal." The very description of "Limited MoU" itself is fishy and confusing.

It was also reported that Swan Telecom planned to invest on a dictated price of Rs.1,000 crore (i.e. 49 per cent stake) in Greenhouse Promoters. However, they have had to shelve it out since the scam controversy broke out, and J. Gopikrishnan published this in *Pioneer* in advance of the completion of the deal. But still there is sufficient documentation.

Unitech, another real estate company, also entered into the telecom fray by a bumper deal. The company also got licence from 22 circles worth Rs.1,651 crore. After acquiring the licence, it sold them to a Norwegian company viz. "TELENOR" a major telecom player in Pakistan and Bangladesh, at a whopping sum of Rs. 6,120 crore. The company had applied for licences in several names. Unitech Infrastructure, Unitech Builders and Estates, Aska Projects, Naham Properties, Hudson Properties, Volga Properties, Adonis Projects and Azare Properties among them. They were able to merge all their licences when Telecom Minister, Mr. Raja signed another dubious notification allowing this to happen.

In the above deal, the entry of a foreign firm having wide operations in Pakistan and Bangladesh into Indian Telecom Industry has been facilitated, which this author believes would pose a threat to India's national security. There is and was a Home Ministry advisory against Etisalat Telenor and in particular against Shahid Bal who was the MD of Swan Telecom.

After Mr. Raja became a Union Minister in 2004, many of his close relatives floated real estate companies. Companies like Green House Promoters, Equaas Estates and Kovai Shelters Promoters have Raja's brothers, nephews and nieces as directors on their boards. The Minister even got his wife, M.A. Parameswari, appointed on the board.

Mrs M. A. Parameswari, wife of Hon'ble Telecom Minister A. Raja joined as director of the company after three years of its incorporation i.e., in February, 2007. The Minister has not disclosed this fact to the Prime Minister nor discloses the source of income and asset allocation and hereby conducted breach of Conduct Rules.

Mrs M.A. Parameswari resigned from the Board on February, 2008 as part of a damage control process envisaged by Hon'ble Telecom Minister A. Raja. However, Mrs Parameswari could not transfer her holding stake from the company on the said date of resignation, giving room for investigators to show explicit violation of the service rules. On a later day, the said shares were transferred to Hon'ble Telecom Minister Raja's nephew and also a government pleader in Tamil Nadu.

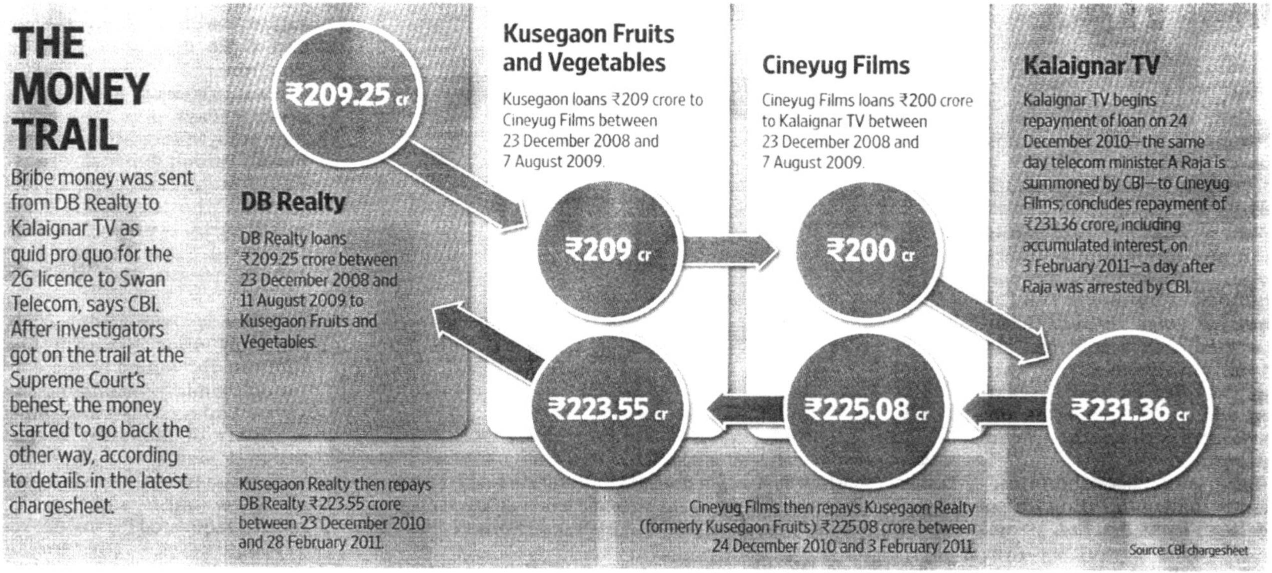

SANDEEP BHATNAGAR/MINT

Karuna kin confirms Kani's active KTV role

RAKESH K SINGH ■ NEW DELHI

In a major revelation, Chief Financial Officer of *Kalaignar TV* and a nephew of Tamil Nadu Chief Minister M Karunanidhi, P Amirtham, has told the CBI that DMK MP Kanimozhi, who is an accused in the 2G spectrum scam, was involved in the day-to-day affairs of the company as its founding director.

The statement is in sharp contrast to Kanimozhi's plea before a designated court here that she be granted bail as she was not actively involved with the operations of the *Kalaignar TV*. The CBI has alleged that Kanimozhi received kickbacks on behalf of former Telecom Minister A Raja as a *quid pro quo* for grant of 2G licences to Swan Telecom.

Amirtham joined the *Kalaignar TV* as general manager (administration) on June 6, 2007 and was appointed as Additional Director on June 12, 2007 but he resigned on July 27, 2007. Later on, he was appointed as CFO on July 27, 2007 and continued on the post till May 28, 2010 and was reappointed as Additional Director on May 28, 2010.

In his statement recorded under Section 161 of the Criminal Procedure Code, Amirtham said, "On being asked, I state that Ms Kanimozhi Karunanidhi was a founder director of Kalaignar TV Pvt Ltd, Chennai. However, she resigned on June 20, 2007 from the board of directors because the necessary clearances from the Ministry of Home Affairs were delayed," he said, adding, "Nevertheless, she used to take keen interest in day-to-day affairs of the company." He, however, claimed that ₹200 crore received by *Kalaignar TV* from DB Group companies was an unsecured loan.

Kanimozhi at Patiala House court in New Delhi on Monday PTI

"On being asked I state that *Kalaignar TV* had taken unsecured loan of ₹200 crore from Cineyug Films Pvt Ltd. In fact, the initial proposal was for acquisition of equity shares in *Kalaignar TV*. However, it did not materialise, Amirtham said in his statement.

The CBI had in its chargesheet refuted the claim that the amount was received as an unsecured loan as there no formal agreement was signed between the two parties and the return of the so-called loan amount to Cineyug Films began the day Raja was asked by CBI to appear for questioning in connection with the 2G scam probe on December 24, 2010.

The CBI had chargesheeted *Kalaignar TV* MD Sharad Kumar, Kanimozhi, Raja, Swan Telecom promoter Shahid Balwa and others for criminal conspiracy, cheating and relevant sections of the Prevention of Corruption Act for paying and receiving illegal gratification as a *quid pro quo* for granting 2G licences that resulted in a loss of over ₹30,000 crore to the exchequer.

The CBI has established that Kanimozhi was an active brain behind the operations of the *Kalaignar TV*.

She had also been in regular touch with Raja regarding launching of *Kalaignar TV*. Kanimozhi also pursued reappointment of A Raja as Telecom Minister (in UPA II) which clearly establishes the strong association of accused Kanimozhi with A Raja in official/political matter.

Continued on Page 4

Karuna kin confirms Kani's active KTV role

From Page 1

The CBI investigation has also reportedly established that pursuant to the criminal conspiracy accused A Raja, accused Sharad Kumar (MD of Kalaignar TV) and Kanimozhi, stakeholders and/or directors of Kalaignar TV accepted and received an illegal gratification of ₹200 crore in Kalaignar TV from the accounts of DB Group companies in the years 2008-09, as a reward in lieu of the undue favours shown by Raja in connivance with other accused public servants in allocation of UAS licences, valuable spectrum and other undue favours to Swan Telecom during 2008-09."

"It is established that accused Raja (being a public servant) in conspiracy with accused Sharad Kumar and Kanimozhi, despite knowing the fact that accused Raja had connections with Shahid Balwa and Vinod Goenka (both of DB Realty) regarding his official functions, obtained for Kalaignar TV a loan of ₹200 crore for a consideration which they knew to be inadequate from Balwa and Goenka, promoters of Swan Telecom," say the chargesheet.

PIONEER : May 11, 2011

Dayalu attended vital Kalaignar TV Board meet

RAKESH K SINGH ■ NEW DELHI

While the CBI may have spared Tamil Nadu Chief Minister M Karunanidhi's wife and a majority shareholder in the DMK-owned *Kalaignar TV*, Dayalu Ammal, the agency has documentary evidence to show that she was part of the Board meeting of the channel that decided to accept the alleged bribe money from a company linked to DB Realty promoter Shahid Balwa.

Ammal was let off by the CBI in the multi-crore 2G spectrum scam on the ground that she was not an active director of the company but the evidence gathered by the agency also suggest that she was a founder director of the company and was a signatory to the opening form of the current account of *Kalaignar TV* at Kodambakkam branch of the Indian Bank in Chennai.

The other signatories of the opening form for the current account bearing number 733560561 of the channel include DMK MP Kanimozhi and Managing Director of *Kalaignar TV*, Sharad Kumar.

Both Kumar and Kanimozhi besides former Telecom Minister A Raja, Swan Telecom promoter Shahid Balwa and a host of Telecom Ministry officials and directors of Balwa-owned company have been chargesheeted by the CBI for payment and receipt of bribe for alleged favours to Swan Telecom in the grant of 2G licences.

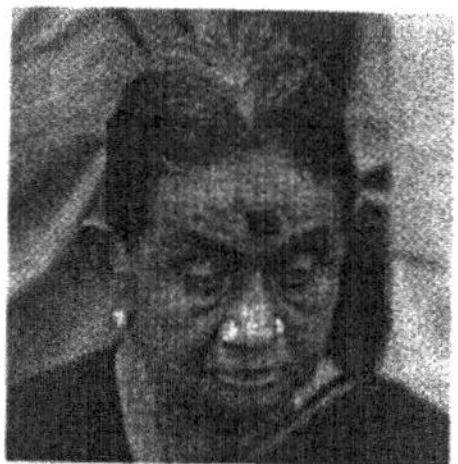

CBI has proof this meeting decided to accept alleged bribe money

Agency had let off majority shareholder and TN CM's wife

DB Group company Cineyug Films had transferred ₹200 crore to the *Kalaignar TV* current bank account between December 23, 2008 to August 7, 2009 which has been dubbed as the bribe money for the *quid pro quo* of favours by Raja to Swan Telecom.

General Manager (Finance) of *Kalaignar TV*, G Rajendran has in a statement to the CBI under Section 161 of the Criminal Procedure Code revealed, "As per the minutes of the meeting of directors of Kalaignar TV Pvt Ltd held on 13.02.2009, Sharad Kumar was authorised to raise fund from Cineyug Films Pvt Ltd upto ₹200 crore. This meeting was attended by Sharad Kumar and Karunanidhi (Dayalu Ammal)."

He also had *Kalaignar TV*'s account with the Indian Bank and said that account No. 733560561 bore the signatures of MK Dayalu, Kanimozhi Karunanidhi and Sharad Kumar. "Cineyug Films Pvt Ltd has transferred a total sum of ₹200 crore in the said account," said Rajendran who is a prosecution witness in the 2G spectrum scam case.

The CBI has instead made Dayalu Ammal, who owns 60 per cent of the *Kalaignar TV* shares a prosecution witness

Continued on Page 4

Related report on P4

From Page 1

and has relied on her statement that she had informed the Kalaignar TV Board that she cannot be expected to give any attention to the company's affairs on account of her age and deteriorating health. She has also claimed that she did not understand any language other than Tamil and that she would attend Board meetings only to suffice quorum requirement.

He also claimed, "We refunded the loan amount along with accrued interest to Cineyug Films as the lender was pressing for refund of the same. The interest rate charged by Indian Bank was higher than that of Cineyug Films. The lower interest rate charged by Cineyug was due to the fact that the amount lent by them was big sum, ie to the tune of Rs 200 crore and the channel had very high credibility in the market."

Countering the Kalaignar TV claim that the said amount of Rs 200 crore was received as an unsecured loan, the CBI investigation has revealed this plea to be "false as no valid agreement to this effect was entered into by the companies, including Cineyug and Kalaignar TV and that no collaterals/securities were ensured to secure the alleged loan amount."

HINDU May 10, 2011

'Accused liable even if loan obtained by fraud is repaid'

High Court's inherent powers must not be exercised to stifle legitimate prosecution: Bench

J. Venkatesan

- 'More than sufficient circumstances exist suggesting hatching of criminal conspiracy'
- 'High court must exercise powers sparingly

NEW DELHI: Merely because the loan dues of a bank or a financial institution have been repaid, the accused cannot be exonerated from criminal liability if the charge against them is that they obtained the loan by fraud or forged documents, the Supreme Court has said.

A Bench of Justices D.K. Jain and H.L. Dattu rejected the contention that the full amount in question having been re-paid to the bank, there was no monetary loss to the bank and, therefore, continuation of criminal proceedings against all the accused, including the appellant, would not only be an exercise in futility but an abuse of the process of law as well.

Justice Jain writing the judgment did not agree with the contention that since the loan amount had been repaid, the charge sheet against the appellant, Sushil Suri, should be quashed at a preliminary stage when he had only been summoned to stand trial.

On the contention that the High Court should exercise its inherent powers under Section 482 Cr.P.C. to quash criminal proceedings at the preliminary stage, the Bench said inherent powers should not be exercised to stifle a legitimate prosecution.

The Bench said: "Although the power possessed by the High Court under the said provision is very wide it is not unbridled. It has to be exercised sparingly, carefully and cautiously, ex debito justitiae to do real and substantial justice for which alone the court exists.

"The High Court should normally refrain from giving a prima facie decision in a case where all the facts are incomplete and hazy, more so, when the evidence has not been collected and produced before the court and the issues involved, whether factual or legal, are of such magnitude that they cannot be seen in their true perspective without sufficient material."

In the instant case, the Bench said the accused not only duped a bank but also availed himself of depreciation on the machinery, which was never purchased and used by them, causing loss to the exchequer, a serious economic offence against society.

"In the present case, having regard to the modus operandi adopted by the accused, as projected in the charge sheet, we have no hesitation in holding that it is not a fit case for exercise of jurisdiction by the High Court under Section 482 of the Cr.P.C. as also by this Court under Article 142 [to do substantive justice] of the Constitution. In the instant case more than sufficient circumstances exist suggesting the hatching of criminal conspiracy and forgery of several documents leading to commission of the offence. We refrain from saying more on the subject at this juncture, lest it cause prejudice to the appellant or the prosecution.

"The gravamen of the allegations against the appellant, as also the co-accused is that the company hatched a conspiracy by forging and fabricating a number of documents, like photographs of old machines, purchase orders and invoices showing purchase of machinery in order to support their claim to avail hire purchase loan."

Dismissing the appeal against the Delhi High Court judgment, the Bench asked the trial court to proceed with the case registered in 1999 as expeditiously as possible without being influenced by any observation made by the High Court or in this judgment on the merits of the charge sheet.

It is also reported that the Company's bankers (Canara Bank, T. Nagar Branch, Chennai) received an amount of Rs.150 crore from Middle East, Hong Kong, Singapore besides India. No proof or clarify on source of the fund and its remittance.

The company also opened a branch office at Singapore in 2006 in order to avoid or escape public scrutiny and cut down direct flow of funds into its Indian counter-part. Hon'ble Telecom Minister Mr. Raja not only violated the existing rules in respect of Green House Promoters Pvt. Ltd. but also promoted another company through his kit and kin viz. Equaas Estate Pvt. Ltd. The said company's turnover was Rs.755 crore on completion of one year. The company has not filed any proper documents with Registrar of Companies as required under Form No. 23AC (to be filed by privately owned companies specifying information on sale of goods manufactured, sale of goods traded, sale of supply of services, etc.).

The CBI has yet to probe it, and has lost a lot of time already. Key figure in the Green House Promoters Ltd was Sadhick Batcha but he has committed suicide and is no more. Another shadowy figure was Raja's nephew, Deepak and he too has mysteriously dropped dead while working out in a gym in Chennai.

The second money trail is from Swan's real owner, DB Realty, to Kalaignar TV, founded on the inspiration of TN CM M. Karunanidhi. *Kalaignar* comes from the Sanskrit word *Kala,* meaning arts, and *Kalaignar* means revered artist, a nick name for Karunanidhi. Here the CBI has made some progress and has sent out Letters Regotary to some countries. But the CBI is handling with aspect of the case with kid-gloves.

Since, according to author's investigations, the bribe money is alleged to have been shared in differing proportions by the political patrons of Raja at the state and central levels, the money trail is the most difficult part of the investigation and prosecution case. But then we need to be determined and never to give up on this. The CBI has to be kept on notice and its toes, which is possible only if the Supreme Court monitoring continues as before.

CBI INVESTIGATION OF THE 2G SPECTRUM CASE

On the basis of the nationwide concerns expressed and specific complaints received by the Central Vigilance Commission (CVC) against

एस. एम. कृष्णा
S. M. KRISHNA

विदेश मंत्री, भारत
MINISTER OF EXTERNAL AFFAIRS
INDIA

सत्यमेव जयते

No.12332/EAM/2010 December 13, 2010

Dear Dr. Swamy,

This has reference to your letter of 17 November 2010 to Hon'ble Prime Minister with a request that the US Government be asked to share bank transfer details regarding the 'Spectrum Deal'.

According to the views provided by the Ministry's legal officers, requests of this nature could be made to the United States under the bilateral Mutual Legal Assistance Treaty. The Ministry of Home Affairs is the designated central authority for the purpose of implementing the Treaty. The procedure for assistance under this Treaty is that the concerned investigating agency or the Hon'ble Court hearing the case should write to the Ministry of Home Affairs to make a request to the United States Government.

I am forwarding a copy of your letter and the comments of this Ministry's Legal and Treaty Division to Minister of Home Affairs for his consideration.

With best regards,

Yours sincerely,

(S.M. Krishna)

Dr. Subramanian Swamy
A-77, Nizamuddin (East)
New Delhi – 110 013

Dr. Subramanian Swamy Ph.D. (Harvard)
President, Janata Party
Minister for Commerce, Law & Justice (1990-91)
Chairman (with Cabinet rank), Commission on Labour Standards and International Trade (1994-96)
Member of Parliament (1974-99)
Professor of Economics, Indian Institute of Technology, Delhi (1969-91)
Faculty, Harvard University (1963-69, 1985-86, 2001-08 Summer)

JANATA PARTY

A-77, Nizamuddin (East), New Delhi - 110 013, India
Phone: +91 46016465 Fax: +91 24357388
Mobile: +91 9810194279 +91 9940205331
Website: www.janataparty.org, www.indiaright.org
Email: swamy@post.harvard.edu
swamy39@gmail.com

PRIME MINISTER'S OFFICE
18 NOV 2010
DAK SECTION

November 17, 2010.

Dr. Manmohan Singh,
Prime Minister of India,
New Delhi.

Dear Prime Minister:

I write this letter to urge you to immediately put Mr. A. Raja, former Telecom Minister & MP under a high level security cover.

My usually reliable friends abroad have informed me that two European women bearing Slavic names have been trying to contact hit men in Dubai to silence forever Mr. Raja since he is key to much embarrassing information for some of those in power today.

Please also direct the EAM ask the US Government to share the bank transfer records regarding the spectrum deal which the US maintains through its communication facility in Fort Meade in Maryland state.

These data are vital for future prosecution and finding out the bribe money trail.

Warm Regards,

Yours sincerely,

(SUBRAMANIAN SWAMY)

L-413/67/2010
Ministry of External Affairs
(Legal & Treaties Division)

Reference note No. 5172/JS(AMS)/10 dated 22 November 2010 from the AMS Division. enclosing a letter of Dr. Subramanian Swamy, President of Janata Party to the Prime Minister regarding the 2G Spectrum scam.

2. Dr. Swamy has mentioned that Mr. A. Raja, a former Telecom Minister and MP faces a threat to his life from abroad and therefore he be provided a high level security cover. This being an administrative issue is to be examined and looked into by the administratively concerned Divisions/Departments.

3. Further, Dr. Swamy has requested the Prime Minister for a direction to the EAM to ask the US Government to share the bank transfer records regarding the Spectrum deal which the US maintains through its communication facility in Fort Meade, Maryland State.

4. Requesting a foreign country regarding information concerning bank accounts in its territory amounts to the seeking of international legal assistance i.e. mutual legal assistance.

5. Seeking and providing of international legal assistance in a criminal matter is governed by international or bilateral conventions/agreements between the counties concerned. There exists a bilateral Treaty between India and USA on mutual legal assistance in criminal matters. The provisions of the Treaty allow the contracting States to seek assistance in criminal cases both at the investigation and at the trial stage. The scope of assistance under Article 1 of the Treaty covers providing of documents, records and items of evidence. According to Article 5.4, execution of a request for assistance will not be declined on the ground of bank secrecy.

6. The Ministry of Home Affairs (MHA) is the Central Authority for the purpose of the implementation of the Treaty. The concerned investigating agency or the court before which the case may be pending could, if necessary, seek assistance by submitting a request for assistance to MHA prepared under the Treaty. Accordingly, the matter may be referred to MHA.

7. This issues with the approval of JS (L&T).

(Dr. V.D. Sharma)
Legal Officer (Gr.I)
03.12.2010

JS (AMS)

2G scam: CBI charge-sheet

Accused and charges against them in the 1st charge-sheet		
1	A Raja, the then MoC&IT	420, 468, 471 IPC and 13(2) r/w 13 (1) (d) PC Act
2	Siddhartha Behura, the then Secretary, DoT	420 IPC and 13 (2) r/w 13 (1) (d) PC Act 1988
3	RK Chandolia, the then PS to MoC&IT	
4	Shahid Usman Balwa, Director, Swan Telecom	420, 468, 471 IPC
5	Vinod Goenka, Director Swan Telecom	
6	Swan Telecom Pvt Ltd	
7	Sanjay Chandra, MD, Unitech Ltd	420 IPC
8	Unitech Wireless (Tamil Nadu) Pvt Ltd	
9	Gautam Doshi, Gr MD, Reliance ADA Group	109 r/w 420 IPC
10	Surendra Pipara, Sr VP, Reliance ADA Group	
11	Hari Nair, Sr VP, Reliance ADA Group	
12	Reliance Telecom Ltd	

irregularities of grave nature committed in the allocation of 2G Spectrum under the UAS licencing and since the replies of the DOT to the Questionnaires of the CVC were not specific, the Commission decided to conduct a direct inquiry on the matter on June 17, 2009.

After completing the Inquiry, the CVC, on October 12, 2009, referred the matter to the Central Bureau of Investigation for detailed investigation on the basis of Commission's Direct Enquiry Report. The CBI, accordingly, filed the First Information Report (FIR) on October 21, 2009.

The Public Accounts Committee asked the reasons for the CBI waiting for the CVC reference of the case and not registering the FIR and investigating the case on its own when so much information had already been in the public domain on the alleged irregularities committed in the allocation of 2G Spectrum. In reply, the CBI stated that CVC had been looking into the various complaints received by it, since January-February 2008 itself, regarding allegations about the allocation of UAS Licences in January 2008. CVC had initiated a direct enquiry under section 8(1) (d) of CVC Act, 2003. After completing said inquiry, CVC sent its report to CBI *vide* its letter dated October 12, 2009.

In the meantime, a Source Information was also processed at CBI *w.e.f.* January 12, 2009 and was pending decision, when it was learnt that CVC was looking into the matter. Accordingly, it was decided to wait for outcome of CVC enquiry. Normally, when CVC undertakes a direct enquiry, CBI awaits the outcome and its report from CVC.

The PAC then wanted to know whether the facts in the CVC reference fell within the purview of the Prevention of Corruption Act. In reply, the CBI submitted in the affirmative and stated that the details of facts mentioned in the CVC letter/report dated October 12, 2009 prima facie indicated abuse of official position by certain officials of Department of Telecommunications, in conspiracy with others. CVC in its letter dated October 12, 2009, vide Para 2, mentioned that "The Commission is, therefore, of the view that the matter requires further investigation to establish the criminal conspiracy in the allocation of 2G Spectrum under Unified Access Services Licence Policy of DoT and to bring to book all wrong doers. The CBI may take early necessary action in the matter and keep the Commission duly posted with the progress." Accordingly, FIR was registered under section 120-B of India Penal Code (Criminal conspiracy) read with section 13(2) r/w 13(1) (d) of Prevention of Corruption Act, 1988 (criminal misconduct).

A perusal of the FIR revealed that it had been registered against unknown persons. Expressing their surprise, the Committee asked in evidence whether it was a general practice in the CBI to lodge an FIR against unknown persons. In reply, the Director, CBI submitted: "Normally, we register a preliminary inquiry in which we establish who are the persons responsible and then, we lodge an FIR."

Asked to state why that practice was not followed while lodging the FIR in the 2G Spectrum case, the Director, CBI stated that the CVC in their Direct Inquiry Report did not name anyone and wanted the CBI to investigate further the irregularities that the Commission found in their inquiry. He further apprised: "We were expecting them (unknown persons) in the Department of Telecommunications, private persons as well as Companies – all the three."

When the Committee desired to know whether identifying only the Departments would suffice, the Director, CBI replied: "They (unknown persons) have been arrested and they are known now."

Referring to the CBI FIR which stated "Thus, the concerned officers of the Department of Telecommunications had a criminal conspiracy with certain persons/companies and by abusing their official position granted Unified Access Service Licences to a few selected Companies at nominal rate by rejecting the application of others without any valid reason thereby causing wrongful loss to the Government of India," the Committee asked whether the CBI had not come to the conclusion while lodging the FIR to identify those persons who caused wrongful loss to the Government. The Director, CBI responded: "That is where we are in the process of investigation and we have made certain arrests."

The Committee, thus, enquired about the date on which the first raid was done by the CBI after lodging the FIR. The Director, CBI replied that the raids started after October 2010. He further stated: "Some searches had taken place immediately after the case had been registered, but not against the Government Officers; Offices were searched and private companies were searched. The Government Officers were not raided initially – immediately, they were not raided."

The Committee asked about the reasons for such a long delay between the lodging of the FIR and the first raid and desired to know whether there was any difficulty in investigating or coming to a conclusion or some resistance to it or whether there were any influences on the Agency not to proceed too quickly. In response, the Director, CBI submitted: "There were a lot of records that had been initially seized; they were being examined plus we had the Radia Tapes which were given to us. We are going through the entire process."

The Committee, thus, queried whether the CBI would share the general impression that there were certain influences which prevented the Investigating Agency to act swiftly. In reply, the Director, CBI, stated that the Supreme Court had asked the CBI the same questions, but they were very satisfied with the progress of the investigations.

The Committee retorted that they were not concerned whether the Supreme Court was satisfied or not and reminded the Director, CBI, that he was duty-bound to come out with the whole truth to satisfy the Committee and in the process the country. In response, the Director, CBI, submitted: "I would like to mention that I had just taken over about two months ago. I was not associated with this case, but I shall certainly go back, check and then, I will satisfy the Committee as to why this delay was there."

In a post-evidence information, the CBI explained the reasons for delay in investigating of RC DAI 2009 A 0045 (2G Spectrum case) which reads as follows:

> During the course of investigation of the case, immediately after registration of the case search warrants were obtained from the Court of Special Judge CBI, Patiala house Court, New Delhi on October 21, 2009 and searches were conducted on October 22, 2009 for collection of incriminating documents in the Wireless Planning and Coordination Wing and in Access Services Cell of Department of Telecommunications, Sanchar Bhavan, Ashoka Road, New Delhi. During searches 59 files of Access Services Cell, which deal with policy issues relating to the Grant of Unified Access Services Licences (UASL) and issuance of UAS Licences, were seized. These documents

pertained to review of Licencing Policy, decision of the Department of Telecom on TRAI Recommendations, procedure adopted by Department of Telecom for issue of Letters of Intent (LOIs) for UAS licences, First–Come-First-Serve Policy, etc. as regards the UAS Licence policy of the DoT and files of DoT regarding processing of 122 UAS Licence applications of 17 companies to whom UAS Licenses were issued in the January-March, 2008, and files regarding grant of UAS Licences to these 17 companies for 122 telecom circles throughout India. During investigation further records of Access Services Cell of Department of Telecommunication relating to issuance of UAS licences by DoT, especially the allocation of UAS Licences during 2003 onwards, were also taken over from Department of Telecom.

Apart from the aforementioned documents 25 files of Wireless, Planning and Coordination (WPC) Wing of Department of Telecommunications were also seized during searches of the said wing of DoT on October 22, 2009. These files pertain to the planning, coordination, availability and allocation of Spectrum to the new UAS licencees during the relevant period. During investigation further records of WPC Wing of DoT were also seized.

During investigation of the case, further searches under section 165 crore P.C. were also conducted during October 23, 2009 to January 19, 2010 at 21 other places at Delhi, Noida, Gurgaon, Jaipur, Mumbai, Mohali, Chennai, Gandhinagar and Bangalore, which include office premises of the various companies which got the Letters of Intent of UASL on January 10, 2008 regarding 2G Spectrum. These companies include M/s Swan Telecom Pvt. Ltd., M/s Datacom Solutions Pvt. Ltd., M/s Idea Cellular Ltd., M/s Unitech Wireless group companies (consisting of M/s Adonis Projects Pvt. Ltd., M/s Hudson Properties Ltd., M/s Unitech Infrastructures Pvt. M/s Aska Projects Ltd., M/s Azare Properties Ltd., M/s Unitech Builders & Estates Pvt. Ltd., Nahan Properties Pvt. Ltd. and Volga Properties Pvt Ltd.), M/s Spice Communications Ltd., M/s Tata Teleservices Ltd., M/s S Tel Ltd,' M/s Loop Telecom Private Ltd., M/s Shyam Telelink Limited and M/s Allianz Infratech Pvt. Ltd., all of which were allotted the UAS licences without any competitive bidding. The premises also included the premises of Auditor and person connected with M/s Green House Promoters Pvt. Ltd., Chennai and other companies allegedly related to kin of Shri A. Raja, then MOC & IT. Voluminous documents were retrieved from these searches. These documents were put to detailed scrutiny and further records from Registrar of Companies, Banks, companies, etc. were also collected from time to time for such scrutiny *vis-à-vis* the flow of funds regarding shareholding of the companies, eligibility of the applicant companies were also sought and examined.

The investigation involved analysis of the issues relating to the Telecom Policy of the Government of India since 2001, and even before, especially in view of the issues raised by then DoT officials that First-Come First-Served policy for issuance of licences, at the prices discovered in 2001, was in vogue since 2003. For this purpose further records of Department of Telecommunications (DoT)—Access Services Cell and Wireless Planning and Coordination Wing (WPC), Telecom Regulatory Authority of India (TRAI) were also taken over and analyzed.

The aforesaid documents were put to detailed scrutiny vis-vis-vis the facts of the case and further documents were collected, and witnesses were examined from time to time, as per needs of the investigation. The documents/files collected during investigation (till Hon'ble Supreme Court decided to monitor the investigation on December 16, 2010) run into more than 1 lakh pages, details of which is mentioned in a separate annexure, i.e. Annexure B. Numerous witnesses had also been examined by then.

It is also worth mentioning that in May 2010 the recordings of around 5,800 intercepted calls of Ms Niira Radia were also received by CBI for examination in connection with the investigation of this case. The same were also being simultaneously analyzed with respect to relevance in the investigation of this case.

Apart from the circumstances mentioned above, it is also relevant to mention that investigating officer of the case also completed investigation of another case (RC DAI 200 A 0014) in early 2010 and was also simultaneously attending to another important case under investigation (RC DAI 206 A 0006 – NTPC Case). Thereafter, he was on a foreign visit during April-may 2010 in connection with Basic (Computer Forensics) Training conducted by IACIS at Florida, USA. Apart from being busy in connection with preparation for said course/visit before such training, he also completed Peer Review Phase of Certified Forensic computer Examiner (CFCE) of 4 months duration in India, after returning from USA, simultaneously with the investigation.

In view of the circumstances mentioned above, there was no significant delay in the investigation of this case and the investigation was progressing. It actually took off on day to day basis, after general scrutiny of the documents was done, in June-July 2010, before Hon'ble Supreme Court decided to monitor the investigation vide order dated December 16, 2010.

A status report dated November 30, 2010 about the investigation of 2G Spectrum case was filed by CBI in a sealed cover before the Hon'ble Supreme Court of India, On perusal of the same Hon'ble Supreme Court of India observed in its order dated December 16, 2010 that "The reports produced before the Court show that the CBI and the Enforcement Directorate have started investigation in the right direction."

However, Hon'ble Supreme Court, keeping in view the statements made by the learned Solicitor General and the learned senior counsel representing the CBI, that the Government of India and the CBI would have no objection to a Court monitored investigation by the CBI, and with a view to ensure that in a serious matter like this, comprehensive and coordinated investigation is conducted by the CBI and the Enforcement Directorate without any hindrance, decided to monitor the investigation of this case, vide and order dated December 16, 2010 in the said matter.

Further, a Progress Report about the investigation of the case was filed by CBI before Hon'ble Supreme Court of India on February 10, 2011, after perusing which, and hearing the arguments on both sides, Hon'ble Court observed in its order dated February 10, 2011 that –

> "we have gone through the reports and note with satisfaction that the Director, CBI has given due importance to the 2G Spectrum case."

The Public Accounts Committee asked when would the CBI be able to complete the investigation. In reply, it was stated that the investigation of the case is in progress and is likely to be completed by March 31, 2011, barring foreign investigation which may take a little longer time. In respect of the main issues contained in the CBI FIR, is likely to file a charge sheet before the designated court by March 31, 2011 (The CBI did on April 3, 2011 file the first charge sheet). On remaining aspects the court shall be requested to allow continuing further investigation under section 173 (8) of Cr.P.C.

The Director, CBI further clarified:

> We will be filling our first charge sheet by March 31, 2011. But that would not mean that the investigation of the case would completely be over. We would still be having supplementary investigation going on and there is a lot of foreign investigation involved. So, till those reports come, we will not call it a complete investigation.' However, the first charge sheet will be filed by March 31, 2011.

Referring to a Press Report wherein it was mentioned that the Agency probing the 2G Spectrum scam opposed judicial monitoring of the case, the Committed asked the Director, CBI to clarify the matter, in response, he submitted: "I do not think we have opposed ... we have welcomed the Court, in fact, we were very keen that it should be monitored by the Court because they were asking for all sorts of monitoring."

The Committee then pointed out that had that been the case, how it was coming out in the press that the CBI said 'no to the Court monitoring the probe. In reply, the DIG, CBI submitted:

> There was a question of capability of the courts to monitor the investigation. This was one issue which was debated. The legal position that the CBI took was that it was beyond the scope of the courts to monitor the investigation. But once it was specific to this

particular case, our Counsel said that in view of the complexity and vast national interest of this case we offer this case to be monitored by the Supreme Court. There are two separate issues, one is the legality issue and the other is specific to this case alone.

In post-evidence information, the CBI further clarified that the Counsel for CBI argued on the issues relating to scope of monitoring of cases by courts, in general, and legal issues as to in what circumstances and in what manner courts can monitor the investigations. However, CBI had no objection to a Court monitored investigation in view of the seriousness of the allegations in this particular matter.

In response to a specific query regarding the number of documents seized and witnesses examined by the CBI so far, it was replied that 1,626 documents running into 1,38,765 pages had already been seized and 115 relied upon witnesses, as mentioned in the charge sheet filed by the CBI on April 2, 2011 had been interrogated.

Drawing the attention of the Director, CBI, to Arun Shourie, the former Telecom Minister's statement that he had met the then Director, CBI, and given him some documents, the name and telephone number of the whistle-blower etc, the Committee asked whether any such record was available and whether the then Director, CBI took up the issue forward or ignored Mr. Shourie's meeting, the documents etc. In response, the Director, CBI, stated that he would get back to the Committee after checking the records.

The source whom Arun Shourie has been publicly referring to, has been in touch with CBI and information furnished by him was considered during investigation. His name is Ashirvatham Achari, a former PS to Minister Raja, and is now a Railway Minister official. He has courageously given a Section 164 Cr. PC statement before the Session Judge, and agreed to be a witness. The nation salutes him for his act of patriotism. For effective prosecution we now need not only patriotic whistle blowers but some accused turning approvers.

Chapter IV

Conclusions: Combating Corruption

Corruption in the public domain represents monetary and other payments to the decision maker for subversion of his decisions, which decisions are required to be made on merits, to thus deprive the meritorious and enable the undeserving to benefit and thus. Corruption is driven by greed and greed is inevitable if social status in a society depends on how much money or wealth one has. This has never been the basis of an Indian society based on *Sanatana Dharma*. But with globalization Indians are fast forgetting this *Dharma* which made us today the only continuing and longest civilization in the world.

The purity of public office is an imperative for the functioning of the Constitution of India and for safeguarding the fundamental rights of citizens for which is required that all public servants including the highest be answerable for their actions and misdeeds. It has now become the major public issue in India today.

The effects of corruption on our society as we know above are in three dimensions:

First, it causes sub-optimality in economic decision making and hence makes for a squandering of scarce financial and natural resources.

Second, it empowers in election to public office those who engage in criminal activities since they are adept in corrupt activities and can finance elections in abundance through bribery and fraud.

Third, if corruption becomes rampant in a society then it enables hostile foreign interests to undermine national security and integrity. Soon freedom of the nation itself becomes a casualty.

On the question of systemic basis of corruption, arising from the Leftist view that freedom and competitive market are more prone to corruption, I am of the view that greed in any system breeds corruption. In a democracy adopting the market economic system, the scope is much more for a free play of greed as we saw in the recent sub-prime loans fraud in the US.

Democracy is a system of governance of the society. Today about 115 countries have some form of democratic governance. Twenty five years ago, there were only 20 countries. This shows that democracy has become the trend, the accepted system of government globally, and it is spreading world-wide. The view of Lee Kuan Yew of Singapore at one end and Communist at the other, that economic development must be first achieved before democracy is possible, has now been decisively rejected.

Moreover, the comparative economic results in East and West Germany, North and South Korea, China before reform and China now, not to mention socialist India then, and India now, have conclusively proved that democracy is a better system of governance than dictatorship and market system is superior to state controlled system.

Devolved democracies also better manage contradictions and conflicts arising out of a heterogeneous society (e.g., India vs. USSR vs. Yugoslavia or Sri Lanka) and provide effective feedback through independent press to enable corrective action by Government (e.g., China famine). It empowers people to question authority and make them accountable in an election.

But democracy is not a spectator sport for the people. There has to be people's involvement in decision-making and in choosing the right decision-makers. The most dangerous development of the last 61 years in India is the trend of hatred of politics amongst the educated people.

For healthy democracy, educated and well-placed persons, without necessarily formally joining politics, must encourage and help good and learned persons to enter the political arena. Without alert citizens there cannot be transparency and accountability, which are the bed-rock of good governance. Today in India we are hurt by opaqueness of decision making process, and we lack a proper system of accountability in all spheres of decision-making. This legitimizes inefficient allocation of scarce resources and encourages corruption. In a comparative economic system framework, India performs poorly in indexes of case of business and corruption.

With the disintegration of the USSR into 16 countries in 1991, comparative economic development theory has changed its focus from a study of alternative systems to alternative governance models of democracy, market system and globalization, i.e., change of focus from dictatorship vs. democracy, and state ownership vs. competitive market, to harmonizing freedom and choice with regulation, how much public sector and how much private, and how the emancipating and enabling power of democracy is to be balanced with the development of a profit-driven and competitive efficient markets i.e. what regulatory democratic institutions must do to promote efficient allocation of resources with good transparent and accountable governance. These harmonizations cannot be achieved unless spiritual values are integrated with the material urges that drive organizations in a new ethos of governance.

With globalization, governance today needs the most sophisticated minds to manage material advancement with being derailed by greed. Hence spiritual values must legitimize the aspiration of qualified persons to enter politics. This was our tradition too laid out in Ramayana and Mahabharata, and in the Freedom Movement. But we have lost that tradition today. Persons with no education or those with low educational qualifications are at the helm of affairs today. The few who are educated lack the necessary moral courage to effect accountability and fight corruption.

Just as democracy is favoured by the overwhelming consensus opinion for governance, development is now globally regarded as best done through the market system. Although democracy and market economy conceptually match each other as favouring the freedom of the individuals, it is a volatile mixture, and of some contradictions. Hence managing these contradictions is a part of good governance and organizational leadership.

For example, democracy empowers the more numerous who are however without much resources i.e., "the poor," while market empowers the well-to-do –"the rich" who are in the minority. Thus, pro-market forces, if selfish, could seek to undermine democracy through crony capitalism or by undermining elections through money power, while the unenlightened and "poor" majority could place curbs on the market through it's voting power.

Democratic development thus needs strong institutions for effective governance. But these institutions should not however be so empowered as to be used to threaten democracy in order to be able to contain disorder, and to deal with market failure.

Institutions must thus work out trade-offs such as through just affirmative action, social security and safety nets to create stake for the poor majority in the market, thus leveling the playing field, and create hope. This will legitimize reasonable profit-making, and thus the harmonization of the market and democracy and resolving the contradictions.

Market-dominant minorities—with their disproportionate capital, skills, business networks, and control over the modern economy—drive globalization. Any backlash against market-dominant minorities, whether the Chinese in Indonesia, Ibo in Nigeria, or political resentment against America at the global level, thus also becomes a backlash against markets, and hence fueling the appeal of the Left politics in these countries.

Thus good governance provides the security for the future stability of the new global system of democracy and market system. This depends on how the market dominant rich minority co-opts the relatively poor majority who dominate the democratic process because harmonization of contradiction is led by example and not by impersonal institutions. We need today both democracy and market, but by harmonization we must make both work. Hence the art of governance is crucial for our future by resolving the contradiction between democracy and market.

This contradiction if not resolved can electorally doom the best of leaders, e.g. P. V. Narasimha Rao. But the fact is that today the economic growth in India is indeed lop-sided and requires fresh dynamic vision for reform. For example, how can we explain the fact that while IIM students earn huge salaries, farmers are committing suicides in thousands in the same country?

Governance norms, if properly enforced can enable India to grow at 12 per cent per year by efficiently using a 36 per cent rate of investment by reducing the current incremental capital output ratio from 4.0 to 3.0. A 12 percent growth rate will mean a doubling of GDP every six years and that of per capita income every seven years. This can take us to the league of the top three nations of world, of US, China and India, and to overtake China in the next two decades hence. *That should be the goal of governance for us today.*

India is not yet an economically developed nation. While it has demonstrated prowess in IT software, biotech and pharmaceuticals, accelerated it's growth rate to 9 per cent per year to become the third largest nation in terms of GDP at PPP rates, it still has a backward agricultural sector hosting 62 per cent of the people of India and in which sector, farmers are committing suicides unable to repay their loans, a national unemployment rate is of over 15 per cent of the adult labour force, a prevalence of child labour arising out of nearly fifty percent of the children not making it to school beyond the fifth standard, a deeply malfunctioning primary and secondary educational system, 300 million illiterates and 250 million people in dire poverty; India's infrastructure is pathetic, with frequent electric power break-downs even in metropolitan cities, dangerously unhealthy water supply in urban areas, galloping HIV infections, and gaping holes on the National Highways.

To become a developed country by 2020, India's GDP will have to grow at 12 per cent per year for at least a decade. Technically this is within India's reach, since it would require the rate of investment to rise from the present 28 per cent of GDP to 36 per cent while productivity growth will have to ensure that the incremental output—capital ratio declines from the present 4.0 to 3.0. These are modest goals that can be attained by increased FDI and by use of IT software in domestic industry. But for that to happen, a more vigorous market centric economic reforms to dismantle the vestiges of the Soviet model in Indian planning, especially at the provincial level is required.

Democracy cannot be sustained as corruption-free unless the electorate is intellectually empowered by informed intelligence, to make moral judgments over the limits of material wants that can slip into greed. Ultimately, then the best ideology for a nation is one that blends the pursuit of materials ends with spiritual advancements.

But reforms are urgently required to be carried out for accelerating India's growth rate to 12 per cent per year. India has many advantages today for achieving a booming economy: a demographic dividend, an agriculture that has internationally the lowest yield in land & livestock-based products, and also at the lowest cost of production, a full 12 months a year of farm—friendly weather, a highly competitive skilled labour force and low wage rates at the national level, the advantages of which has already proved to the world by the outsourcing phenomenon. We have a young population (average is 28 years compared to US of 38 years, and Japan of 49 years) that be the base for it by ushering innovation in our production process.

Since the world view of economic development has now completely changed economic development is no more thought of as capital-driven, but as knowledge-driven. For application of knowledge, we need innovations, which means more original research which needs more fresh young minds out—the cream of the youth—to be imbibed with learning and at the frontier of research.

This requires adequate empowerment of mental faculty endowed with multi-dimensional intelligence. It is not adequate to foster cognitive intelligence only. There are other dimensions of intelligences recognized now viz., emotional,social, moral and spiritual. Our vast youth population is our demographic potential dividend if equipped with multi-dimensional intelligence.Thus, intelligence should not only be used for material progress but also harmonise it with ethical behavior and spiritual values.

Thus, cognitive intelligence is necessary for technical competence and intellectual articulation; emotional intelligence for the ability to perceive, apprise, and express emotion adaptively to create empathy in others, and to regulate emotions in ways that assist thought; moral intelligence is the mental capacity to determine how universal human principles should be applied to our personal values, goals and actions; and social intelligence is knowing how to use our neurological Wi-Fi to motivate others since our thoughts, emotions and body language impact on the responses of others who interact with us, just as laughter, anger, rebuke, praise, optimism, pessimism, honesty, crookedness, etc., each affects the behaviour of others bilaterally and multilaterally.

This is view of Integral Humanism as propounded by Deendayal Upadhaya or what we have for centuries have called as Sanatana Dharma. The social structure called *Varna*, till it degenerated into a birth based social cartel, was also designed to downgrade wealth as the indicator of status as it has become in the current Globalisation process.

Materialistic progress alone does not guarantee national security of a nation. What is essential is the character and integrity of its citizens. Hence, besides the objective of acquiring knowledge and getting employment that require cognitive intelligence, the youth must be motivated in other dimensions of intelligence that of emotional, moral and social. These concepts have been developed in the eighteen chapters of Bhagavat Gita that has been interpreted in modern context by Sri Chandrashekharendra Sarasvati of Kanchi Mutt, Swami Chinmayananda, and Swami Dayananda Sarasvati of Arsha Vidyalaya. In the United States, as the *Business Week* magazine has recently reported, these concepts have become highly popular in the corporate world, and have been incorporated in the best-selling books written by Daniel Goleman, Deepak Chopra, and Anthony Robbins among others.

Thus, cognitive intelligence is necessary for technical competence and intellectual articulation; emotional intelligence for the ability to perceive, apprise, and express emotion adaptively to create empathy in others, and to regulate emotions in ways that assist thought; moral intelligence is the mental capacity to determine how universal human principles should be applied to our personal values, goals and actions; and social intelligence is knowing how to use our neurological Wi-Fi to motivate others since our thoughts, emotions and body language impact on the responses of others who interact with us, just as laughter, anger, rebuke, praise, optimism, pessimism, honesty, crookedness, etc., each affects the behaviour of others bilaterally and multilaterally.

In brief, out National Policy for integrating spiritual values and organization leadership can be achieved by measures by which we can create a modern mindset in the youth of India, not only to motivate the youth to acquire technical competence, but to develop emotional, moral social and spiritual values that will make that person a self-reliant individual of high character, patriotic, and possessing a social conscience.

Business ethics and organizational leadership has been founded on that pool of talent.

Such an army of evolved youth will be the asset of the nation, and then collectively the demographic dividend for the nation can be reaped by us for the glory of the nation Bharat Mata. Hence, a well structured national policy for development of multiple intelligence is vital for making India global power two decades hence. This then would be a basis for our national renewal and renaissance.

Our goal has to be thus the efficient use of resources, human and physical, hardware and software by an able and human spiritually guided and ethically organizational leadership in a framework of competitive market economies.

With such spreading corruption, are freedom and market system the facilitator of such fraud and corruption? Is there any value to focusing on individual cases of corruption however big rather than on the systemic basis for such corruption?

The answer that focuses on both is necessary. A simple mathematical analysis based on probability of detection, the cost to the corrupt of such detection, averaged by the expected value of the gain from the corrupt act, proves that even if the probability of detection is low (as generally it is), if the cost to the corrupt of detection is a some multiple of the gain from the corrupt act then every rational person would choose not to bribe or to accept a bribe. This is because the expected value of any corrupt transaction then becomes negative. Hence, focusing on individual cases and making an example of them is useful for fighting corruption.

If thus Indian society, reared on *Satyam, Shivam, Sundaram,* is not able to make an example of most glaring case of corruption of this first decade of the 21st century then the nation cannot look forward to becoming developed again. Instead of *Satyam, Shivam, Sundaram,* our new motto will be *Satyam, Spectrum* and *Scandals.*

The question that remains is: what governance principles should be adopted not only to rescue the Indian economy from the current tail-spin induced by corruption but also to rapidly progress to a developed and corruption-minimal nation status in the next two or three decades?

Hence, concisely stated, for this to be achieved on a long-term basis, the Indian economy should be founded on a harmonization of efficient organizational leadership and abiding spiritual values which we call as *Sanatana Dharma.* That can be nurtured only bottom up, i.e. educate our growth accordingly—to synthesize material pursuits with spiritual values which lauds simplicity and eschews greed.

Ultimately, it will also be decided by how we vote in elections. But we need a new ideology to combat the cancer of corruption in our system. For this we need a new breed of Indian leaders-educated, courageous, and rational risk takers. That we can get only if the ethos of our people changes from the purely individualist pursuit of material pleasures and goals, to an integral outlook.

In brief, our National Policy for integrating spiritual values and organization leadership can be achieved by measures by which we can create a modern mindset in the youth of India, not only to motivate the youth to acquire technical competence, but to develop emotional, moral social and spiritual values that will make that person a self-reliant individual of high character, patriotic, and possessing a social conscience. Business ethics and organizational leadership has be founded on that pool of talent.

Such an army of evolved youth will be the asset of the nation, and then collectively the demographic dividend for the nation can be reaped by us for the glory of the nation Bharat Mata. Hence, a well structured national policy for development of multiple intelligence is vital for making India global power two decades hence. This then would be a basis for our national renewal and renaissance.

Our goal has to be thus the efficient use of resources, human and physical, hardware and software by an able and human spiritually guided and ethically organizational leadership in a framework of competitive market economies.

But this goal cannot be achieved unless there is accountability in governance such accountability requires transparent and ethical reporting of the finances of an organization.

The question that remains is: what governance principles should be adopted not only to rescue the Indian economy, from the current tail-spin foretelling a possible enormous fiscal crisis, but also to rapidly progress to developed corruption-minimal nation status in the next two or three decades?

Annexures

By Speed Post A.D.
Right to Information

PRIME MINISTER'S OFFICE

South Block
New Delhi – 110 101
Dated: [illegible] February-2011

No. RTI/185/2011-PMR

To:

Dr. Subramanian Swamy
A – 77, Nizamuddin (East)
New Delhi -110 013

Subject: Application under Right to Information Act, 2005

Sir,

Reference is invited to application-dated 14.1.2011, received on 17.1.2011, on the above noted subject. The matter was referred to the office for providing inputs. Signed statement furnished by the office is enclosed (1+6) along with documents.

2. Under the Right to Information Act, information can only be provided on the basis of available records of this public authority. You may note the input provided by the office on this matter.

3. For the purpose of Section 19 of the Right to Information Act, 2005, Shri Amit Agrawal, Director, is the appellate authority in respect of this office.

Yours faithfully,

Encl: 7 pages a/a

(Sanjukta Ray)
Deputy Secretary and
Central Public Information Officer
☎ : 2307 4072

RTI Matter
RTI/185/2011-PMR

Subject: RTI application of Dr. Subramanian Swamy, President, Janta Party

Request	Inputs
(1) Copy of the letter written by Dr. Swamy to the Prime Minister regarding the national security concern of Etisalat DB Telecom Company acquiring the license allotted to Swan Telecom	Copy of a letter dated 10.12.2010 of Dr. Subramaniam Swamy, addressed to the Prime Minister, which includes reference to security concerns and M/s Etisalat DB, running into two pages (F/A), may be provided, upon payment of requisite fee, if any
(2) Copies of all filing notings concerning the action of the Prime Minister on this aforesaid letter	Copy of the file notings (F/B), running into four pages, may be provided, upon payment of requisite fee, if any

15/2/11
S. O. (ES-I)

Dr. Subramanian Swamy Ph.D (Harvard)
President, Janata Party
M... er for Commerce, Law & Justice (1990-91)
Chairman (with Cabinet rank), Commission on Labour Standards and International Trade (1994-96)
Member of Parliament (1974-99)
Professor of Economics, Indian Institute of Technology, Delhi (1969-91)
Faculty Harvard University (1963-69, 1985-86, 2001-08 Summer)

JANATA PARTY
A-77, Nizamuddin (East) New Delhi - 110 013, India
Phone : +91 46016465 Fax : +91 24357388
Mobile : +91 9810194279 ; +91 9940203333
Website www.janataparty.org; www.indiaright.org
E-mail : swamy@post.harvard.edu
swamy39@gmail.com

December 10, 2010.

Dr. Manmohan Singh,
Prime Minister of India,
South Block,
New Delhi.

Re: Cancellation of all 2G Licences

Dear Prime Minister:

This letter is in continuation of my earlier letters on the same subject.

There is now much evidence within your Government itself that Etisalat DB, the new name for Swan Telecom, and one of the favoured few which got the UASL 2G licenses for 15 circles in 2008, is a company that is a partner with the Pakistan Government's Telecom Company: the PTCL (incidentally which is dominated by ISI, a pro-terrorist intelligence agency of the Pakistan army). Etisalat is also connected to China's PLA. Etisalat DB's Shahid Balwas is a close associate of Dawood Ibrahim (the underworld 'Don' and criminal who is a proclaimed offender). Balwas is also close associate of one of your Cabinet Ministers.

These data are available with your Home Ministry. The Home Ministry has also information that Etisalat DB has Telecom Surveillance Software that will enable it to track movements of anyone who takes a SIM card from it for its service.

This also is the position of Unitech Wireless which is another undeserving licensee, and which has now sold its controlling shares to Telenor which is also operationally based in Pakistan.

Hence to safeguard our national integrity, you must use your residuary extraordinary power vested in you as PM, to cancel all the 2G licences awarded, and order an auction for Indian bidders. The Supreme Court judgment in the Petrol Pump allotment matter also empowers the government. Therefore, Mr. Sibal's 60 day notice to 2G Spectrum allottees is foolish in this background.

In this context, it is of concern that financial sleaze operator, Ottavio Quattrocchi, who has a temporary respite from incarceration thanks the indulgence of yours and your predecessor NDA governments, has become again active in India's business fixing, sometimes operating from Malaysia on behalf of a large East Asian nation, sometimes from Milan for European interests. He leverages his son's presence in India and extraordinary access to the Gandhis (Sonia and Rahul). It is essential that he be declared an'undesirable alien'. I believe the CBI maintains such a list of undesirable persons and circulates that list to bureaucrats to ensure that no one entertains any persons on that list.

I also draw your attention to the baneful influence of one Ms. Farida Ataullah, a Pakistani with dubious connections (during the Benazir Bhutto tenure as PM she was her 'bag person'), who has been a close friend of Ms. Sonia Gandhi for decades-- so much so that she was Chief Guest of Honour at a select gathering at the wedding of Ms Gandhi's daughter, Priyanka in the mid 1990s. She lives in Dubai and co-ordinates all kinds of nefarious activities in and out of India.

Perhaps because of her influence, an important member of the core group of the Congress Party called the Mumbai and Maharashtra police officials to his suite in Oberoi Hotel Mumbai after the 26/11 terrorist attack, and directed that "Indian collaboration" in 26/11 should <u>not</u> be probed.

All these facts put together paint a grim picture of the national security scenario in the country. Pakistan was defeated four times in open military warfare by us but because of corruption in high places today flowing from the well known "Gangotri", Pakistan may succeed in undermining our national integrity through such well placed persons and effect a soft subversion of the Indian nation.

I write this letter to you place my concerns on record. As a public person who has been elected to Parliament five times and held Cabinet rank posts twice in the Union Government, I have a duty to inform you of these developments that I have been apprised of by my trusted friends in India and abroad. Please verify for yourself these facts and accordingly discharge the oath of office that you have sworn to uphold.

Warm Regards

Yours sincerely,

(SUBRAMANIAN SWAMY)

Internal

Dr. Subramanian Swamy, President, Janata Party, has addressed letter dated 10.12.2010 [FR] on the subject "Cancellation of all 2G licences", in continuation of his earlier letters on the same subject. While the subject cited is one of the issues covered in the letter, the letter also raises other matters in the context of their alleged implication on security.

2. Broadly speaking, the following three issues have been raised:

(i) Dr. Swamy has stated that there is much evidence within the Government itself that Etisalat DB, which got the Unified Access Service (UAS) 2G licence for 15 telecom circles in 2008, is a company which is a partner with Pakistan Government's telecom company, PTCL (dominated by the ISI). Further, Etisalat is connected with China's PLA and Etisalat's Shahid Balwas is a close associate of Dawood Ibrahim and also one of the Union Cabinet Ministers. Dr. Swamy has further stated that these data are available with MHA, which also has information that Etisalat has telecom surveillance software that will enable it to track movements of anyone who takes a SIM card from it. He has further added that this is also the position of Unitech Wireless, which has sold its controlling shares to Telenor, which too is operationally based in Pakistan.

Against this background, Dr. Swamy has opined that, in order to safeguard national integrity, the Prime Minister should use the residuary extraordinary power vested in him as Prime Minister, to cancel all 2G licences awarded and order an auction for Indian bidders. He has further stated that the Supreme Court judgment in the petrol pump allotment matter also empowers the Government. He has opined that "Mr. Sibal's 60-day notice to 2G spectrum allottees is foolish in this background."

(ii) Dr. Swamy has further added that in this context, it is of concern that financial sleaze operator Ottavio Quattrochhi, who has a temporary respite from incarceration thanks to the indulgence of the present and predecessor NDA Governments has again become active in India's business fixing on behalf of a large East Asian nation, sometimes from Milan for European interests. He leverages his son's presence in India and extraordinary access to Sonia and Rahul Gandhi. Dr. Swamy has opined that it is essential that Ottavio Quattrochhi be declared as an "undesirable alien" and has added that he believes that the CBI maintains such a list of undesirable persons and circulates the same among bureaucrats to ensure that no one entertains any person on the list.

(iii) Dr. Swamy has also invited attention to the influence of Ms. Farida Ataullah, a Pakistani with dubious connections (during the Benazir Bhutto tenure as Prime Minister she was her 'bag person') and one who has been a close friend of Smt. Sonia Gandhi for decades – she was the Chief Guest of Honour at a select gathering at the wedding of Smt. Gandhi's daughter, Priyanka Gandhi. Ms. Ataullah lives in Dubai and coordinates all kinds of nefarious activities in and out of India. Against this background, Dr. Swamy has stated that perhaps because of Ms. Ataullah influence, an important member of the Core Group of the Congress Party called Mumbai and Maharashtra police officials to his suite in Oberoi Hotel, Mumbai after the 26.11.2010 terrorist attack and directed that "Indian collaboration" in 26.11 should not be probed.

3. In conclusion, Dr. Swamy has stated that all these facts, put together, paint a grim picture of the national security scenario, adding that Pakistan may succeed in undermining / national integrity through such well-placed persons and effect a soft subversion of the Indian nation. He has stated that he is writing the letter to place his concerns on record and as he has the duty to inform the Prime Minister of these developments that he has been apprised of by his trusted friends in India and abroad. He has requested that the Prime Minister may verify these facts for himself and, accordingly discharge his oath of office.

4. Two earlier letters of Dr. Swamy on the same subject are of 14.4.2010 [1/C, which had been considered on *pp.* 1-4/N] and 6.12.2010 [9/c].

5. On the letter dated 6.12.2010, Prime Minister desired that it be acknowledged and that the M/o Communications & IT be asked to examine. The letter was acknowledged by PS(I) to PM and Prime Minister's desire for examination was conveyed to DoT *vide* ID note dated 16.12.2010 [10/c].

6. Prime Minister has desired on the instant letter that the Principal Secretary examine and discuss.

7. The issue in paragraph 2(i) relates to DoT, and may be referred to DoT for examination. The issue in paragraph 2(ii) relates to the CBI, and may be referred to DoPT for examination. The issue in paragraph 2(iii) relates to the Home Ministry, and may be referred to that Ministry for appropriate action.

8. Submitted for consideration of the suggestions in paragraph 7 above, and/or any other orders as may be deemed appropriate.

Sd/-
(Director)
21.12.2010

Joint Secretary — May kindly approve.

Sd/-

Secretary — Principal Secretary may like to discuss this with PM.

Sd/-

Principal Secretary — Please discuss with me early.

Sd/-

Secretary

From pre-page

9. This was discussed with Principal Secretary.

10. It was felt that the issues raised by Dr. Swamy in paras 2(i) and 2(ii) may be sent to DoT and DoPT respectively for examination and submitting their views in the matter.

11. The issues raised in para 2(iii) may be sent to MHA for action as appropriate.

Sd/-
Secretary
23.12.2010

Principal Secretary — Pl. brief PM before the action proposed is taken.
Sd/-

PS to PM — PM has been briefed, pl.
Sd/-

Principal Secretary
Sd/-

Secretary
Sd/-

Joint Secretary
Sd/-

Director — IDs pl.
Sd/-

Section

Department of Economic Affairs
FIPB Unit
******

New Delhi, September 29, 2010

To

M/s Etisalat DB Telecom Private Limited
C/o Pratap Ghose,
5th Floor, Infinity Towers,
Mindspace
Link Road, Malad (W)
Mumbai – 400 064

Subject: Application seeking approval for transfer of 1,33,17,245 equity shares from a person resident in India to a person resident outside of India.

******

Sir,

I am directed to refer to your letter dated December 3, 2009 on the above mentioned subject and to state that your proposal has not been acceded to for the reason that MHA has not supported the proposal.

Yours faithfully

(Vijay Singh Chauhan)
Director (FIPB)
Telfax: 011-2309 4045

Nature of proposal	Deferred (January 18, 2010, February 12, 2010, March 15, 2010, April 9, 2010, July 12, 2010 and July 30, 2010)
Name of the Applicant	M/s Etisalat DB Telecom Pvt. Ltd., Mumbai
Name of the Foreign Collaborator	M/s Emirates Telecommunications Corporation, UAE subsidiary Etisalat Mauritius Limited.
Activity	Existing activities: Providing Unified Access Services
Foreign Equity	Existing 49% : proposed 54.27%
Projected inflow	₹ 380.49 crore

Background

1. M/s Etisalat DB Telecom Private Limited (Company), a company incorporated in Mumbai, is stated to have obtained licenses for provision of Unified Access Services for the areas of Andhra Pradesh, Delhi, Gujarat, Haryana, Karnataka, Kerala, Maharashtra Mumbai, Punjab, Rajasthan, Tamil Nadu, Uttar Pradesh (East) and Uttar Pradesh (West). The company proposes to offer a whole range of services on its network including Unified Access Services, ISP Services, internet telephony services originating in India, Internet Services, broadband services, national long distance calls, international long distance calls.

The equity of the company is held in the following manner:

Name of the shareholder	No. of equity shares	%	Indian/ Foreign
Tiger Trustees Private Limited	11,55,20,463	45.73	Indian
Genex Exim Ventures Private Limited	1,33,17,245	5.27	Indian
Etisalat Mauritius Limited	11,29,94,230	44.73	Foreign
Delphi Investments Limited	1,07,91,000	4.27	Foreign

2. M/s Etisalat DB Telecom Private Limited has a WOS in the name of M/s Allianz Infratech Private Limited, Mumbai. Pursuant to an order of de-merger by the Hon'ble High Court of Delhi, for Unified Access Service Licenses in relation to 20 service areas have been de-merged to Telespice Wireless Private Limited. Only 2 service areas viz., Madhya Pradesh

and Bihar circles remain with the subsidiary. The investment by the company in the subsidiary has been made on March 17, 2009 pursuant to and in accordance with the provisions of Press note 2 of 2009 read in conjunction with Press Note 4 of 2009.

3. Etisalat Telecommunications Corporation (Etisalat) was incorporated in 1976 in United Arab Emirates (UAE). Etisalat UAE and, together with its group companies and subsidiaries (Etisalat Group) is also engaged in international telecommunications operations. Members of the Etisalat Group include Etisalat's direct subsidiary, Etisalat International India Private Limited, UAE and its step down subsidiary, Etisalat Mauritius Limited, Mauritius. Etisalat Mauritius (purchaser) was incorporated on October 16, 2008 with registered office in Mauritius. Etisalat propose to purchase the shares of the company through the purchaser.

Post transfer of shares, the equity of the company will be held in the following manner:

Name of the shareholder	No. of equity shares	%	Indian/ Foreign
Tiger Trustees Private Limited	11,55,20,463	45.73	Indian
Etisalat Mauritius Limited	12,63,11,475	50	Foreign
Delphi Investments Limited	1,07,91,000	4.27	Foreign

Proposal

4. M/s Etisalat DB Telecom Private Limited sought the approval of FIPB for the following:

(i) Purchase by Emirates Telecommunications Corporation, UAE through its subsidiary Etisalat Mauritius Limited of 1,33,17,245 fully paid up equity shares of ₹ 10/- each of Etisalat DB Telecom Private Limited from Genex Exim Ventures Private Limited, for an aggregate consideration of not less than ₹ 380,49,73,846/- or at a price per share or not less than ₹ 285.72;

(ii) Subscription by Etisalat Mauritius Limited of up to five fully paid up equity shares of ₹ 10/- each of Etisalat DB Telecom Private Limited at a price per share which is not lower than the price per share valued in accordance with the guidelines issued by the erstwhile Controller of Capital issues;

(iii) Such purchase and subscription of shares would result in Etisalat Mauritius Limited holding up to 50% plus ten equity shares in Etisalat DB Telecom Private Limited (directly) and (b) in Allianz Infratech Private Limited (indirectly);

(iv) As a result of the above, the total foreign shareholding in Etisalst DB Telecom Private Limited would be 54.27% and the total foreign shareholding in Allianz Infratech Private Limited (a WOS of Etisalat DB Telecom Private Limited) would be 54.27% pursuant to the mirror image rule set out in Press Notes 2 and 4 of 2009

Policy/ Need for FIPB Approval

5. As per extant FDI policy, in telecommunication sector, foreign equity beyond 49% requires the approval of FIPB.

Earlier Deliberations

6. The proposal was considered in the FIPB's 149th FIPB Meeting (held on January 18, 2010), 150th Meeting (held on February 12, 2010) and 151st Meeting (held on March 15, 2010) and 152nd Meeting (held on April 9, 2010) and was deferred each time on the request of MHA. DIT has communicated that the proposal relates to DoT, therefore they have no technical comments to offer. DoT has conveyed its no objection to the proposal, subject to the following conditions:

(i) Observance of Press Note 3 of 2007, 2 of 2009 and 4 of 200

(ii) Observance of license conditions for provisions of UASL, ISP, NLD & ILD

(iii)Observance of lock-in guidelines of DoT issues vide letter No. 20-100/2007-AS.I dated July 23, 2009 and

(iv) Security clearance of investors by MHA including concern on their operation in Pakistan

DEA has conveyed its no objection to the proposal subject to the compliance of Press Note 3 of 2007, Press Note 2 of 2009, Press Note 4 of 2009 and Press Note 3 of 2009 Shares' Transfer/Issue/Pricing guidelines of RBI/SEBI, FEMA 20/2000, security clearance from MHA and Guidelines of the Administrative Ministries. DIPP has conveyed its no objection to the proposal subject to compliance of the provisions of Press Note 3 of 2007. DoR has not supported the proposal on the grounds of treaty shopping. MHA has conveyed its no objection to the proposal, subject to (a) addressal of the following mentioned security concerns:

- (i) Attempt by Etisalat to mount a telecommunication Surveillance application software on Blackberry within UAE in 2009;
- (ii) Its presence in Pakistan and Afghanistan;
- (iii) Its Backend technical tie up with M/s HUAWEI which is a company founded by a PLA officer and the company having the capability to remotely manipulate the equipments, it supplies to its clients;
- (iv) That Shahid Usman Balwa should not be associated with the company either as Director or in any other capacity.

The Board directed that the letter of MHA be shared with DoT for their comments. The Board further directed the FIPB Secretariat to intimate the MHA concerns to the company and give them an opportunity to present their position. The Board accordingly deliberated the proposal and deferred it.

7 As per the directions of the Board in its meeting held on April 9, 2010, FIPB Secretariat shared the concerns of MHA with DoT and also with the company. The para-wise comments of DoT are as under:

(i) Etisalat DB Telecom Pvt. Ltd. Mumbai is separate entity and has to abide by telecom license conditions which have a number of security conditions including remote access conditions.

(ii) For their presence in Pakistan and Afghanistan, MHA has to suggest security conditions. In case of Unitech Wireless M/sTelenor was also having presence in Pakistan and MHA proposed in that case that any personnel who have worked in Pakistan, should not work in India. FIPB may consider similar condition in this case also.

(iii) DoT has already amended the license conditions of telecom licensees and they have to get security clearance of Licensor before placing any order on foreign suppliers. In this case also, any supply of equipment from foreign vendor would be only after getting security clearance of DoT who in turn consults MHA.

(iv) This is the first case in which MHA has objected for Indian Director in the company. Since the applicant has also been written by FIPB to submit their reply, FIPB may decide accordingly. As far as DoT comments are concerned, our recommendation is subject to security clearance by MHA only.

The company vide their letter dated June 29, 2010 have stated that they are in touch with Emirates Telecommunication Corporation and requested time for 2 weeks to respond to the queries raised by FIPB in its letter dated April 27, 2010.

8. The proposal was again considered in the FIPB Meeting held on July 12, 2010 and July 30, 2010 and was deferred. The Board observed that the objections of DoR are generic in nature and can be overruled. Point-wise response of MHA on the detailed comments furnished by DoT is awaited. The Board directed that the matter may be revisited by MHA and may offer further comments for decision on the matter. The Board accordingly deliberated the proposal and deferred it.

UP-DATE

The applicant in response to FIPB letter dated April 27, 2010 has furnished para-wise reply as under:

1. Etisalat DB Telecom Private Limited is a separate legal entity governed by the laws of India and the terms & conditions including security and Remote Access conditions of the telecom sector licenses granted by the Department of Telecommunications, Government of India. The company is committed to comply with conditions with respect to any service including VAS and Blackberry Service that it provides in India as well as meet security requirements imposed upon it.

Emirates Telecommunications Corporation (Etisalat) is a Statutory Corporation incorporated by Law No. 1 for the year 1991 in which the Federal Government of the United Arab Emirates owns 60% and controls its board and management and is a publicly listed entity. Etisalat has set up Etisalat Group to manage its international expansion and operations in over 17 countries across the globe and follow high standards of corporate governance and compliance. Etisalat investment in India comes as part and parcel of its international expansion policy. The various affiliates/subsidiaries of Etisalat operating in different countries/jurisdictions follow the local laws & regulations governing the business in the relevant geographies. As you may appreciate, these obligations include, inter alia, obligations to comply with relevant directions on matters relating to public interest, safety and/or national security.

2. They wish to state that no remote access to the company equipment has been agreed to be provided to Huawei by the Company. However, it will be appropriate to state that Huawei is one of the leading manufacturer of telecommunication equipments in the world and even public sector undertakings such as MTNL and BSNL amongst various other telecom service providers have purchased equipments worth billion dollars and which has been deployed in India. Whenever any remote access facility to any vendor is extended it will be governed by license conditions and permission shall be obtained as per License condition.

3. It is true that the Etisalat Group has a subsidiary in Afghanistan and 23.4% voting share interest in Pakistan Telecommunication Company Limited (PTCL) in Pakistan, as intimated in he Company's FIPB Application. The company is a separate legal entity and they shall ensure that no person employed by Etisalat/nominated by it on the Board of Directors of such Afghanistan subsidiary or PTCL will be sent/stationed in the Company.

Deliberations

DIPP has reiterated its earlier stand and has supported the proposal. DoR has reiterated its earlier stand and has not supported the proposal on the grounds of treaty shopping. MHA has not supported the proposal as it has not agreed with DoT observation and reiterated its concerns expressed earlier in the 152nd Meeting. The Board accordingly deliberated and recommended the proposal for rejection.

Recommendations

The Board recommended the proposal for rejection.

*******************************(End of item No. 53)*************************

Name of the operator	Percentage of equity transferred	Value of equity transferred	Name of the Company.	
			Seller	Buyer
1. M/s Swan (Now Etisalat DB Telecom)	5.27% (proposed)	`380.50 crore	Genex Exim	Etisalat Mauritius
2. M/s S Tel	5.61% (proposed)	238.5 crore(i) (ii)	Sky city Foundations (Indian) Telecom Investment (Foreign)	BMIC, Mauritius (Foreign)
3. M/s Unitech	67.25 %	`6120 crore	Unitech Limited (Indian)	Telenor Asia (Foreign)
4.M/s Tata Teleservices	27.31%	`12924 crore	TTSL (Indian)	NTT Docomo (Foreign)
5.M/s Tata teleservices (Maharashtra) (TTML)	20.25%	`949 crore	TTML (Indian)	NTT Docomo (Foreign)
6.M/s Sistema Shyam Teleservices Ltd (SSTL)	63.71%	`210.33 crore	Shyam Telelinks (Indian)	Sistema Joint Stock (Foreign)
	Fresh Issue	US$ 678 million (` 3051 crore)	SSTL (JV with 74% FDI)	ROSIMUSHCHE STVO (Foreign)

Out of the above six, three companies viz. M/s Swan Telecom, M/s S Tel and M/s Unitech were new entrants in the telecom sector. The fact that these operators could draw huge foreign investments, even before establishing a foothold in the Indian telecom market would suggest that acquiring UASL and with it, allotment of 4.4 MHz of GSM spectrum for roll out, was the main factor which attracted the foreign investment.

5.5.2 The Unitech Wireless Services, claimed in their letter to DoT on 4 November 2008 that M/s Telenor was partnering with them at a stage when about 6 months of effort and `2100 crore of expenses had already been put in and the entity's value was not only that of spectrum. However, considering that Telenor is an established international provider of a high quality

SUNDAY HINDUSTAN TIMES, NEW DELHI
JANUARY 30, 2011

Singh gave info to scam-tainted firm

NAILED MHA official is charged with passing secret information to Etisalat, a firm named in the 2G scam

Vijaita Singh
vijaita.singh@hindustantimes.com

NEW DELHI: Tainted IAS officer Ravi Inder Singh, arrested by the Special Cell of Delhi Police for "compromising national security", was also allegedly passing on secret information to UAE-based telecom major Etisalat DB, the police said. The company's name had figured in the 2G spectrum scam, it added.

Police found transactions of over ₹3.85 crore in Singh's bank accounts and also seized two documents of properties in Greater Noida and Gurgaon. His income is below ₹50,000.

In the chargesheet filed against Ravi Inder Singh, director with the internal security wing of Ministry of Home Affairs (MHA), the Special Cell of Delhi said the accused was taking both "sexual and monetary favours" to provide information about the files pertaining to security clearances to US-based Telecordia and Etisalat DB.

Ravi Inder Singh

Singh, a 1994-batch IAS officer, and a middleman Vineet Kumar were arrested on November 22, 2010 following inputs from the Intelligence Bureau. The police also said in the past three years they have found details of transactions over ₹3.85 crore from four bank accounts including two accounts in the name of Singh's wife.

"The information regarding the files was passed by Vineet Kumar to the officials of the two companies," the chargesheet filed at Tis Hazaari courts said.

It also said Singh took keen interest in the clearance of these files even though he was not authorised to do so. Police had intercepted 12,000 telephone conversations between Singh and Kumar as part of the undercover operation.

According to investigators, Sanjeev Arora, a top official with a telecom firm, tipped off Singh about his phones being tapped. Arora is now a witness in the case. Police said Kumar flushed SIM cards and sensitive documents to dodge the probe.

DELHI
THE HINDU • BUSINESS LINE
FRIDAY, JANUARY 14, 2011

PMO wants new 2G players put under security scanner

Thomas K. Thomas
New Delhi, Jan. 13

The Prime Minister's Office has directed the Department of Telecom to examine whether 2G licences issued to Etisalat DB and other new players should be cancelled because of security concerns. The PMO note follows a complaint letter from the President of Janata Party, Dr Subramanian Swamy, alleging that Etisalat had links with Chinese and Pakistani intelligence agencies.

"Dr Swamy has stated that there is much evidence within the Government itself that Etisalat DB, which got the Unified Access Service 2G licence for 15 telecom circles in 2008, is a company which is a partner with Pakistan Government's telecom company PTCL (dominated by the ISI). Further Etisalat is connected with China's PLA. Dr Swamy has further stated that these data are available with Ministry of Home Affairs, which also has information that Etisalat has telecom surveillance software that will enable it to track movements of anyone who takes a SIM card from it. The above issue may be examined by the DoT and views sent to this office," stated the PMO note to DoT. Dr Swamy has also

DoT asked to examine allegations against Etisalat

mentioned that Uninor should also be investigated, as its majority stake holder Telenor has operations in Pakistan.

The security scanner adds a third angle to the ongoing investigation as the DoT is already examining whether 2G licences should be cancelled or not as some of the new players, including Etisalat DB, have failed to meet the roll-out obligation. Investigation is also on whether these companies gave false information to the Government on their eligibility for acquiring the licences. The Comptroller and Auditor General has said five companies including Etisalat's Indian joint venture were not eligible for the 2G licences given in 2008.

Meanwhile, the UAE Ambassador to India, Mr Mohammed Sultan Al Owais, and the Chairman of the Etisalat Group, Mr Mohammed Hassan Omran, met Mr Kapil Sibal, Minister of Communications and Information Technology, earlier this week in a bid to clear the air.

tkt@thehindu.co.in

3. IB, after examining the representation submitted by Shahid Usman Balwa, one of the Directors of M/s Etisalat DB Telecom Pvt. Ltd Mumbai, in its report dated 18.10.2010 has furnished the following inputs:

(i) In November 2009 a mobile phone of Mumbai had come to adverse notice for being in contact with a Hawala Operator, who in turn was in touch with **a Pakistan based LeT activist**. The said mobile was registered in the name of **D.B. Reality Pvt. Ltd.** (Dynamix House, Yashodham, Gen. A.K. Vaidya Marg, Goregaon, Mumbai) and being used by **Shahid Usman Balwa**.

(ii) Earlier in 2008, enquiries had indicated **Shahid Usman Balwa** and his father **Usman Ebrahim Balwa** being close to **Chhota Shakeel** for the past several years.

(iii) Balwa's partner viz. **Vinod K. Goenka** (s/o **Krishna Murari Goenka and b/o Pramod K. Goenka**, both Directors in **Shahid Usman Balwa** promoted **M/s BD & P Hotels (India) Pvt. Ltd.**, Mumbai) had come to notice for association with **Dawood Ibrahim**.

(iv) **Krishna Murari Goenka** was FIR named accused in the murder case of builder Rajesh Chandrakant Patange (October 29, 2003), who named him before succumbing to his bullet injuries. Krishna Murari Goenka, however, was neither arrested nor charge-sheeted in the case.

(v) One **Tariq Abdul Karim Mechant** @ Tariq Praveen @ Patel @ Andha @Tariq Bhai, **a close associate of Chhota Shakeel**, who was arrested in March, 2003 had disclosed in his interrogation about close association of **Krishna Murari Goenka** and his son **Pramod K. Goenka** with 'D' company. He has further disclosed that in 2003, **Parmod K. Goenka** negotiated certain property deals with **Jabid Moti**, a local politician of Karachi and close associate of **Dawood Ibrahim, on behalf of Dawood.**

(vi) **Zameeruddin Ghulam Rasool Ansari** @ Kalia @ Jamil @ Zameer @ Kasam @ Moin s/o **Ghulam Rasool Ansai**, a **henchman** of **Anis Ibrahim**, arrested by Crime Branch of Mumbai police in September 2004 from Bandra, revealed during interrogation that **Pramod K. Goenka** (brother of **Vinod K. Goenka**), owner of Kenwood builders, **was** very close to **Anis** and **Dawood** and that both of them had made heavy investment in his company.

(vii) During his interrogation in 2005, **Abu Salem Abdul Qayyum Ansari** @ Abu Saman @ Captain **also** disclosed that **Pramod Kumar Goenka** was present at the wedding of Humayun, younger brother of Dawood (Karachi/December 1997).

In view of the above report of IB, the following is proposed:-

(i) Considering the clear adverse report against Shahid Usman Balwa, we may our earlier decision and as such, accordingly, treat this receipt disposed off.

(ii) Considering the adverse inputs of IB against Shri Vinod K. Goenka, file is submitted for orders whether security clearance granted to him earlier needs review.

அ. இராசா
ए. राजा
A. RAJA

मंत्री
संचार एवं सूचना प्रौद्योगिकी
भारत सरकार,
इलैक्ट्रॉनिक्स निकेतन, 6, सी.जी.ओ. कॉम्प्लेक्स,
नई दिल्ली-110 003

MINISTER
COMMUNICATIONS & INFORMATION TECHNOLOGY,
GOVERNMENT OF INDIA.
ELECTRONICS NIKETAN, 6, C.G.O. COMPLEX,
NEW DELHI-110 003

D.O. No. 20-215/2009-AS.I(Pt.)

18 JUN 2009

Dear Thiru. Swamy,

This has reference to your letter dated 29.11.2008 addressed to Hon'ble Prime Minister regarding allotment of licences in 2G mobile services etc. In this regard, it is clarified that the roaming agreement of Bharat Sanchar Nigam Limited. (BSNL) with M/s. Swan Telecom have been taken by the BSNL Board/Management after due diligence and considering BSNL's business interest at every step and there is no role of any individual BSNL official in the matter.

The transfer of officials in Wireless Planning & Coordination (WPC) Wing are done as per Government of India norms i.e., generally any officer having more than 3 years of public dealing is considered for change of seat. Accordingly, Thiru. R.J.S. Kushvaha, JWA and Thiru. D. Jha, DWA who have been working in WPC Wing for more than 3 years were transferred with the approval of the competent authority.

The issue of alleged violation of substantial equity' clause i.e., clause 8 of UAS Licence Guidelines dated 14.12.2005 by M/s. Swan Telecom Pvt. Ltd. on the date of their applications for grant of UAS licences, has been raised by Dr. Arvind Gupta in his Writ Petition (Civil) No.; 7815 of 2008 before Hon'ble High Court of Delhi in the matter of Dr. Arvind Gupta v/s. Union of India and the matter is presently sub-judice.

Contd..2/-

The reasoning of continuance of 'First-Come-First-Served' basis Policy for grant of Unified Access Services (UAS) licence and facts about SWAN and UNITECH deal are enclosed at Annexure-I and II respectively.

With regards,

Yours sincerely,

[A. RAJA]

Encl: As above.

Dr. Subramanian Swami,
President, Janata Party,
A-77, Nizamuddin (East),
New Delhi-110 013.

ANNEXURE-I

The reasoning of continuance of 'First-Come-First-Served' basis Policy for grant of UAS licences is as follows:-

(I). On 25th January 2001, the guidelines for issue of licence for Basic Service under NTP 99 was announced wherein the licensing of Basic Telephone service was opened on continuance basis on receipt of application and subject to fulfillment of eligibility conditions. As per para 26 of the guidelines, the licensees were to be allocated spectrum for wireless access system in local area on first-come-first-served basis.

(II). TRAI in its recommendation dated 27.10.2003, after discussing various options including the option of 'Auctioning' regarding entry fee for UASL licence, recommended that for fixing the entry fee for migrating to UASL Regime, the entry fee for fourth cellular operators shall be the entry fee for migration to UASL Regime.

(III). TRAI recommendations were placed before GoM (Group of Ministers). The recommendation of GoM were considered by the Cabinet. As per the Cabinet decision dated 31.10.2003, the recommendations of Group of Ministers (GoM) on Telecom matters chaired by the then Hon'ble Finance Minister, inter-alia, on issues as quoted below was approved:

".....The scope of NTP-99 may be enhanced to provide for licensing of Unified Access Services for basic and cellular licence services and unified Licensing comprising all telecom services. Department of Telecommunications may be authorised to issue necessary addendum to NTP-99 to this effect.

The recommendations of TRAI with regard to implementation of the Unified Access Licensing Regime for basic and cellular services may be accepted.

DoT may be authorised to finalise the details of implementation with the approval of the Minister of Communications & IT in this regard including the calculation of the entry fee depending on the date of payment based on the principle given by TRAI in its recommendations."

(IV). Based on the above Cabinet decision, an addendum to NTP-99 was notified on 11-11-2003. Also on 11.11.2003, "Guidelines for Unified Access (Basic & Cellular) Services Licence" was issued wherein Government had decided to move towards a Unified Access Services Licensing regime. The guidelines, inter-alia, others stipulates that "With the issue of these Guidelines, all applications for new Access Services Licence shall be in the category of Unified Access Services Licence."

(V). On 14.11.2003, TRAI once again clarified that the entry fee of the new Unified licensee would be the entry fee of the 4th cellular operator. Also, on 19.11.2003, TRAI recommended that if the licensor has to issue any unified access license to new applicants, the TRAI feels that spectrum to these licensees may be given as per the existing terms and conditions relating to spectrum in the respective license agreement. The UAS License Agreement was finalised in consultation with TRAI in January 2004.

(VI). On 17.11.2003, DoT decided to accept and process the UASL applications similar to the manner adopted for Basic Service License. On 24.11.2003, Hon'ble MOC&IT approved the approach of granting of UAS licences on First-Come-First-Served basis as the announced guidelines had made it open for new licences to be issued on continuous basis at any time and spectrum was to be allotted subject to availability.

This in effect implied that an applicant who comes first will be granted the spectrum first so it had resulted in grant of licence on First-Come-First-Served basis.

(VII). After enhancement of FDI in telecom sector from 49% to 74%, DoT on 14.12.2005 issued Guidelines for Unified Access Services (UAS) licences. These guidelines, interalia stipulate that:

- Licences shall be issued without any restriction on the number of entrants for provision of Unified Access Services in a Service Area.
- The applicant will be required to pay one time non-refundable Entry, annual Licence fee @ 10/8/6% of Adjusted Gross Revenue (AGR) for category A/B/C service areas respectively and spectrum charges on revenue share basis as specified by WPC wing.

(VIII). Since introduction of UAS licensing regime in 2003, 51 new UAS licenses have been issued till March 2007 based on the policy of continuous award on First-Come-First-Served (FCFS) and spectrum was also allocated based on FCFS basis under a separate Wireless Operating License, subject to availability.

(IX). Fast changes were happening in the Telecommunication sector. In order to ensure that the policies keep pace with the changes/developments in the Telecommunication sector, the government contemplated to review certain terms and conditions in the Access provider (CMTS/UAS/Basic) license. Accordingly a reference was made to TRAI on 13.04.2007 stating that the policy on Unified Access Service Licensing was finalized in November 2003 based on the recommendations of TRAI and 159 licenses have been issued so far for providing Access Services (CMTS/UASL/Basic) in the country with 5-8 Access Service providers in each service area. The Access Service providers are mostly providing services using the wireless technology (CDMA/GSM). As per the present policy, any Indian company fulfilling the eligibility criteria can apply for UAS license. These are increasing the demand on spectrum in a substantial manner. Therefore, TRAI was requested to furnish their recommendations on the issue of limiting the number of Access providers in each service area and review of the terms and conditions in the Access provider license mentioned thereof.

(X). TRAI revisited the issue of new licences, allocation of spectrum, entry fee, spectrum charges etc. through a open consultation process with all the stake holders. Finally, TRAI in it's recommendation dated 28th August 2007 on "Review of license terms and conditions and capping of number of access providers" has, inter-alia, recommended as below:

- No cap be placed on the number of access service providers in any service area.
- Keeping in view the objective of growth, affordability, penetration of wireless services in semi-urban and rural areas, the Authority is not in favour of changing the spectrum fee regime for a new entrant. Opportunity for equal competition has always been one of the prime principles of the Authority in suggesting a regulatory framework in telecom services. **Any differential treatment to a new entrant vis-à-vis incumbents in the wireless sector will go against the principle of level playing field.** This is specific and restricted to 2G bands only i.e. 800, 900 and 1800 MHz. This approach assumes more significance particularly in the context where subscriber acquisition cost for a new entrant is likely to be much higher than for the incumbent wireless operators.
- **It is therefore recommended that in future all spectrum excluding the spectrum in 800, 900 and 1800 bands should be auctioned so as to ensure efficient utilization of this scarce resource.** In the 2G bands (800 MHz/900 MHz/1800 MHz), the allocation through auction may not be possible as the service providers were allocated spectrum at different times of their license and

the amount of spectrum with them varies from 2X4.4 MHz to 2X10 MHz for GSM technology and 2X2.5 MHz to 2X5 MHz in CDMA technology. Therefore, to decide the cut off after which the spectrum is auctioned will be difficult and might raise the issue of level playing field.

(XI). The recommendation of TRAI that there should be no cap on the number of access provider in any service area, was accepted by the Government in October 2007, after due deliberation.

(XII). Through a Press Release dated 06.11.2007, the Department made it clear that the pending applications to grant of New Unified Access Services Licences will be process as per the existing policy.

(XIII). The guidelines issued for UAS Licences on 14.12.2005, in consonance with NTP 99 & TRAI recommendations are the extant guidelines for grant of new UAS licence. These established policy regarding issuance of license, allocation of spectrum and charges thereon have been followed since November 2003 by the successive Governments till date.

(XIV). The basic aim of a government policy is expansion of telecommunication services at an affordable rate in the whole country in a competitive environment so that customer is able to enjoy the fruit of latest technology in terms of data and voice so as to protect his own interest specially in rural areas where other means of communications may not be available, at the same time by following the existing practices and processes, revenue of the government has not been compromised. Any initial entry barriers such as high initial one time charges for license/spectrum by way of auction would have hampered the competition and retarded the fall of tariffs in the sector which would have been detrimental for the rural masses and expansion of such services.

(XV). It will not be out of context to mention that in 1994-95 licenses were granted for operation of basic and mobile telephone services by way of auction for license fee. Very high license fee were quoted by the service providers which resulted in practically nil growth of services till 1999 when a migration package was offered to migrate from high fixed annual license fee to a revenue sharing arrangement. The growth of telecom sector is established, without doubt, by such a measure. The competition has forced the tariffs to come down drastically from Rs.16 to Rs.1 per minute over the period of time with the expansion of mobile telephones from 1.2 millions in March 1999 to 346.89 millions at the end of December 2008. There is a continuous increase in the receipt of licence fee. Moreover, increase in subscriber base has also seen increase in collection of service tax from telecom services.

(XVI). In case license/ spectrum is auctioned, it would not have been possible to charge the higher spectrum usage charges of the order of 2-6% and maintenance and administration cost which is typically of the order of 0.5% to 1%could be recovered in a judicial manner. Low entry barriers with graded spectrum usage charges with quantum of spectrum does not put an initial burden on the operator as well as subscribers as one time initial charges would have to be recovered along with the interest from the subscriber and would have resulted in higher tariffs for subscribers.

(XVII). Every phase of introduction of new operators with present approach has seen reduction in tariffs, expansion of subscriber base and provision of more Value Added Services for subscribers with increased revenues of the Government. Such telecom facilities are in the interest of the general public leading to indirect and direct employment, growth in GDP and thereby improving the health of the economy.

ஆ. இராசா
ए. राजा
A. RAJA

डी.ओ.सं. 71 सं.एवं सू.प्रौ.मंत्री/2010
D.O. No. .... MOC & IT/2010
मंत्री
संचार एवं सूचना प्रौद्योगिकी
भारत सरकार,
इलैक्ट्रॉनिक्स निकेतन, 6, सी.जी.ओ. कॉम्प्लेक्स,
नई दिल्ली-110 003
MINISTER
COMMUNICATIONS & INFORMATION TECHNOLOGY,
GOVERNMENT OF INDIA,
ELECTRONICS NIKETAN, 6, C.G.O. COMPLEX,
NEW DELHI-110 003

21 APR 2010

Respected Sir,

Vanakkam.

I am herewith presenting for the kind attention of the Hon'ble Prime Minister the following facts regarding.W.P.(C) No. 2442/2010 filed by Dr. Subramaniam Swamy before the Delhi High Court.

2. The allegations made by him are all taken out of the news published in the magazine called "Pioneer", which is the party magazine of Bharathiya Janata Party. Dr. Subramaniam Swamy has chosen to call the articles published in the said magazine as "investigative reports". The term investigative reports attributed to the said magazine, particularly in respect of the news item in question can only be described as a misnomer. The various news items in question are absolutely motivated and malafide exhibiting a deliberate attempt to malign me. This malicious exercise had been started by this magazine against me since the year 2008. Dr. Subramaniam Swamy had deliberately chosen to place reliance on these reports because his intention in filing the above said Writ Petition before the Delhi High Court is not in any way different from the motive or intention behind the said reports published in the said magazine. Long before he filed the above said case before the Delhi High Court, Dr. Subramaniam Swamy, had been giving interviews particularly in a T.V. channel called "Jaya TV" operating from Chennai that he would be filing the case in the Delhi High Court.

3. It is brought to the kind attention of the Hon'ble PM that excepting the following two allegations viz., Allegation No. 9(g) and under the caption "persons involved" in the same paragraph under sub-para (e) all other allegations are subject matters of a suit filed by me for defamation against a bi-weekly called "Junior Vikatan" before the Madras High Court in C.S. No. 366/2009, in which as a counter to the application filed by me

for the grant of injunction in O.A. No. 420/2009, the Printer and Publisher of the said bi-weekly magazine have raised all these allegations not only in the reports published by them in the said magazine, but also in their counter affidavit to my application for injunction culled out from the said Newspaper "Pioneer". It was on the basis of the pleadings between the parties in the said application for injunction pending disposal of the said suit that a Division Bench of the Madras High Court by order dated 1.10.2009 in the OSA No. 230 & 231/2009 was pleased to grant an order of interim injunction pending disposal of the aforesaid suit subject to certain conditions (**Copy enclosed - Flag 'A'**). The averments contained in my affidavits / counter affidavits and related papers thereto will reveal the strong denial of those allegations which are now being perpetrated by Mr. Subramaniam Swamy in the present petition (**Copy enclosed - Flag 'B'**). As a matter of fact, the magazine 'Junior Vikatan' neither preferred appeal as against the order of the High Court nor filed any new credentials or documents to substantiate the allegation. The suit is still pending and as such subjudice. The said judgment of the Division Bench of the Madras High Court has been reported in (2009) 5 L.W. 117.

4. It is also relevant to point out that this magazine "Pioneer" had published false news information regarding the subjects discussed between the Hon'ble Home Minister of India and the Hon'ble Chief Minister of Tamilnadu and when a lawyer's notice was sent on behalf of the Hon'ble Chief Minister of Tamilnadu, the said magazine has expressed unqualified regrets and had the same published in their newspaper. This is brought to the notice for the purpose of showing the news worthiness of this newspaper "Pioneer".

5. Weighing the credibility of the newspaper 'Pioneer' in terms of quality of worthiness and quantity of circulation, I did not institute any such legal proceedings as I did in the case of 'Junior Vikatan' and therefore this optional and intentional omission cannot be permitted as a shelter for Mr. Swamy whose public credibility is known to all.

6. Further, I have come across on verification of documents that the companies viz., Green House Promoters (P) Ltd., and Equaas Estates (P) Ltd., have also separately filed Criminal Complaints C.C. No. 9602/2009 and 9603/2009 respectively against the bi-weekly magazine "Junior Vikatan" and the said complaints have been taken on file and the same are pending before the XVII Metropolitan Magistrate, Saidapet, Chennai-15 (**Copy enclosed - Flag 'C' & 'D'**). The accused in the said complaints "Junior Vikatan" have taken notice and also appeared in person.

7. Similarly, regarding Para 9(g), the allegation that "Earlier while serving as Minister for Environment & Forests Respondent No. 2 had appointed his nephew Dr. R. Sridhar as Deputy Director in the Ministry of Environment and Forest by flouting the Norms of Appointment". The real facts pertaining to the aforesaid allegation is that the said Dr. R. Sridhar applied for the post of Deputy Director pursuant to the Notification of inviting applications. He became successful on his own merits. I was in no way connected with the said appointment and at the time of his appointment I was also not the Minister of Environment and Forest as alleged.

8. As regards the other allegation under the caption "persons involved" sub para (e) viz., "Mr. A. Kaliaperumal (Brother of Respondent No. 2) arrested by the CBI in January 2010 on an FIR filed following the directions of the Chief Vigilance Commissioner on this matter", the said allegation is false and when this is false, one can estimate the veracity of the said publication, the so called Pioneer magazine, a party magazine of BJP and their motive in making such false publication. There was no proceedings taken against him by the CBI and therefore the question of his arrest, filing of FIR etc., are totally false.

9. With regard to another allegation in para 12 on page 20 which refers the order of Hon'ble Supreme court in S'Tel Vs Union of India, the petitioner Mr. Swami cannot rely upon it for his case as this case was filed to assail the cut off date chosen by the government to issue license, admitting the policy and procedure for issuance of license and allotment of Spectrum. It is pertinent to note that affidavit filed by M/s S'Tel itself admits that the order is not arbitrary after verification of Spectrum availability.

10. In any event it was never pleaded by S'Tel that the government suffers exchequer loss or undue favour to any company enabling them for unlawful enrichment. However to avoid legal repercussion on administrative domain of the government, the matter has been referred to the Law Ministry for further clarification. Thus the Order of the Supreme Court does not offer any sustenance or strength to the petitioner for either criminal interpretation of scam or exchequer loss.

11. It is clear that there are some 'vested interests' including the above named Petitioner in filing the case against me before the Delhi High Court and they are bent upon bringing down my image as well as the image of the Government of India on such false news and premises.

12. Since the matter is coming before the High Court of Delhi on 18.5.2010 for hearing, I am placing on record the aforesaid facts for necessary further course of action with relevant copies of documents referred.

With regards,

Yours sincerely,

(A. RAJA)

Dr. Manmohan Singh,
Hon'ble Prime Minister of India,
South Block,
New Delhi.

May 10, 2011.

Mr. A.P. Singh,
Director,
Central Bureau of Investigation,
CGO Complex, Lodi Road,
New Delhi.

Dear Mr. Singh,

I write this letter to ask whether you have conducted any further inquiry arising out of the charge against the former Telecom Minister Mr. A. Raja { stated on page 59 of the Final Report under Section 173, Cr P.C. submitted in the Court of the Special Judge (CBI), New Delhi in the matter registered on 21.10.2009} since he is alleged to have deprived the Government exchequer of huge revenues because he deliberately and dishonestly gave away the licences of 2G Spectrum at an entry fee cum spectrum price that was determined in 2001.

While it is true that the Finance Ministry at the level of the Finance Secretary had raised the question of revising this price, however, vide the decision taken and notified by the Cabinet Secretariat on December 7, 2006, empowering the Finance Minister and the Minister for Communications & IT to jointly determine the Spectrum price which by TRAI recommendation of 2007 ought to include an entry fee for obtaining the licence as also a price for Spectrum allotment, and a further charge subsequently for its usage.

According to the records, Mr. P. Chidambaram and Mr. A. Raja both then Ministers of the respective portfolios of Finance and Telecom, had corresponded with each other, and subsequently met and finalized the entry fee at around Rs.1651 crores and decided consequently to provide the spectrum allotment bundled free with the licence of several megahertz.

This being so, if Mr. Raja is culpable for fixing a very low price for the 2G spectrum licence, then because of this joint determination, Mr. P. Chidambaram is also prima facie culpable on the same charge as Mr. Raja.

Hence, please inform me at the very earliest and before the Supreme Court summer vacation period begins, of any step that you may have taken to date.

Yours sincerely,

(SUBRAMANIAN SWAMY)

THE HINDU

News » National

Vahanvati took part in meet on 2G spectrum in 2007

Meeting was attended by Pranab, Raja

The former Solicitor-General, G.E. Vahanvati, who is now Attorney-General, had participated in the discussions held in the first week of December 2007 with the then External Affairs Minister, Pranab Mukherjee, on issues relating to 2G spectrum allocation and in that meeting the former Communications Minister, A. Raja, also participated.

The office of the Attorney-General gave this information to Central Public Information Officer R.K. Gupta of the Department of Telecommunications, in response to an order passed by the Central Information Commission on an application from rights activist Subash Chandra Agrawal seeking a number of questions, including whether any discussion was held with the then External Affairs Minister and if so to provide him details.

Initially the CPIO of the department declined to divulge such information. However, the CIC asked him to revisit the matter and to furnish the information sought by the applicant. It was in this context the CPIO wrote to the office of the Attorney-General to ascertain whether Mr. Vahanvati [as the then Solicitor-General] had participated in the meeting.

A.S. Malhotra, PPS to the AG, in his reply to Mr. Gupta's letter dated March 15, said: "The offices of the Solicitor-General [and the AG] do not have a CPIO." Hence as PPS to the then Solicitor-General and now the AG for India, he had obtained the necessary information to give the response.

On whether discussion was held with the then External Affairs Minister, he said: "Yes. In the first week of December 2007, there was a discussion held with the then Union Minister for External Affairs in relation to the issues raised in the proceedings filed by [Cellular Operators Association of India] COAI before the TDSAT in relation to allocation of spectrum. The Minister for Communications and IT was present. The contentions of the COAI and those of the DoT were explained to the Minister. The meeting lasted about 15 minutes."

Mr. Malhotra, however, said no minutes were prepared or any written advice was given. He said a brief note was prepared by Mr. Vahanvati and handed over to the Minister. Mr. Agrawal had sought the details about the participation of Mr. Vahanvati in the discussions relating to spectrum allocation as according to him it was in violation of the Law Officers (Conditions of Service) Rules.

On the directions of the Central Information Commission in another order the Union Law Ministry provided Mr. Agrawal information stating that the Attorney-General Vahanvati appeared for the BCCI (in the appeal filed by the former BCCI president, A.C. Muthiah) in his private capacity in the Supreme Court and that he obtained prior permission to do so.

Keywords: 2G spectrum issue, Vahanvati

POINTS MADE IN SUPREME COURT ON MAY 13, 2011 BY THE AUTHOR FOR MAKING P. CHIDAMBARAM AS ACCUSED IN 2G SPECTRUM SCAM

1. In Your Lordships' Order of December 16, 2010 in paras 2(ii) & (iii) it is directed that that the CBI will make sure that no one no matter how highly placed in office, is above the law and legitimate investigation.

2. In its charge sheet against A. Raja [p.59-63 reproduced in my Application No 8 in SLP 24873 of 2010 in pages 11-19], the CBI holds Raja guilty of causing a huge loss to the government[page 14]

3. The charge is phrased as: " Cheating the Government Exchequer by Non-Revision of Entry Fee"

4. However, the averment of the CBI in the last para [on p. 14 and continuation on p.15], that this was despite the warnings of the officials of the Ministry of Finance, is not the whole truth.

5. The whole truth is that the civil servants of the MoF did put up a fight for an upward revision of the price till November 22, 2007, a strange silence descended thereafter in Finance Ministry Secretariat on the pricing issue as if from a directive from above.

6. The final decision to fix the entry fee on a Telecom licence, and the spectrum one time charge, as well as spectrum usage charge, were in fact subsequently jointly determined by the two Ministries at the Minister's level.

7. This mandate to jointly decide the entry fee and spectrum pricing is sourced to the Cabinet decision of October 31, 2003 [see Justice Shivraj Patil Committee Report [p. 49 para 2.49 (ii)] and the Revised Terms of Reference of December 2006 for the GoM set up in February of 2006.

Patil Committee Report [p. 49 para 2.49 (ii)] and the Revised Terms of Reference of December 2006 for the GoM set up in February of 2006.

8. In the Note dated January 15, 2008 written by the then Finance Minister P. Chidambaram to the Prime Minister [p.28 para 6, and para 7], the then FM points out that the spectrum licence pricing decision is exclusively for him and Raja to decide.

9. He also clarifies the concept of pricing in the 2G matter. On para 9[p.29] he makes clear that the entry fee decided by Raja at 2001 level would not be revised.

10. Incidentally in December 2006, the PM on the urging of the then MoC&IT, Dayanidhi Maran, had revised the terms of reference to exempt this joint decision being approved either in a e-GoM or in a full Cabinet meeting.

11. Hence from then on the MoC&IT and MoF were empowered to decide the licence entry fee and the two spectrum charges, *and their joint decision was final.*

12. The same finality emerges from the Finance Minister's letter to the MoC&IT dated April 21, 2008 [p.33].

13. I have personally verified that the DoT had informed in answer to a question by the PAC, that the two Ministers had met for this purpose at least three times, that is on 30/1/08, 29/5/08, and 12/6/08 and decided on: the 2001 discovered rate for the entry fee, zero amount for the one-time Spectrum allotment fee, and an already agreed formula for annual spectrum charge, and then informed the PM in a joint meeting on July 4, 2008.

14. On my RTI replies, I have been informed that the Minutes of these meetings do not exist.

15. But a close reading the Prime Minister's statement to the Rajya Sabha on February 22, 2011 [p. 39] and also the text of the PM's speech to Editors of the Electronic Media on 16.2.11 [p.32] confirms this unequivocally.

16. The Draft Report of the Public Accounts Committee has also come to the conclusion on the culpability of Mr. Chidambaram in fixing a low entry fee and a zero spectrum price.

17. Hence, *prima facie* it is obvious that if Mr. Raja can be charged for causing loss to the exchequer, then Mr. Chidambaram's culpability has to be investigated by the CBI without fear or favor.

18. Hence my prayer[on p. 7-8] to direct the CBI to investigate Mr. Chidambaram in the 2G Spectrum Scam..

Index